GO TO THE PRAIRIE

Andrew Taylor Still, M.D., D.O.

Frontiersman, Visionary and
Founder of Osteopathic Medicine

Marshall D. Walker, D.O.

Go To The Prairie

© 2014

Marshall D. Walker

ISBN - 13: 978-1505206623
ISBN - 10: 1505206626

*Front cover photo of Andrew Taylor Still, ca. 1857,
used with permission of
Museum of Osteopathic Medicine^{SM},
[1994.1593.02].*

Warwick House Publishers
720 Court Street
Lynchburg, Virginia 24504

Dedicated
to
Donna Walker

For her patience with me,
and for the multiple roles she has endured,
as a wife, English teacher, writing critic, and friend.
Her former students need to know she did not spare me from
the dreaded red pencil—highlighting all my errors
to help me achieve a better story.

CONTENTS

ABOUT THE AUTHOR

The author, Marshall D. Walker, DO, FAODME, began his medical career as a navy hospital corpsman at San Diego, California, and was initially stationed at Camp Pendleton Naval Hospital. He finished his final year at sea as a third-class hospital corpsman aboard the Destroyer Tender, U.S.S. *Dixie* (AD 14), after completing a West Pac Cruise.

He entered civilian life with a desire to attend medical school and return to active naval service as a medical officer. With his wife Donna teaching English and daughter Michelle in grade school, he was able to complete his medical training at the Kansas City College of Osteopathic Medicine in 1972.

Dr. Walker resumed his naval career as a lieutenant in the medical corps and spent the next five years at Naval Regional Medical Center, San Diego, California. He completed an internship and surgical residency program in otolaryngology, graduating in 1977. His final assignment in the Navy was Honolulu, Hawaii, where he practiced at the Makalapa Naval Clinic and performed ENT surgery at Tripler Army Hospital. He separated from active naval service after achieving the rank of Commander.

Dr. Walker spent twenty years in private ENT practice in Wichita, Kansas. After a short retirement, he began a second career in medicine as a medical educator. During the past sixteen years he has served as the Director of Medical Education for Riverside Hospital, Wichita, Kansas; Medical Center of Independence, Kansas City, Missouri; and Via Christi Hospitals, Wichita, Kansas. He has been a Board of Trustee member since 2010 for the Kansas City University of Medicine and Biosciences, and served as the thirteenth president of the institution during 2013. He is presently the Chairman of the Board of Trustees.

ACKNOWLEDGMENTS

I would like to express my appreciation to editor, Joyce Maddox, at Warwick House Publishers in Lynchburg, Virginia. She was understanding and patient with me as a new writer. She connected to the story and drama that occurred during A.T. Still's lifetime. My appreciation also to Amy Moore of Warwick House Publishers for her expertise in designing my book for publication.

It was apparent to me that if this book were going to be successful, the osteopathic profession would have to be interested in its own history and support an effort to familiarize our students with the roots of where the profession has been and where it is going in the future. I had the manuscript reviewed by a number of osteopathic physicians to get their critique and feedback regarding the material. Those reviewers were: Stephen Shannon, DO, President and CEO, AACOM; Marc Hahn, DO, President and CEO, Kansas City University of Medicine and Biosciences; Robert Cain, DO, Vice President of AODME; John Dougherty, DO, FAODME, Senior Associate Dean, KCUMB; Mike Johnston, DO, Vice Dean, KCUMB. All were helpful in offering suggestions to improve the story and encouraged me to finish the manuscript and have it published. Their encouragement resulted in my commitment to finish the book.

The ATSU Museum in Kirksville, Missouri, was always willing to help me with materials and pictures to document the history that I was trying to capture. Jason Haxton, the curator of the museum, was invaluable with his historical knowledge. Furthermore, he was always supportive with unfailing enthusiasm about the content of the book and provided additional historical facts. His staff was always courteous when I needed help.

Carol Trowbridge, author of the book *Andrew Taylor Still, 1828-1917,* took the time to review my manuscript and make some helpful suggestions to improve the accuracy of the story. Thanks, Carol, for your help and depth of knowledge regarding the Still family.

My personal friends, Ron Stephen, retired USAF, Colonel and osteopathic CEO administrator; Karen Every, Table Rock Lake, Golden, Missouri, were kind enough to look at the manuscript and give a non-osteopathic physician critique and opinion. Thank you both for your help, time, and encouragement.

I would like to express my appreciation to the Kansas State Historical Society for allowing me to use their materials in researching the period when the Still family lived in Kansas. The Wichita Public Library also provided resources from their historical collection room and was always willing to retrieve documents not out on display.

Finally, I would like to acknowledge Sarah Miller Braet, osteopathic student coordinator, for her time and help in completing the manuscript.

GO TO THE PRAIRIE

Andrew Taylor Still, M.D., D.O.

Frontiersman, Visionary and
Founder of Osteopathic Medicine

The Still Family
Used with permission of ATSU Museum.

PROLOGUE

They came to the Plains in search of freedom for all, unaware that even the wind gets lost in the prairie. This great expanse of prairie ran through the central part of the United States and was known only as the Kansas Territory. It was a peaceful place sometimes, but it could be unstable in a moment's notice with a thunderstorm blowing up quicker than a hawk swooping down on a rabbit. One minute the sky was bright blue with the fresh spring day glowing above the gentle clouds that floated over the treetops on the land below. Suddenly, and without warning, the clouds bunched up, causing their white puffy appearance to disappear, creating a darkness that captured these previously friendly floaters. The sun vanished. Lightning flashes produced hot pokers between the ground and sky, and what had only moments before been a restful scene of tranquility turned into an ugly, threatening cauldron. The storm would come. Rain bounced off the ground, running in sheets along the baked earth. The sheets of water ran into grooves, gouged out by previous storms, and what had been flat water spread out over the prairie's surface turned into water shoots that careened down slopes, hills, and valleys until the torrent-swollen streams converged. The churning wall of liquid power propelled the water into the riverbed below, taking along everything that stood in the way. Once the power of the water began to flow, there was no way to stop it.

Hail might be added to the assault of the storm, varying in size from gravel to ice shards as large as an orange. Many trees stood bare, stripped naked without bark, when Mother Nature blasted the countryside with her rasp of frozen water.

If the air from the northwest was cold enough and collided with moist, warm air from the southwest, the condition might spawn the ugliness of a tornado. The twister would hurl itself down from the sky that only minutes before had been calm. With clouds coalesced into a dark, black, boiling stew, its tongue hanging down to the ground, it licked the land clean of everything it touched and spit debris for miles over the countryside as if showing contempt for the land, property, and the lives that it had consumed.

There was nothing that would satisfy the hunger of the tornado. It devoured houses, barns, animals, and the people who lived there.

The pioneers, who had come and claimed a few acres, had cleared homesites, and hammered nails into the wood, could not have known that they might someday be in the way of a storm. They filled these shelters with their meager possessions: cooking pots and pans, clothing, blankets, and the few luxuries that they could carry with them on wagons. Some of these families produced fragile babies who grew into children inside these walls. These buildings were truly held together by the glue of their blood and the bonds of their beliefs. A tornado, however, could suddenly take this collection of work and time, and the souls that produced this temporary reality, without showing any mercy or remorse. It destroyed all.

After the storm rolled through, the sun appeared, the winds settled down, and the sky turned blue again. The prairie was once again peaceful. The dead would be buried. The scars on the land would disappear over time. Where a structure once stood, the wild grass, weeds, and trees would grow and erase the memory and the history. In a generation or two, all would be forgotten as if nothing had really ever happened.

This tug-of-war battle with the weather has gone on forever in the Kansas prairie with a constant fight to decide which condition is going to prevail. It is not vengeful, it is not hateful, but it is frightening and deadly when these invisible forces meet to decide whose turn it is to dominate for the moment.

This land has been chosen to be the fighting ground for Mother Nature to settle the battle between warm or cold, wet or dry, breeze or calm. Which majestic force of nature will prevail and triumph is beyond the ability of man to control. But even more compelling was why this same soil had been chosen as the place to begin the fight over slavery and freedom.

On this prairie, in the year 1852, the human storm began to brew. This storm was being created over the fundamental questions of freedom or slavery. The slavery conflict would be the power behind this driving force. And like the winds that forever struggled over the prairie, this battle over slavery was to be defined in the Kansas Territory.

The conflict had a history in legislation. In 1820, the Missouri Compromise had been adopted by Congress, and Missouri had been admitted as the last slave state. Slavery, according to law, was now prohibited forever, from all territories north of thirty-six degrees and thirty minutes. Thirty-four years later, in 1854, the Missouri Compromise was stricken from the federal law books and in its place the Kansas-Nebraska Bill was substituted. This new bill permitted slavery to cross the 36'30' line if the people in the Territories decided they wanted slavery to be introduced there. The mechanism for making this decision would be the ballot box and a majority vote would rule.

Unlike nature's storms that are controlled by the laws of physics, the storms of slavery were driven by the emotions of hate, greed, fear, and anger. This decision caused the people of the prairie to begin to coalesce like the clouds. They were forced to choose one side or the other. As the emotions grew, the air turned dark and violent. The storm suddenly began to blow from every direction. And as the power of the storm increased, men's lives would turn and be driven at times by a force that they did not understand.

The Prairie was sparsely inhabited. The pioneers were busy scratching out a meager existence and a few families had brought their slaves with them when they entered the Territory. Most of the pioneers came to stake their claims and work the land themselves. The political unrest, however, began to change the climate with the potential expansion of slavery grant- ed in the new Kansas-Nebraska Bill. Without warning, the air began to thicken, and words began to rumble like claps of thunder until the conflict condensed enough energy in the bowels of the political storm to cause it to move. The furor moved slowly and directly for the Kansas Territory, taking time to gather up great momentum and strength until nothing could stand in its way. It could not be stopped. The fury and the awful damage that the tu- mult possessed headed toward the unsuspecting pioneers who had recently made their homes in the Territory.

For the most part, people came and went as their will and needs led them, but some were destined to make their mark on history as they stood in the storm's path. One of the families destined to go to the Kansas Territory was the Stills. Their journey would eventually lead them directly to the center of the tempest.

They would personally witness and suffer the results as the intensity of the slavery upheaval increased. The hail stones were turning into lead bul- lets, and the gorges were running with blood rather than water. They would experience the nightmare. Once the blood started flowing, there was no way to stop the hemorrhage.

CHAPTER ONE
Andrew Taylor Still

A thousand miles away from the Kansas Territory in the most western tip of Virginia, in an area shaped as sharp as an arrowhead, lay the small town of Jonesville. Just outside of this small community and nestled in the foothills of the Cumberland Mountains, was a log cabin, located on a five-hundred acre farm.

If a calendar had been hanging on one of the four walls of the cabin, the numbers indicating the year would have been 1828. The family who occupied and lived a robust life in this small one room cabin was well known in the area primarily because of the master's occupation. The father of the family was Abraham Still, who was a Methodist minister. Since Abram served the church as a circuit rider, his face was a familiar one in the area. Abram, as he was called by those who knew him, was always among the people in Jonesville and traveled far into the remote areas of the Blue Ridge Mountains. As a circuit rider, he was responsible for delivering the Methodist doctrine to the people of this region, regardless of where they lived, even when it meant traversing the dangerous mountain paths on horseback. Abram and his horse's shadow could be seen dancing along the ground in the setting sun as he rode along the mountain trails. It could have represented a silhouetted symbol and the only hope of the Christian faith for the mountain people. His Bible, strapped inside his leather saddle bag, bounced along and slapped the rear of his horse, echoing the rhythmic sound of the cadence. Abram's mission required him to ride out frequently to the surrounding Cumberland Mountains and preach his extemporaneous sermons. It was his responsibility to spread the church's message to those who otherwise would have no access to the Gospel.

While Abram was performing his duties as a circuit rider, his wife Martha Still remained at home. She had the responsibility for the care of their two sons, Edward, age three, and James, age two. Martha was pregnant with a third child and gave birth to another son on August 6, 1828. The child was named Andrew Taylor Still.[1]

---

1   Carol Trowbridge, Andrew Taylor Still, 1828-1917, 20.

Family picture of Abram, Martha, Edward, James, Andrew.
Used with permission of Museum of Osteopathic Medicine^{SM}, [1985.1056.03]

Restored Still cabin housed at ATSU museum.
Used with permission of Museum of Osteopathic Medicine^{SM}, [SM0172]

The intensity of their work resulted in Abram and Martha sharing an active six years of marriage. Besides Abram's time-consuming ministry, they were raising three sons and sharing the work of running the farm. Abram had been appointed to other important committee positions in the Methodist Church. He served the church, holding offices requiring different levels of responsibility, including organizing committees. These committees were aggressively attempting to expand the Methodist Christian doctrine across the country. While Abram had the opportunity to serve the church in many different capacities, the ministry he loved the most was circuit riding and taking the church to those in the remote hills and wilderness of the Blue Ridge Mountains. Abram had to frequently leave his family, which meant the children and the farm had to be managed by Martha Still. These circuit rides on horseback could require him to be absent for up to six weeks at a time because of the number of people who lived in the remote hills and valleys. [2]

Martha Still had adjusted and became comfortable with this lifestyle after she and Abram were married in 1822. When the newly-wedded couple settled in this beautiful area of Virginia, they were initially spared the separation of Abram's circuit riding for almost two years. However, in 1824 Abram's new circuit-riding responsibilities began for the church. For Martha, it meant a challenging life with little help with the chores, meager comforts, lonely isolation, and frequent pregnancies. In addition, she was raising the three boys, counting Andrew, often without her husband's male influence. Martha's life was filled with the increasing responsibilities of caring for the farm, the small children, and having to feed this expanding family. The time required for her to care for the family, the five-hundred-acre farm, and farm animals was daunting. She also began to worry about the children's future education and what that would mean for the boys, since there was only limited schooling in Jonesville, Virginia.

Abram had his own struggles to face when he rode out to begin a circuit tour. It was at times a rigorous endeavor he encountered on horseback. He would occasionally be forced to sleep in the open overnight and have little food available to eat during the trips in the remote areas of the mountains.

Abram Still, like many of the other Methodist missionaries, carried along with the word of the Gospel, the only medical care available to these backwoods areas. Many Methodist missionaries had taken time to learn about medical treatment. One of the medical text books they utilized was written

---

2   Charles E. Still, Jr., Frontier Doctor Medical Pioneer, 2.

6

by John Wesley, the founder of the Methodist Church. Abram's medical bible was the *Primitive Physicks: An Easy and Natural Way of Curing Most Diseases (1747)*, written by Wesley in an attempt to bring medical knowledge to the common person. The book was a composite of expertise of the medical authorities of the day such as Thomas Sydenham and George Cheyne. Included were treatments commonly used by the apothecaries of the times.[3] While Abram embraced the Wesley tradition of bringing medical care into the wilderness, he also blended and used the heroic Benjamin Rush treatments of bleeding, purging, and harsh medications as part of the therapy in his treatment of the sick. He carried the Bible to save the soul and used his medical knowledge to help save the body from disease. Abram and the Methodist ministers brought in their saddle bags the only treatment available in the wilderness and offered to the sick: simple and inexpensive medical treatment.

By the early 1830s, the Wesleyan methods of medical care had been used for almost a hundred years. This method offered the patients a shift from opium, steel, bark, and quicksilver and substituted a philosophy of disease prevention through exercise, cleanliness, rest, and temperance in both food and drink. Wesley's philosophy advocated the simple medical remedies that had been passed down for generations. This philosophy challenged the new medical recommendations as being technical, complicated, and harsh. The newer heroic treatments seemed to Wesley's proponents to be experimental and in reality unavailable to most of the people.[4]

Abram Still embraced the Wesley philosophy but he also used Rush's medical treatment and blended the two for use in his medical practice. This philosophy would later be passed down to his sons as the best way to practice medicine. The Wesleyan medical philosophy, however, was the one that was encouraged by the church missionaries. They continued to encourage the church's philosophy rather than the newer medical treatments. As a result, the Wesleyan medical practices were condemned by organized medicine since its philosophy threatened the authority of the emerging medical profession.

With Abram's medical knowledge and treatment skills, he developed the ability to administer the religious faith to the sick and dying, and provide care to those who were physically suffering, as well. He often found himself in these dual roles, like many of the isolated clergymen. Often the

---

3   Trowbridge, Andrew Taylor Still, 1828-1917, 15.
4   Ibid.

missionaries were the only educated people who visited these remote regions and their presence represented someone with authority who might offer medical comfort. The needs of the isolated frontiersmen were often spiritual and physical and were usually inseparable. Abram had to witness their agonies in whatever manner he found them. He dedicated his life to helping the people he served and, since he provided his medical skills, he was considered "their doctor." He was a comfort to his congregation in the wilderness.[5] Abram was the only one they had to provide their medical care but this added even greater responsibility to his ministry. It resulted in his being called away from his family even more.

The Still family worked hard in an effort to maintain the farm outside of Jonesville. When the boys became old enough to attend school, Martha's worries about the quality of their education proved to be justified in the classroom they traveled to by foot and horseback.

The description of the Jonesville school experience, given by Andrew many years later, suggested that the school was a single classroom and the pupils were taught the basic lessons in a collective manner. The teacher was characterized as an older man who had very little patience with the students. He would beat the children if they disappointed him in any way. The beatings were often severe. Sometimes the children were sent home at the end of the day with bruises and marks on their bodies from the vicious spankings he had given them. Martha Still had seen the injuries inflicted on her sons' bodies but was not sure how to stop the teacher from his brutal treatment of the pupils. If anything, the beatings had become worse and more frequent. Out of desperation, Martha began to appeal to Abram to ask for a new position which would allow them to move away and protect the children from this kind of brutal punishment. Andrew described this terrifying experience in his autobiography. His words were filled with emotion when he verbalized what he and the other children had experienced at the hands of the cruel teacher. The frustration of being tortured by an adult, who had been placed over him as an authoritative figure, had not been dimmed in his mind even as the years had gone by.[6]

"In due time I was sent off to school in a log school house, taught by an old man by the name of Vandeburgh. He looked wise while he was resting from his duties, which were to thrash the boys and girls, big and little, from 7 a.m. till 6 p.m., with a few lessons in spelling, reading, writing, grammar,

---

5   Lamps on the Prairie, 31.
6   Still, Autobiography, 17-18.

and arithmetic. Then the roll-call, with orders to go home and not fight on the road to and from the schoolhouse, and be on time at seven next morning to receive more thrashings, till the boys and girls would not have sense enough left to recite their lessons. Then he made us sit on a horse's skull-bone for our poor spelling, and pardoned our many sins with the 'sparing rod,' selecting the one suited to the occasion out of twelve which served in the walloping business, until 6 p.m."[7]

The children experienced daily terror as they sat at their desks while the professor paced up and down the aisles. Andrew's painful introduction to education had a lasting effect on him and the memory of this traumatic experience followed him to his grave.

The Stills had other stresses that entered the family while in Jonesville. Martha delivered their fourth child, a daughter, in 1830. The girl was named Barbara Jane. Approximately two years later, another addition, a fifth child, named Thomas, was delivered in 1833. This brought the number of children to five. When Abram was home from his circuit riding it meant that a family of seven shared a one-room farmhouse. These over-crowded living conditions, along with the lack of educational opportunities, reinforced Martha's persistence about leaving Jonesville, Virginia.

As a result, Abram requested a change in location from the Methodist church. He was appointed to new ministerial duties in New Market, Tennessee. In the summer of 1834, Abram, Martha, and their five children loaded two wagons hitched behind oxen, which would pull the family and their possessions toward the west to relocate in Tennessee. It would take a month for the Still family to reach their new destination.[8]

When they arrived at New Market, they encountered a very pleasant community with modern schools and facilities, including a framed house with several rooms waiting for them. The home they would occupy was described as also having a *"well-kept front yard and a small vegetable garden."*[9]

The educational commitment of the small town and the new school building on the hilltop was what impressed Martha. This had been her dream for the children and what she had been wishing for all these years. The fine brick school, named Holston Academy, overlooked New Market. The Academy was supported by the Methodist church and served the

---

7   Still, Autobiography, 17-18.
8   Still, Jr., Frontier Doctor, 4.
9   Ibid., 5.

community as an education center for the elementary and secondary grades. This meant that the Still children for the first time were in a more civilized and relatively cultured environment and given the chance to receive a formal education. They were also blessed with a dedicated educator by the name of Henry Saffel who headed the school and emphasized quality and sound course work.

As Andrew described, *"In 1834 my father was moved from that place of torture, which was at Jonesville, Lee County, Va., to Newmarket (sic.), Tenn. Then in 1835 I was entered for further schooling with two older brothers, as a student in the Holston College, which was under the control of the M. E. Church, and was located at New Market, Tenn. The school was conducted by Henry C. Saffel, a man of high culture, a head full of brains, without any trace of the brute in his work."*[10]

This was the educational opportunity that Martha had wanted so much for the three older boys. Their daughter, Barbara Jane, would not be able to attend the Academy since girls were not permitted admission. Abram Still would be associated with the Holston Academy as part of his duties in New Market. He would serve as the agent for the Academy which would require him to recruit potential students and to work as a fund raiser.[11]

In Martha's eyes, things could not have been better. She thought they finally had everything that a family could hope for. Her life in town was comfortable and Abram was at home to help her without the six-week absences she had lived with for the past ten years. Even when a sixth child came in 1836, another boy, named John Wesley, it must have seemed relatively easy with so much community attention available during the pregnancy and the birth of the baby. She had never experienced such luxury, security and support as that which surrounded her in New Market.[12]

This wonderful life for Martha and the children would last only three years because Abram was unsatisfied with his new position. He believed his calling and ministry was serving God in the wilderness and carrying His message to those in the isolated areas of the country. In New Market, the job had become almost totally an administrative position, contacting prospective students, and raising money for the school. He wasn't preaching as often as he wanted nor as he had been promised when he came to New Market.[13]

---

10   Still, Autobiography, 18.
11   Still, Frontier Doctor, 7.
12   Ibid.
13   Ibid., 7-8.

There was speculation that the curtailment of his preaching assignments was related to his attitude regarding slavery issues, which had spilled over into his sermons. Abram Still was a staunch abolitionist. Slavery was common in the fields of Tennessee and Abram's belief that slavery was wrong was not well received in New Market and the surrounding countryside.

Abram eventually became bored and restless with his administrative position. He yearned to ride out on horseback and to reach isolated families with his extemporaneous sermons as an evangelist. He longed to once again build Christianity in the wilderness, and he missed his calling in the wild. Everything else in Abram's life was secondary to his spiritual zeal for the church—including the comforts and the education that his family enjoyed in New Market.[14]

Abram requested a change of duties and asked the Methodist Church for another assignment again in the wilderness as a church circuit rider. The Methodist Church honored his request and sent him to spread the Gospel in the sparsely populated areas of northern Missouri. This meant that Martha and the children would have to give up their comforts in New Market, Tennessee. They began packing up their belongings for the trip into the wilderness of Missouri. Andrew summed it up for the children in the family, *"We bade adieu to the fine brick college at Holston, and at the end of seven weeks' journey reached our destination, and found we were in a country where there were neither schools, churches, nor printing presses, so here our schooling ended until 1839."*[15]

---

14   Still, Frontier Doctor, 7-8.
15   Still, Autobiography, 18.

CHAPTER TWO
The Northern Missouri Wilderness

Abram, Martha Still, and their six children had only recently become a family who had learned to enjoy the luxuries of living in the civilized environment of New Market, Tennessee. Now, they were a transformed frontier family headed straight for the untamed wilderness of northern Missouri. They would be living with only the necessities and comforts available to them, which were dictated by the packing space in the two wagons hauling them farther west. They were leaving the comfortable life they had experienced in New Market and the conveniences of residing in a community. What they now faced would be living with only a few essentials that they could carry in the wagons to provide for their basic needs. That would be no easy task because they were a family traveling with six children whose requirements varied drastically, with ages ranging from one to thirteen years. They were heading for an almost totally uninhabited area of the country. There would not be a four room, framed house with a vegetable garden in front waiting for them when they arrived at their destination. Nor would there be schools for the children for the continuation of their education. With each turn of the wagon wheels, they were moving toward northern Missouri and a life of isolation, relative loneliness, and a situation of making do-with-what-you-have. It was a life Martha Still knew all too well. She also realized that her new life potentially could become a far greater challenge than she had experienced in the past in Jonesville. She would be returning to a life of bearing the majority of the responsibility of caring for the children alone—with little help from Abram—and this time without a comfortable house or crops waiting to be harvested to sustain them. How they were going to survive in the wilderness, where the food would come from, and how they were going to cope with the isolation were questions yet to be answered. The only financial help they had was seven hundred dollars paid in cash in advance by the Methodist Church to get them started in establishing a foothold for the church.

They also had Abram's daydreams to listen to in his effort to build enthusiasm for the long trip ahead. Abram only looked at the bright side of going to northern Missouri. He dwelled on things that were full of speculation and promises. He talked about the inexpensive land available for farming. He tried to win the support of their oldest son, Edward, who had reached the age of thirteen, with the promise of helping him start his own farmstead, and convinced all of the other boys they were going to a place where hunting would be plentiful.[16]

The opportunities available in northern Missouri would depend on the perspective of each member of the family. Obviously, Abram was happy, excited, and could not wait to return to the horseback ministry that he loved. The older boys looked forward to the hunting, fishing, and adventure. At their ages, the adventurous and exciting frontier life, without having to attend school, would have had strong appeal. Since Barbara had not been enrolled in school, she probably was more concerned about not having any girls to associate with other than her mother. And the baby's needs were Martha's concern.

The immediate challenge that faced them was the hundreds of miles they had to travel to get to their destination; the major rivers they had to cross to get there; and the weather they would encounter during their trek.

The Still family had learned to travel together by ox-driven carts three years previously when they moved from Jonesville, Virginia, to New Market, Tennessee. But that trip had taken only a month to reach their destination; this one would take almost twice as long to travel the longer distance. There were other major differences between the two trips. They were aware that at the end of this journey there would not be an entire community waiting for them with comfortable accommodations for their recovery, support and help upon their arrival, and the security of having a small community to count on for their needs.

They were grateful that at least the weather during the first part of the trip had been comfortable and they moved along unimpeded with horse-driven wagons. As the family approached the Mississippi River, they could hear sounds coming from the steamboats going up and down the waterway. When they came to the riverbank not far from Cairo, Illinois, they were able to see the *"largest moving object they had ever seen"* as the steamboats came rumbling by them. They would have to cross the Ohio River where it emptied into the Mississippi near Cairo. That meant locating a loading dock and going aboard a horse-drawn ferryboat. After crossing the Ohio River, they were able to set up camp along the banks of the

---

16   Still, Frontier Doctor, 9.

Mississippi River, on the Illinois side. The trip had gone reasonably well up to this point.[17] And then the rain started.

The weather had changed from fair to a torrential rain. The roads became quagmires. The wagons "*for the next twelve days...wallowed through one mud hole after another...The boys spent most of their time standing knee-deep in mud, pushing the wagons toward the Mississippi River crossing. By the time the Still wagons had reached a place on the river opposite Saint Louis, the wagons, horses, and most of the family were caked with black Illinois soil...It took nearly two days to get the caked mud off the horses and wagons, and the children needed several scrubbings before they were allowed to put on their Sunday clothes.*"[18]

At this point in their journey they were a family who had achieved approximately the midpoint of their destination, had successfully made it through the muddy passage caused by the heavy rain, and were now ready to cross the Mississippi River from its east bank to enter the city of Saint Louis on the west side of the river. After reaching Saint Louis the Still family attended services at the Methodist Church. A minister by the name of Reverend Harmon delivered the sermon that Sunday. The message during the sermon must likely have been very inspirational. Abram met with the minister after the service and their conversation must have included questions about Abram's mission for the Methodist Church in northern Missouri. Undoubtedly the money that had been given to Abram by the church had entered the discussion. The resident minister asked Abram to loan him some of the money *"without security, payable in six months."*[19] Despite the fact that Abram had just met the minister, he felt compelled to give him the entire seven hundred dollars. This stipend was every penny he had to make the journey and to start a new home. He gave away all of the money he had, to a total stranger, and placed his entire family in peril—even with the possibility of starvation. Later, the decision to loan this money would turn out to have severe consequences.

It would be up to Martha to navigate the family through the dilemma. They were in the middle of their journey to northern Missouri and suddenly they were broke. She earlier had the foresight and discipline to save money secretly for a number of years—just in case they ever ran into hard times. By hiding small amounts, here and there, she had managed to accumulate three hundred dollars of her own. Now, every dime she had saved would

---

17   Still, Frontier Doctor, 9.
18   Ibid., 10.
19   Still, Autobiography, 51.

be needed for their housing and subsistence needs. Andrew later wrote: *"Mother had a little bag of money ($350), and that was our pile for the wilderness life before us for six months or longer."*[20]

When the journey finally ended in Macon County, Missouri, *"Even before they moved into their new home and before the wagons were completely unloaded, Abram was on horseback, off doing what he loved so much: riding to isolated farm families, bringing the word of God to northern Missouri ...What was left of Martha's nest egg was quickly spent on staples to carry the family through the early part of the winter. Too soon the cold arrived in Macon County...During the long cold winter of 1836-1837, with little food to eat...The family's second daughter, Mary, was born...adding another mouth to feed."*[21]

The only way the family survived this ordeal and the cold, hard winter of 1836-1837 was by the hard work provided by Martha and the children. Each member had to contribute toward their survival. The boys had to be mentally and physically tough well beyond their ages. If it were not for their perseverance as hunters, the risk of starvation would have been even more profound. Nothing was wasted from the animals they killed to eat. The meat from the deer, wild turkey, and prairie chickens made up their meals. Martha learned to tan the deer hides and sew and construct the heavier clothing required in this rugged part of Missouri. The animal skins and pelts that were not used for making their own clothing were sold; and the money the boys received was used for replenishment of basic food and supplies for the family to survive. They all suffered a great deal during the worst of the winter months.

When the pain of the cold wind finally eased and the early signs of spring approached, they realized they had survived the ordeal and they rejoiced. They showed their thankfulness to the Lord: *"One evening, when Abraham was home, the entire family spent the time on their knees offering prayers of thanksgiving for their deliverance."*[22] The suffering during those winter months was directly related to Abram's seven-hundred dollar loan to the St. Louis minister. As a result, the family was unable to purchase the things they needed to get through the terrible winter. Andrew later expressed the agony of this painful struggle and the grueling efforts he shared with his family at the age of nine. Years later, his feelings were still filled

---

20   Still, Autobiography, 51.
21   Still, Frontier Doctor, 11-12.
22   Ibid., 13.

with bitterness when he wrote *"Brother Harmon did not pay father for eight years, then only paid the principal. By this time father learned that some preachers were not of God, but dirty liars, just the same as some other people are. He was very much disappointed and disgusted to learn that a professional minister would play a confidence game and rob him of the money he had brought with him to support his family while in his missionary work in the wilds of North Missouri. Hard times soon began to close upon us. Money all gone, clothing worn out, and winter on us with all its fury. Our show for shoes was to tan deerskins and make moccasins, or go barefooted-deerskin pants or naked legs. Labor by day was worth twenty-five cents, so you see money meant much work."*[23]

It had been a long and bitter winter and the family was fortunate to have survived.

When the spring of 1837 arrived, the family must have welcomed the flowers and buds popping out of the ground and on the trees. The white frozen landscape was finally melting away and being replaced with a fresh green-colored blanket. It was time to go to work in northern Missouri. The Stills had to continue to rebuild their lives and prepare for the future. There were acres of ground remaining to be broken with plows and crops to be planted. Animals had to be found and bought. Pigs and cows were needed for the family's immediate and future needs. This was the time to plan and prepare for the next winter—to plant seeds that would produce vegetables and fruits to be harvested and stored for food well in advance of the cold weather's arrival. They began preparing immediately to meet these needs for the living conditions in the wilderness and to prevent the suffering they had experienced during their first winter in Missouri. This work had to be done, and it meant that the Still boys had to do the majority of the hard physical labor. The farm work required them to toil from sun up to sun down. They had to plant and care for sufficient crops to support the livestock and the family. It was absolutely essential for survival. And it left no time for anything else. As a result, the Still's children had no time for schooling for the next two years.

When the Still boys were not working the teams of animals behind a plow, they were honing their hunting skills. They continued to learn more about guns, ammunition and hunting dogs. Andrew had a particular interest in hunting dogs and over time he developed and refined his skills on how to judge the qualities of these animals. He became an expert on the subject.

---

23   Still, Autobiography, 51-52.

It was not hard to understand his interest in dogs since they played such a large role in whether a hunt would be successful. After he arrived in northern Missouri he was able to obtain three hunting dogs. His dogs were well bred and trained. He also had his own rifle. Andrew described this frontier period of his early life in detail. *"That autumn we felled trees in the woods, and built a log cabin eighteen by twenty feet in size, seven feet high with dirt floor, and one whole log or pole left out of the side wall to admit light, through sheeting tacked over the space so we could see to read and write. ...I was like all boys, a little lazy and fond of a gun. I had three dogs—a spaniel for the water, a hound for the fox and a bulldog for bear and panthers. My gun for many years was the old flint-lock, which went chuck, fizz, bang; so you see, to hit where you wanted to, you had to hold still a long time—and, if the powder was damp in the pan, much longer, for there could be no bang until the fizzing was exhausted, and fire could reach the touch-hole leading to the power-charge behind the hall [sic]. All this required skill and a steady nerve, to hit the spot."*[24]

Andrew's reputation for having the ability to judge dogs grew over time and his innate ability to see anatomical details was appreciated in his selection of the dogs he considered to be of good quality. Other people asked his opinion when it came time for them to select a dog.

"I was called a good judge of dogs, and quoted as authority on the subject. A hound, to be a great dog, must have a flat, broad, and thin tongue, deep-set eyes, thin, long ears, very broad, raised some at the head, and hanging three inches below the under-jaw. The roof of his mouth had to be black, the tail long and very slim, for good coon-dog. Such kind of pups I was supposed to sell for a dollar each, though I usually gave them away. When I went to the woods, armed with my flint-lock and accompanied by my three dogs, they remained with me until I said, 'seize him, Drummer!' which command sent Drummer out on a prospecting trip. When I wanted squirrels I threw a stick up a tree and cried: 'Hunt him up, Drummer!' In a short time the faithful beast had treed a squirrel. When I wanted deer I hunted toward the wind, keeping Drummer behind me. When he scented a deer he walked under my gun, which I carried point front. I was always warned by his tail falling that I was about as close as I could get to my game without starting it up from the grass."[25]

---

24   Still, *Autobiography*, 18-21.
25   Ibid., 21-22.

At this time in America, the country experienced both a political change in the presidential office and a technological change in weaponry. Andrew moved from a flintlock to a cap-explosion rifle that was much easier to load and fire. It also was extremely accurate. He described the changes in his weaponry as making it possible for him to become an expert marksman. *"This old-fashion flint-lock hunting was under the Van Buren and Polk's administration; but when Harrison—" "old Tip"—came in, I possessed a cap-lock gun. Now I was a man." "Big Injun me." To pull the trigger was "bang" at once, and I was able to shoot deer "on the run." Shot-guns were not in use at that time, but the frontiersman became very expert with the rifle. I could hit a hawk, wild goose, or any bird that did not fly too high or too fast for my aim. I killed a great number of deer, turkeys, eagles, wild-cats, and foxes. My frontier life made me very fleet of foot."*[26]

From the description given by Andrew of his early days in Missouri, it would appear that he was very happy, independent and was given the freedom to explore the woods that surrounded his family's farm. His growing up in the woods required him to develop skills out of necessity. He was expected, along with his brothers, to be resourceful, almost responsible for his own care, and was looked upon by the rest of the family as a capable hunter who could provide the meat for the dinner table. His resourcefulness in hunting at the end of a long work day was later documented.

"the following winter we caught a mink, and concluded to go to market with its fur as we must have a five-cent bar of lead before we could shoot other game. So I saddled my horse Selim, and went to Bloomington (nine miles) to exchange my mink-skin for lead. The barter was made with my good friend Thomas Sharp...and soon the hide was with his other furs, from coons and possums. I then started home to tell Jim, (his brother) *that I had found a permanent market for mink-skins at five cents apiece. In a short time I shot a deer, and had a buckskin to add to the fur trade, and took my 'big' fifty cents in powder, lead and caps."*[27]

Andrew knew he was fortunate to have the woods at his back door and had a profound respect for nature and the life he enjoyed in northern Missouri. He explained his feeling about learning from nature by later writing *"The lad of the frontier enjoys many thrilling adventures with wild animals of which the city boy can know nothing save what he reads in books. If he is observing he learns more of the habits and customs of the wild*

---

26   Still, Autobiography, 22.
27   Ibid., 22-23.

animals he comes in contact with, than he can gain by a course in natural history, for he has the great book of nature constantly spread before him... It was invaluable in my scientific researches. Before I had ever studied anatomy books I had almost perfected the knowledge from the great book of nature. The skinning of squirrels brought me into contact with muscles, nerves, and veins. The bones, the great foundation of the wonderful house we live in, were always a study to me long before I learned the hard names given to them by the scientific world."[28]

Andrew described one of his early hunting adventures that illustrated his mental development in processing information regarding comparative anatomical details through analytical observations.

"[W]hen I was eight years old... 'bang' went a big gun from the back of our house, about a quarter of a mile away. My mother came running to us, and said: ...I expect Judge Cochran has killed a buck. He said he was going out to look for deer at the spring-lick where they came to drink the water that flowed out of the hill, and promised us venison for supper... Soon the Judge was in the dooryard... He said the deer was lying over at the lick, and he would saddle up a horse and bring it in... I jumped on behind the judge, and away we went. In a few minutes we were at the lick, and dismounted by the dead deer, which was the most wonderful thing I had ever seen. It was about five feet long, from end of its nose to the tip of its tail, near four feet high when standing, and its tail was about one foot long. Its feet and mouth were very much like those of a sheep, except the feet were very sharp-pointed. Its hair was about the color of an Irishman's whiskers. Its legs and feet were very nice and trim, not much larger than a broomstick, but about three feet long. I thought, Oh! how fast he could run, before he departed this life, to cheer our table. A deer can jump as far in one jump as a boy can in six, or about fifty or sixty feet when running down a hill. He can jump over a man's head and never touch his hat."[29]

Andrew, in his description of the deer that was killed for the family to eat, demonstrated his innate and astute ability for comparative anatomy even though seen through the eyes of an eight-year-old boy. The characteristics of each detail of the dead deer such as the dimensions of size, color, the shape of the hoof, limb diameter, similarities and dissimilarities compared to other animals he had seen, were mentally noted. Andrew didn't just see a dead deer lying at the salt lick that day, he saw a wonderful animal

---

28   Still, Autobiography, 34, 43-44.
29   Ibid., 34-36.

specimen and he began doing something unconsciously that would characterize his genius. He began to mentally categorize every anatomical detail and the relationships of everything he saw.

Despite his isolation, Andrew would become well educated by the woods. His great book was nature and it was always open to his sharp comparative eyes which stored the details in a very organized fashion. He had an unquenchable fascination about how things were put together and what made them work. He studied the animals in a way that must have been very meticulous and time consuming.

After the hunt, he dissected the animals in such a way that he looked for variations in their form and structure and memorized the anatomy. The dissected structures and interrelated parts were categorized and Andrew noted each detail carefully. He seemed to welcome the complicated challenge of learning about the bones, muscles, and joints and all the anatomical details that made up these animals. He tried to correlate his findings and wondered if he could apply the information he had learned from the animal dissections to human anatomy. Hunting served a dual purpose for Andrew. It filled his family's table with meat at mealtime, and the animals provided an anatomy lesson. The hunting of the animals also provided physical exercise while the dissections stimulated and disciplined his intellect and curiosity. *"His interest in learning from nature kept widening."*[30]

Sometimes the hunt mainly supplied adventure. As Andrew recalls a particular hunting experience, *"An adventure I once had with a wounded buck about twelve years later, when I was almost a young man. One day I was out with my gun and three dogs, when I heard a noise come thrashing through the brush towards me, and soon a buck came in sight. He had nine points on each horn, and was more than three times as large as the one Judge Cochran killed. I began to realize the danger of an encounter with such a monster, if I missed my mark. Realizing that if I killed him I was safe, and if I missed him he would kill me unless my dogs could save me, I raised my gun when he was within a few feet. Bang went my gun, and down went the deer… I walked toward the deer, supposing him dead, but when I got very close, to my amazement he raised his head… so I climbed a tree…and had the presence of mind enough to take my gun with me. From my perch I loaded and fired until I killed him. My three dogs were pulling away at him…and I had to use great caution to shoot the deer without killing my dogs, for they and the deer were fighting for life. I have since seen*

---

30   Still, *Frontier Doctor*, 13-14.

men grapple in a death struggle, but I don't believe I ever witnessed a more desperate encounter. I was not the first man who had shot him, for when I skinned him I found several balls that had penetrated his hide, all failing to reach a vital point. "[31]

Andrew's daily life growing up in northern Missouri, are a reminder that his life was one of heavy toil and labor. His daily routine and the amount of work and responsibility assigned to him and his brothers is a stunning reminder of the difference between the teenage years they experienced compared to most of their contemporaries. The teenage years so often described in the civilized part of America were filled with daydreams, schooling challenges, and the misadventures in the growing-up process. Andrew and his brothers on the other hand were working on the farm in the role of hardened farm laborers. There was little, if any, time for figuring out what they wanted to be when they became adults. The boys were already working and functioning physically as adults, and in their case, it meant hard labor every day. By Andrew's description, there was no time for wistful teenage daydreams.

"My father owned a farm and raised a large amount of corn, and had a great many horses, mules, cattle, sheep, and hogs to feed on it, so our crops were consumed at home. We had so much corn to husk and crib that we were compelled to commence very early, in order to get it stored away before cold weather. When we were all in our teens, my eldest brother nineteen, the next seventeen, and myself about fifteen, we gathered corn from early morn till late in the evenings, fed the stock, ate our supper, and prepared for a good hunt for coons, foxes, possums, and skunks. We always took a gun, an ax, a big butcher-knife, and flint and steel to make fire. We had a polished cow's horn which we could blow as loud as the horns that overthrew the walls of Jericho. As brother Jim was a great talker, we made him chief horn-blower. He went into the yard, and bracing himself, tooted and tooted and split the air for miles, while the dogs collected around him and roared and howled. You never heard such sweet music as brother Jim and the dogs made. Shortly after the melodies began, we were in the line of march, front, middle, and rear rank, and soon journeyed to the woods to hunt opossums, polecats, coons, wildcats, foxes, and turkeys. Our dogs had a classic education, hunting and killing all classes of varmints." [32]

---

31   Still, Autobiography, 36-38.
32   Ibid., 39.

As a boy, Andrew was strong and healthy but suffered intermittently with severe headaches. He would experience excruciating pain when one of them came upon him but he also feared the drug treatment that his father had given him during one of his attacks. The drug was Calomel. It was a mercury compound and a drug used to treat many different diseases and afflictions. Some patients reacted to the drug with severe gastric pain and bloody diarrhea. It also changed the color of the tongue and throat to a gray ashen color and loosened teeth as a long term complication. Almost everyone treated with the drug experienced uncontrollable salivation described as profuse drooling. It stimulated secretions in the mouth dramatically. Those who had been given the drug for treatment were said to have been "salivated."[33]

The drug had produced many of these side effects in Andrew. He had suffered the *"salivation treatment"* and would later complain, *"it loosened my teeth...I lived in a day and generation when people had no more intelligence than to make cinnabar of my jawbone."*[34] At that time Andrew may have suspected in his own mind that the treatment was harmful, even if his father thought the medicine was useful. He must have made a firm commitment following the "calomel" experience that he would rather bear the pain of the headaches and suffer because he never took the calomel medication again.[35]

By accident, following the unpleasant drug treatment, he learned a method to control his painful headaches in a very unusual way. Andrew later explained what happened on that day and also shared his fears about Calomel and many of the other drugs used by his father and other doctors to treat patients. *"Early in life I began to hate drugs. One day, when I was about ten years old, I suffered from a headache. I made a swing of my father's plow-line between two trees; but my head hurt too much to make swinging comfortable, so I let the rope down to about eight or ten inches of the ground, threw the end of a blanket on it, and I lay down on the ground and used the rope for a swing pillow. Thus I lay stretched on my back, with my neck across the rope. Soon I became easy and went to sleep, got up in a little while with headache gone. As I knew nothing of anatomy at this time I took no thought of how a rope could stop headache and the sick stomach*

---

33   Trowbridge, Andrew Taylor Still, 17.
34   Ibid.
35   Ibid.

which accompanied it. After that discovery I roped my neck whenever I felt one of those spells coming on. "[36]

Andrew had found a way to obtain relief from the headaches. At this time in his life he did not understand how or why applying rope pressure to the back of his neck could make the headache pain go away but it worked every time and brought him relief. He did not understand the significance of this observation. However, it would later change his life and the way he would approach treating patients without the use of drugs and to offer them an alternative to relieve their symptoms. His experience with Calomel and the side effects it produced probably began Andrew's phobia about drugs. He had experienced firsthand what it was like to be poisoned with the mercurial compound called "calomel." The drug would later be shown to be severely toxic to humans by causing severe damage to tissue, especially the kidneys and central nervous system. Andrew's reaction to calomel would later cause him to question other drugs that physicians were using to treat disease. His distrust of medical treatment continued to be reinforced as he observed his father's use of Rush's *"bleeding, purging, and blistering"* methods.[37]

When Andrew reached his teenage years he was full of energy and desired to prove his manhood. Most of his adventures with danger had taken place in the woods while he and his brothers hunted wild animals. One episode was different from the others he remembered. It particularly stuck out in his mind. Andrew, like most teenagers, must have felt the need to prove himself worthy of having been brought into the world. Like most nineteen year old young men, Andrew looked up to the men in uniform, as a role model for courage. In 1847, the United States was involved in the War with Mexico, and the soldiers were seen passing through Missouri on their way to the California Trail to fight in the conflict. Andrew wanted to enlist in the Army and join the battle. He later described this time in his life.

"During the year 1847, when the United States and old Mexico were fighting like two she-tigers, I wanted to go fight Mexicans. Being under age, my father would not consent to my going into the service. One day while riding on horse-back, I was boiling over with fight, my blood was at its highest heat, and I felt that I could thrash all such fellows, as Sampson, John Sullivan, Fitzsimmons, and Corbett, I raised my head and looked in front of me about one hundred paces. I saw something lying across the road

---

36   Still, Autobiography, 32.
37   Trowbridge, Andrew Taylor Still, 19.

which I took to be a fence-rail or a pole about three or four inches in diameter. I gave no further thought to it until I traveled about the distance to where I thought I had seen it. I looked backward and forward in search of my pole, but it had disappeared, and as it was very hot that day, I began to wonder if I had been asleep and had seen a pole in my dream. A few more steps brought me up to a place in the road which was very dusty, and I was dumbfounded to see the track of the snake in the road."[38]

"The imprint in the soft dust was about an inch deep and something over a foot wide. On discovering it was a snake-track without mistake I knew I could get war and plenty of it without going to Mexico. I rode out into the weeds, which were about a foot high, in the direction I thought I was most likely to find him. I found Mr. Snake coiled up; coil, snake, and all would easily have filled a half-bushel. He raised his head two feet above the ground, and fixed his eyes on me. His head measured about three inches across, just back of the eyes. I knew well enough if this snake was ten feet long he could jump his length. To run was cowardice, to fight was dangerous. The thought came into my mind, how will it look in a young man who wants to fight all Mexico to back out and run from a snake? I had seen the snake, and could not tell mother it had run off and I could not find it. In desperation I took the stirrup-strap off my saddle, to which was attached a very heavy iron stirrup, and with a great amount of emotion in both legs approached, the general commanding the opposite side. He had ordered music by the band, which band was twenty-nine rattles fastened to the rear rank of his whole army. I gave the command in a low whisper to strike. With a circuitous swing with the strap and stirrup, which weighed about one pound and a half, I unjointed the general's neck and took his whole army prisoners. I lined it up on dress parade, and found he was three full steps long and one foot over, with twenty-nine rattles, which equals seven inches, making the snake a fraction over ten feet long. Thus ended the greatest snake fight I ever had."[39]

These years in northern Missouri, which consisted of hard work, labor, and adventurous hunting, occurred between 1837 and 1847 and corresponded in Andrew's life to age ten through twenty. According to Andrew there was also some intermittent schooling during this period. The continued interruptions in his education were due primarily to the amount of work he was required to perform and directly related to his father's broad

38   Still, Autobiography, 46.
39   Ibid., 46-47.

church responsibilities. The areas assigned to his father to be covered through his traveling ministry were *"five different circuits: Macon, Goshen, Waterloo, Edina, and Spring Creek."* There was also another interim move to Schuyler County, Missouri, *"for a couple of years so Abraham could spread Methodism farther to the north and west."*[40] These uproots resulted in many different teachers taking part in Andrew and his brothers' education along the way.

Andrew attempted to explain this broken education in his autobiography. *"In the year of 1827(sic), [1837], my father was appointed by the M.E. conference of Tennessee as a missionary to Missouri. Then my father and six or eight others hired a man by the name of J. D. Halstead to teach us as best he could during the winter of 1839-40. He was very rigid, but not so brutal as Vandeburgh. The spring in 1840 took us from Macon County to Schuyler County, Missouri, and I received no further schooling until 1842. This institution of learning was conducted by John Mikel....he was good to his pupils, and they advanced rapidly under his training. The summer of 1843 Mr. John Hindmon...taught a three months term, during which mental improvement was noted.*[41]

In 1845, Andrew entered a school at La Plata, Missouri, taught by Rev. Samuel Davidson, and in the summer of 1848 attended school, *"wholly to the science of number, under Nicholas Langston, who was a wonderful mathematician. I stayed with him until I had mastered the cube, and square root in Ray's third part Arithmetic."*[42]

These broken time periods of formal schooling spent with multiple educators had an accumulative affect on Andrew's intellect, but the major educational interest that was shaping his life centered on medicine. Beginning in 1849, Andrew began to pursue his educational goal of learning about medicine and its application by observing the practice of medicine from his father. Andrew would acquire these skills by accompanying his father when he rode out to call on the isolated parishioners in the wilderness. This kind of medical training was referred to as the preceptor method and was the way that one eventually earned the distinction of being recognized as a medical doctor. The time required to serve the preceptor as a student was typically two years. During this time *"the student doctor mixed medicines,*

---

40   Still, Frontier Doctor, 11.
41   Still, Autobiography, 18-20.
42   Ibid., 21.

observed patients, and learned the therapy. This practical experience was supplemented by reading the medical books in the physician's library."[43]

There were few formal medical schools in the country and only six years had gone by since the first major operation utilizing anesthetics had been performed at Massachusetts General Hospital in 1846. Medical training was in its infancy and only a limited number of printed medical books were available. During the time period that Andrew was learning how to treat and care for the sick at his father's side, there were no licenses necessary or requirements that had to be met to practice medicine. Furthermore, there were no procedures available to officially earn a formal medical degree. Andrew would earn his own reputation by working with his father, providing medical care during the years they spent in northern Missouri. He would become known as a medical doctor by the time he reached twenty.

Also by the time Andrew had reached twenty, he had other things on his mind. His eye for the ladies became his primary focus. He was not long in this pursuit when he spied Mary Vaughn. Andrew Still fell in love with this woman and wanted to devote his life to her. "*The school boy days, the days of youthful trials and sports, passed like vanishing joys, and I arrived at man's estate. I will omit my later schooling, and medical training, and merely state that, like my 'Father who art in heaven,' I thought it not good to be alone, and began to go on dress parade, to see how the girls would like the looks of a young soldier. Like Bunyan, I shouldered my arms and marked time, until a loving eye was fixed on mine. Behind that eye was the form of Mary M. Vaughn, the daughter of Philamon Vaughn. She was to me beautiful, kind, active, and abounded in love and good sense. She loved God and all His ways.*"[44]

Andrew proposed marriage to Mary and a date was set. His exuberance at being her husband and his hard work to be her provider was passionately described. "*After a few words by Rev. Lorenzo Waugh at her mother's house on January 29th, 1849, her name was changed to Mrs. M.M. Still...I took my wife to our new home, on eighty acres of land one mile from my old home.*"[45]

Despite a colossal effort in their first year of marriage to produce a bountiful harvest on their new farm, the work ended like so many other dreams—in disaster. A hail storm reduced his corn crop into utter ruin. In only a few minutes, the months of backbreaking plowing, planting,

---

43   Trowbridge, Andrew Taylor Still, 53.
44   Still, Autobiography, 55.
45   Ibid.

weeding, and care were wiped out. Not only the corn, but every living creature including the birds, rabbits, and squirrels were destroyed. *"I was young and stout, worked early and late, put in sixty acres of corn and kept it clean. It was a beauty, all in silk and tassel. I was proud of it. I began to feel that I would soon have a crib filled with many thousand bushels. The morning of the 4th of July (the day we love to celebrate) came, and I was full of joy and hope. At 3 p.m. a dark cloud arose, which at 4 showered three inches of hail over every acre of my corn not leaving a single stalk nor a blade of fodder in all my sixty acres. Nor did it leave a bird or a rabbit alive on my farm. All were dead."*[46]

Andrew and Mary's corn productivity had failed but there was another major productive event that occurred in their first year of marriage. On December 8, 1849, a daughter by the name of Marusha Hale Still, was brought into the lives of this married couple.[47]

Andrew and Mary's dreams of beginning their married life with a successful farm had been wiped out in only a few minutes, but Andrew accepted this failure and he later wrote *"The Lord loveth whom He chasteneth. I had no corn, and he, whose crop was not torn to shreds like mine, would have some to sell, so after all, things, as usual, were about evened up. I taught school that fall and winter at $15 per month, and thus ended my first year of married life."*[48]

While Abram and Martha Still watched Andrew and the other children mature into adults, their lives continued to be filled with conflict. The horseback ministry that Abram had returned to in northern Missouri was exactly what he desired. He would once again establish himself as a dedicated Methodist missionary and an excellent medical care giver in the wilderness. Abram would be well received and admired among the isolated parishioners he served. Many of the people he ministered to depended on him for their medical care.

But, what Abram had not considered in his move to Missouri, was how the passage of the Missouri Compromise Bill in 1820 would eventually affect his ability to function as an abolitionist-minister in northern Missouri. The law meant that slavery had been officially legalized seventeen years before Abram's arrival and would become an accepted practice in all of the

---

46   Still, Autobiography, 55-56.
47   Trowbridge, Andrew Taylor Still, 202.
48   Still, Jr., Autobiography, 56.

state. Over time, slavery would become a part of the growing farming community's labor force in northern Missouri, as well.

Abram had always been a staunch abolitionist. He first became familiar with slavery through his father's farm located in Asheville, North Carolina. At the time he did not view these black workers as slaves but later witnessed some of them being treated in an inhumane manner. Abram could not rationalize this behavior because it was inconsistent with his Christian beliefs. He felt obligated to take a stand against this practice. Later he began to challenge its morality and carried this belief into his sermons. This stance put him at odds on multiple fronts. First and foremost were the philosophical conflicts with the slave owners. Secondly, were the members in his congregation who viewed slavery differently. Some members believed slavery "*was of divine origin.*"[49] Moreover, the Methodist Church itself had not proclaimed a formal position regarding slavery in states that had legalized its practice.

Since most of the farming was done in the southern part of Missouri, Abram had thought it unlikely that slavery would become much of an issue in the area he was to serve. He had been mistaken. There had been an increasing movement of farmers into northern Missouri because the land was inexpensive and the weather and soil conditions were suitable for growing tobacco. However, the tobacco crop was labor intensive because it required constant worming and weeding. This work meant the use of slaves to produce a crop that was in great demand. A field of tobacco *"was as good as cash"* and these farmers were not about to give up a successful agricultural business because a Methodist minister had taken the view that the use of slaves was inconsistent with Christianity.[50]

This influx of new people meant setting up many new churches to accommodate the farmers and Abram was directly involved in this expansion. He was required to preach at these new churches and his sermons were full of antislavery comments. This view was not well received by many in the congregation. The more complaints he received from the laity, the more fire he put into the sermons. The initial polite suggestions from the church members to tone down his antislavery rhetoric eventually grew into disruptions of his sermons and threats of physical violence, including *"tar and feathers."* This anger against Abram and his sermons, which characterized

49   Still, Frontier Doctor, 15.
50   Trowbridge, Andrew Taylor Still, 34.

the slave owners as *"godless,"* escalated into threats against his life with a bullet.[51]

Andrew described the situation in Missouri and the effect it had on his father at that time: *"He was a man of strong convictions, which he maintained at all times and places. He took a bold stand for abolition...the latter part of the struggle was full of bitterness, and tar and feathers were strong arguments at that time and were freely used, but not being strong enough, they finally gave place to ropes and bullets."*[52]

This slavery issue had also escalated for the Methodist Church nationally and created a major division among its membership. The dissension finally reached such fervor in 1844 that the church split into two separate units: the Methodist Episcopal Church South and the Methodist Episcopal Church North. [It was a division that would last almost a hundred years.] Since Missouri was a legal slave state, the majority of the churches, eighty-six out of one hundred, gave their allegiance to the southern side.[53]

Abram was finally given an ultimatum. He was asked to either join and support the proslavery position of the new southern church or leave it. The end result was that Abram lost his job because he would not budge from his position against slavery. However, he was not abandoned by the northern church and unofficially was assigned to the Iowa Methodist church conference for the next three years. In 1848, the Methodist Church North reorganized in northern Missouri and Abram was appointed to the position of presiding elder. Despite the northern church's support for Abram and the shuffling around to protect his life, the church was acutely aware of his constant danger and the threats to kill him. These threats were becoming intense and more frequent. The Methodist Church had to protect Abram even if Abram refused to recognize the imminent danger. The church desired to send Abram to a place that would offer him and his family the safety they deserved. They were aware of his almost certain death if he remained in Missouri. Finally, in 1850, Abram agreed to go to the Indian Territory of eastern Kansas and serve as the Presiding Elder of a newly proposed Shawnee Indian Mission school to be constructed.[54]

Once again, Abram had to face his wife Martha Still and convince her to move once more—this time to the Kansas Indian Territory to work

51   Still, Frontier Doctor, 15-16.
52   Still, Autobiography, 54.
53   Trowbridge, Andrew Taylor Still, 34.
54   Still, Frontier Doctor, 17.

with the Shawnee Indians. This was not going to be easy. In fact, it was the same tribe of Indians that had almost wiped out her entire family several years earlier. Among those massacred were her Grandfather Moore, Grandmother Moore, and all but two of their seven children. Martha's father James Moore was one of the lucky survivors and an Indian captive for years following the attacks. Martha had told the family story about Abb's Valley many times and could not believe that Abram could possibly be suggesting she go to the Kansas Territory and live among the same savages who had destroyed her family. The story of Abb's Valley would now need to be resurrected once again as a reminder of what had happened to her family and a warning of what could happen again. The details of the story were evidence that the encounters between her family and the Shawnee had resulted in tragedy.

CHAPTER THREE
Abb's Valley
1784

The story was one that all of the Still family must have known by heart. It was about their mother's father James Moore, who had shown unbelievable bravery and courage during his ordeal. The Still children knew they had been blessed with the same brave genetic material from the Moore's side of the family. During their childhood, they would have been able to brag about their grandfather and they had the opportunity to experience a full measure of pride when the Abb's Valley story was told. The story had all the essential components to make it one filled with excitement. They all must have known every painful detail of the massacre. It had happened when their grandfather James Moore was only a boy himself.

Martha's saga regarding the massacre of her father's family occurred in the Appalachian Mountains in the area of Abb's Valley, located in the heart of Shawnee Indian Territory. James Moore was only fourteen years of age at the time the events began. The Moore family had moved to Abb's Valley and had settled on land that was part of the Shawnee Indian hunting grounds. Obviously, the Indians were hostile toward the encroachment on this land and intermittently raided the settlers in an attempt to drive them off.

The Indians were not willing to give up their hunting grounds in the valley and many people had been massacred and tortured by the Indians in an effort to drive the settlers from the area. The Moore family didn't scare easily. Instead of running away from Abb's Valley to safety, they built a fortress to live in and to serve as a place to do battle.[55]

Even though James Moore was only fourteen, he was treated and respected by his family as being independent and often given adult responsibility. This included farm work and care of the animals. It was James' involvement in caring for the farm animals that set the stage for the rest of the story.

---

55   James Moore Brown, The Captives of Abb's Valley: A legend of Frontier Life, 39-43.

About the middle of September 1784, James Moore was sent to bring back a horse from a pasture located about two miles from the farm house. He was not afraid to go into the wilderness to retrieve the horse and had made the trip alone before. But this time he had an unusual premonition. That day while he was alone in the woods, he sensed fear of the unknown and he worried about his vulnerability. He was not afraid of snakes, or getting lost, but instead he was dwelling on the fear of the unknown—creatures that were wild beasts and imaginary.

Despite his uneasiness he continued to move along toward the horse he was sent to halter and bring back home. Suddenly, the air was filled with the sounds of war whoops as three Indians charged toward him. He was instantly captured without being harmed and taken prisoner. He would soon learn that his captors were Shawnee Indians. One of them was an Indian Chief named Black Wolf, and he was accompanied by two young Indian warriors. James was not afraid of the Indians and knew that they would have killed him if that were their intention. He realized that he would probably be forced to go with them as their captive to the Shawnee village.[56]

Although he had been captured by the Indians, he was mentally relieved since his dread of being attacked by some imaginary wild beast had not occurred. He apparently felt safe with them although he refused to cooperate with the Chief to help catch one of his father's horses. Black Wolf had given James some salt to help lure one of the animals close enough to be caught. Instead of catching the horse as it came to eat the salt James held in his hand, he scared the animal away so it would run off and avoid being captured. Black Wolf quickly gave up on having James catch any of the horses and instead tied a rope around James' neck and led him away like an animal. It would later turn out that he might have been better off if he had obeyed the Indians and caught the horse to aid them on the long trek that was just beginning.

The Shawnee Indians and their captive headed out on foot to an Indian campsite in Michigan which was located a thousand miles away. The Indians led James with a leash made of rope and began the journey northward. The warriors were self-reliant and carried few provisions which forced them to use their ingenuity to hunt and trap food each day on their journey. If the Indians failed to procure food, they all went hungry. That hunger could last for days at a time. However, they were at home in the wilderness and daily

56   Brown, The Captives of Abb's Valley, 44.

hardships were their way of life. There were no guarantees, no one else to rely on, and life was truly lived or lost, day by day.

As they traveled, James began to carefully mark the trail by breaking off the tops of bushes and kicking up leaves with his toes, but Black Wolf was not fooled by these tactics. He threatened James with death as he swung his tomahawk close to his head. James knew there could be no further efforts to escape or sabotage the journey or he would be killed. That night they camped in a thicket and had no food or fire since the Indians were unsure whether they were being followed.[57]

By this time, James must have known that he was not going to fool the Indians and survive the tomahawk that threatened his life unless he accepted his fate and cooperated. Cold, wet, hungry, and exhausted from the day's travel, he lay bound like a dog on the forest floor with one of the ropes tied to Black Wolf.

Morning came and the Indians resumed their trek. They came to a pass where they had hidden a cast-iron oven that James would be required to carry for the rest of the journey. James resisted this task until the chief offered him the load he had been carrying. James could not even pick up the heavy load off the ground. He quickly learned that they had not demanded him to do more than they required of themselves. If James had stolen his father's horse, as the Indians had requested, he probably would have been spared carrying the heavy oven because the horse would have been used to pack out the spoils as they headed back to Michigan.

Eventually it became necessary for James to stand up and challenge one of the young Indians. The Indian had taken his hat away from him. He must have known it was time he showed bravery by defying his captives. He resisted the act of having his personal possessions taken away and his defiance resulted in greater admiration and respect by his captors.

It would be difficult for anyone who had never gone hungry to imagine the difficulties of traveling over a thousand miles on foot with nothing to eat except what might be found along the way. These men went hungry almost every day and were sometimes forced to survive only on the inner bark of the yellow poplar trees. They were able to kill a bear on the third day of travel, but the meat was in such poor condition the Indians left it untouched. They were more fortunate on the fourth day of escape and killed a buffalo. Because of their starvation and physical condition, the Indians

---

57   Brown, The Captives of Abb's Valley, 44-45.

knew better than to attempt to eat the rich meat. Instead they only made a broth out of the animal's intestines which they drank to relieve their hunger.

The broth was prepared again that night and the meat was saved until the following morning and eaten for breakfast. The discipline shown by the starving Indians on the day they killed the animal is hard to imagine.

They were only one day away from the Ohio River when they stopped to rest. James was tested during this break in their journey to see if he might try to escape. He was sent off to a stream below their campsite for water. During his trip down to the stream, he took the opportunity to kneel and pray and to put his life totally in the hands of the Almighty. He found a great sense of peace following his prayer and shed tears of joy for the comfort he had gained spiritually. When he returned he had tear stains on his cheeks. These stains resulted in James receiving the Chief's displeasure for showing weakness. A tomahawk was swung over his head once again to make sure James understood there was to be no more tears.

James Moore was learning the Indian world was vastly different from his past. His tears had been viewed as an embarrassment. He would slowly earn their respect and trust as the days passed. Through prayer, he had gained the strength necessary to survive the ordeal. He would no longer feel alone with his captors and he experienced an inner peace with having his Lord travel with him over the mountains.

They resumed their travel and came to the Ohio River crossing the water on a raft. James soon found himself in the camp of the Shawnee Village in Michigan.

James had survived the journey to the Shawnee camp. Tired, bruised, and with sores on his feet, he was hidden and protected from any cruelty from the rest of the tribe. He would soon be presented to the main Shawnee Chief at a council meeting, which would bring him some protection and allow him to be assimilated into the Shawnee tribe.[58]

At this point, James began his life as an Indian and learned how to live like they did in the wild. He would have to endure many hardships along with them. James would join the young Indians and become part of their hunting party. This hunting party would live away from the village until midwinter in very uncomfortable conditions that resulted in bathing every morning in ice covered creeks, sleeping in small miserable huts with only very thin blankets available for cover and warmth. All suffered together equally and James received the same treatment as the others. They found

---

58   Brown, The Captives of Abb's Valley, 53.

very little game to kill and survived almost entirely on parched corn. James could not have known that he would spend two years living under these hardships. However, during this time spent with the hunting party he was fortunate to befriend a French trader named Bateeste Ariome and was eventually released from slavery. After his release, he was taken to Canada by Ariome, who would treat him like his own son.

Mr. Ariome was also kind enough to have one of his friends, a fellow trapper, who was heading toward Abb's Valley, carry a message to notify James' family that their son was alive and living with him. Finally, the Moore family learned the fate of James who by this time had been missing for two years. They rejoiced that James was alive and well and was being cared for by a civilized man. All they had to do now was to figure out how to go north, reclaim him, and bring him back to Abb's Valley.

The saga about the Moore family was far from over. In fact, the worst was yet to happen. In 1786, in the middle of the summer, Chief Black Wolf and forty of his warriors headed back to Abb's Valley to attack the rest of the family. The Indians hid in the valley the night they arrived and prepared to attack the family at dawn.

Through the night, the Indians quietly crept into Abb's Valley, hiding out until daylight, before beginning the attack. It had been a restless night for the family, with the animals stirring in the barn and the dogs barking unceasingly. None of the family paid any attention to the warnings thought to be caused by a wild animal that had been prowling in the vicinity. At daylight, the Moore family rose early, and began the normal work for the day. It was the busy season of harvest. Two hired men were reaping wheat a few hundred yards from the house. Mr. Moore, James' father, was outside giving salt to some young horses while the rest of the family began eating breakfast inside the cabin. Two of the children, William and Rebecca, were sent out to the well to fetch the morning water. One of the smaller children, Alexander, was playing out in the yard. There were other smaller children who remained inside the cabin. These included John, Jane, and a baby, named Margaret. The baby was being attended to by one of her sisters, named Mary. They had a visitor with them that morning by the name of Martha Evans. There was also a servant in the home, named John Simpson, who would usually have been helping with the monumental tasks of feeding everyone. He was sick that day and had remained upstairs. Mrs. Moore sent her daughter, Mary, to the fence to call the men in for breakfast. As Mary's shouts echoed across the valley, the sounds of her calls were drowned out by the war whoops of Chief Black Wolf and the forty warriors in the Shawnee War Party.

The Indian attack had begun.

Mary ran back to the house and slipped inside before the heavy door was slammed and dead-bolted shut. Her mother had panicked when she saw the Indians attacking and had not waited for the rest of the family to run inside for protection before securing the door. The rest of the family had been trapped outside in the open yard.

Mr. Moore started to run toward the house and would have made it inside if the door had not been bolted shut. When he stopped amid the total confusion that surrounded him in the yard, he was killed after being struck by several of the bullets that had been fired at him. One of the warriors then ran up to Mr. Moore and tore off his scalp with a tomahawk.

William and Rebecca, the two children who had gone for water, were overtaken before they reached the house and were struck down by a volley of bullets. Alexander, who had been playing near the house, must have seen the massacre going on in front of him. A bullet dropped the little child to the ground. Hopefully, he was spared seeing the scalp ripped from his father's head and held by Black Wolf, high in the air, like a bloody trophy.

Inside the block house was utter panic. The Englishman in the upstairs loft had already been struck and killed by a bullet. In an attempt to hide the children from the onslaught, they were at first hidden under a plank in the cabin floor, but the baby's crying spoiled the hiding spot. Only the visitor, Martha Evans, remained in the hole as the plank was replaced.

The Indians charged the house to capture the rest of the family who were hiding inside. Two large fierce guard dogs were attacking the Indians as they worked feverously to hack down the front door of the house. Mrs. Moore knew there was no way to stop their capture or death and she knelt with all of her children and prayed to the Lord that His will be done. She unbarred the front door of the house to accept their fate.

Mrs. Moore and the remaining children were now at the mercy of the Shawnee. Chief Black Wolf glared at her and the children as he entered the fortress with his warriors. The live captives were held in the block house with the other dead family members strewn around the barn yard.

After the Indians entered the house, they saw the warm breakfast still waiting on the table. They sat down and finished the uneaten food. When they were done, they began hauling everything outside they wanted, and prepared to burn the rest. They had decided to leave nothing that might

36

encourage anyone to rebuild. All of the livestock except what they would take with them was killed. Finally, a torch was used to finish the process of destruction.

The only one untouched that morning was Martha Evans, the visiting neighbor, who had managed to hide well enough to avoid discovery. She later gave up her hiding place and was also captured.

News of the massacre spread to the surrounding neighbors and the towns in the countryside by the two men who were reaping in the field that day. A company of men formed to return to see what was left of the Moore's homestead and to bury the dead. A decision was made by the men to not pursue the Indians who had caused the destruction of this family.

The Indians had gotten away with the massacre and had not received a scratch in the skirmish. However, they had not counted on an unsuspected enemy. The Indians had taken three horses with them from the Moore's farm. One of the horses, named Yorick, was vicious and had never been broken for riding except by the Moore's horse trainer. On the second day of the escape toward the Shawnee Village, the Indians decided to use Yorick for riding and one of them mounted the horse. He was thrown and stomped to death almost instantly. Two more of the Indians attempted to ride him and were stomped and bitten savagely as the horse killed them both.

The horse was killed in retaliation. After the delay, the Indians and captives continued their escape on foot across the mountains of Virginia. The women and children were expected to keep up or be killed.

The captives were led over the same trail that James Moore had been led over only two years before. They were treated harshly on the trek back to Ohio. Those who couldn't keep up were soon singled out. One of the children, named John, was ill the day of the attack, and eventually fell behind the others. A warrior picked him up and, when they were out of sight of the others, split the boy's head open with his tomahawk. The warrior finished the slaying by cutting off his scalp. Later that day, the warrior proudly showed the boy's mother what was left of her son as the scalp of her child dangled on the warrior's belt as a trophy.

The Indians knew this act of brutal punishment was sure to speed up the steps of the captives by showing them what would happen to anyone who dared slow down the War Party. The women and children were tied like animals at night so that they had no chance to escape. Mrs. Moore tried to keep up and was probably careful not to indicate that the baby she was carrying was affecting her progress by slowing her down. The warriors knew better and must have watched her struggle with the baby, named Margaret. Even though exhausted, she refused to give in as she fought to support the weight of the child. It was only a matter of time and the Indians must have been anxious to speed up the journey. A warrior rode up to the mother and grabbed the baby girl from her arms. He took the infant and ran toward the forest swinging the baby over his head by her ankles and struck her head into the side of a tree. He continued to flail away until *her brains dashed out against a tree, and the lifeless body thrown away.*[59] The child's body was left for some scavenger to devour at a later time.

The Indians led the two remaining captive women from this spot along with Mary and her sister Jane, who only three days before had been safe at home and underfoot at the time of the attack.

After the long trek to Ohio, Mrs. Moore was taken with her daughter, Jane, to one of the Shawnee villages, and her neighbor Martha Evans and Mary Moore were taken to another village. What occurred after that was impossible to know, but Mrs. Moore and her daughter's introduction to the village was of the worst treatment. Both she and her daughter were tortured and finally burned at the stake. Martha Evans and the little child Mary Moore were hidden by the Shawnee squaws until the rage was over and the raiding party forgot about them and headed back out on the trail for more scalps.

Martha Evans soon took favor with the village chief and by pacifying and amusing him was able to barter for Mary and her life. Their life was a difficult one, essentially working as Indian slaves, but they were alive, and compared to the fate of Jane and Mrs. Moore, were well cared for.[60]

Martha Evans, the visiting neighbor on the day of the attack, and the child named Mary, were the only remaining survivors. Eventually they would come to the same fate as James Moore. They would be taken to Detroit and sold as slaves. Unknown to them was the fact that James Moore was close by in Canada.[61]

The captives had not been forgotten by their friends and family in Abb's Valley. Many of them searched for months trying to find the Indians and any of the captured family that might still be alive. The hunt for the victims all ended without results. One man who was not easily discouraged was Thomas Evans, Martha Evans' brother. He never gave up the search for his sister who had been visiting the Moore family on the day of the attack. He

---

59   Brown, The Captives of Abb's Valley, 75.
60   Ibid., 79-80.
61   Ibid., 86.

had been searching for his sister and the missing Moore family for almost two years and refused to accept the notion that they had all been killed. He had no way of knowing that the only survivor of the Moore family was the child, Mary Moore, and his sister Martha Evans.[62]

Thomas Evans' relentless pursuit eventually was successful in locating the survivors from both raids. He was able to buy freedom for all of them, James and Mary Moore, and his sister Martha Evans. The ordeal was finally over.[63]

At this point, James Moore was sixteen years old. James didn't want to return to the valley after being set free from slavery and learning the bloody details of what had become of all of his loved ones. He had spent two of his teenage years as a Shawnee, hunting and trapping in the Canadian wilds. He had learned to be happy where he was. But it probably was seeing his little sister, Mary, who changed his mind. He was her brother and the only other family member who had survived.[64]

James returned with the women to Abb's Valley. There he rebuilt the cabin and eventually married Barbara Taylor. As a result of that marriage, Martha Moore, was born. It was Martha Moore who would later marry Abram Still, in 1822, and from this marriage Andrew and his brothers and sisters would be brought into the world.[65]

This was the family story that was handed down about Martha Still's father and their fate at the hands of the Shawnee. At this point, the story would have been told once more and fear of the Shawnee Indians would be reinforced among her own family.

Despite Abram Still's reassurances that they would not be in any danger from the Shawnee Indians in the Kansas Indian Territory, Martha was uneasy with the proposal. The shadows of her father's saga still haunted her and could not be forgotten.

The Stills were, however, a hardy family and had inherited their spirit and courage. That legacy meant living a life of not being afraid to face the unknown wilderness, nor having to be familiar with the path that lay in front of them.

The result was that Martha Still, despite her misgivings, would be going with her husband to the Kansas Territory. Almost all of the other members

---

62   Brown, The Captives of Abb's Valley, 94.
63   Ibid.
64   Ibid., 94-96
65   Ibid., 134.

39

of the Still family would also be going with them or would join them later at the new mission being planned for construction on the Wakarusa River. Even after having made the decision to go to the Kansas Territory, Martha must have felt as if she were being delivered to the tents of her family's torturers.

By making the decision to go to the Kansas Indian Territory, however, the Still family unknowingly had accepted an assignment that would be filled with even greater conflict and turmoil than any of their previous missions. They were being thrust into a location that would soon become the most politically charged and dangerous spot in the country because of the slavery issue. It was as if they had thrown a dart at a map hanging on a wall, with their eyes closed, and had, by accident, hit a bull's eye of future conflict. They were now heading directly to the center of that target.

CHAPTER FOUR
The Kansas Territory

The Kansas Prairie belonged to the Indians. It was given to them by the United States government and the words used in the treaty stated this land would always be theirs *"so long as grass should grow or water run."*[66]

With this treaty, the Indians truly believed the Plains would be theirs forever. The government had tied this knot with a treaty based on the laws of nature. Before them grew an ocean of grass, and water flowed in endless streams into their rivers from the melting snows of the mountains to the west. It would be theirs for eternity.

At the time of the treaty, the prairie was almost a totally uninhabited place except for the Indian tribes that lived in the eastern half of the Territory. In many areas of the Prairie the only living things were the wild animals seen grazing on the bluestem grasses or birds flying about in the air. The land was truly unspoiled and uniquely beautiful.

The prairie grass that covered the land was thick, plentiful, and so high that the blades obstructed both the view of what lay ahead and also hid the terrain beneath its roots. The very nature of the grass surrounded everything that penetrated its waving walls creating a backdrop as if attempting to hide the past, and present. It even shrouded the future events upon the soil in which it grew. The thick grass created a density that could at times prevent seeing ahead more than the depth of a blade or two. Once the grass was entered it could hold the intruder captive and lost until the other side was reached ending the imprisonment. This curtain hid everything including deadly rattlesnakes and other potential risks. The Prairie was capable of creating an unsettling effect on the frontiersmen and settlers who dared the adventure.

For the white man, the prairie had been a land that was only traversed. It was a place where men were on their way to somewhere else and the ground was worn with trails as they made their way through these central plains. The trails had been traveled so often that the wagon wheels cut and gouged endless tracks deeply into the Kansas soil. These trails became

---

66   Anna Arnold, A History of Kansas, 1931, 43.

permanently etched in the land and created the gateways to the west and were named for their destinations—Santa Fe, Oregon and California.[67]

The trails, however, were the most recent evidence of newcomers in the region. Exploration of the prairie had a rich history with the first Europeans arriving from Spain in search of gold. Other countries, including France and England, were inspired to join the hunt for hidden treasure with the hope of finding the precious metal. The messages that were sent back home from the explorers who came and survived the Prairie's hardships, were always the same—no treasure found. They found instead a rich soil for growing crops and a land plentiful with animals, including herds of buffalo.

Only the Indians recognized that the soil and animals were the true treasures of the Prairie. These riches were worthy enough for them to stay and call it home.

Unlike many of the other white men passing through, the Still family would soon be making the Kansas Prairie their home. The initial ingredient for this adventure had begun in 1848 during the time period Abram Still served as the presiding elder responsible for the Methodist Episcopal Church North, which included an area that encompassed what would eventually become the Kansas Territory. His first efforts to aid the Shawnee Indians who resided in the area was to assign Thomas B. Markham as a missionary to serve a faithful band of about twenty Indians who had chosen to resist the owning of slaves.[68]

Later, in 1851, Abram requested funding to build an Indian educational church mission in the Territory. The grant was approved and he was appointed superintendent in charge of the project and would direct the construction of the building.

Abram had recognized the need for the Methodist Church North to come to the Indian Territory. The 1844 dissolution of the main body of the Methodist Church into two fractured pieces had resulted in the survival of only one Methodist mission school in the Territory. It was a Southern Methodist Mission School, which represented the proslavery position.

Abram's proposal for a Northern Mission School to be constructed in the Kansas Territory next to the Wakarusa River would primarily serve these Indians. This Indian tribe did more than protest the owning of slaves. They had chosen to leave the Methodist Church South for the same reasons Abram had left his church in Missouri over the slavery issue.

---

67   Arnold, A History of Kansas, 39.
68   Goode, Outposts of Zion, 295.

These Shawnee Indians were known as the Fish Tribe and were led by Chief Paschal Fish, Jr., who believed that owning slaves was immoral. It was this small tribe that would become the nucleus for Abram and the Methodist Church North to begin to rebuild the slave-free Methodist religion. Luckily, Abram Still was never discouraged by being in the minority. He was willing to serve this group of Indians, which had now grown to a tribe of about one-hundred, who had chosen to resist the owning of slaves.[69]

Prior to Abram's arrival in the Indian Territory, the main body of the Shawnee had already been sequestered into the Kansas Territory's Methodist Episcopal Church South. This meant that *"the Methodist Episcopal Church South controlled all Indian education in the Kansas Territory."*[70] The church school was named the Indian Mission Manual Labor School, and was under the leadership of the Reverend Thomas Johnson who represented slavery and the southern camp. He was held in high esteem by both the southern church and by the proslavery men of the Territory. He not only proclaimed the right of individuals to own slaves, he owned and utilized slave labor at the mission. Johnson had defied the Missouri Compromise Bill even before it had been struck down. He demonstrated his attitude toward the bill by openly owning slaves north of the 36'30' line. The action put him in conflict with those against slavery, and he would later be described by the early abolitionists in the area as *"vulgar, illiterate, and course."* The Indian Mission Manual Labor School was his and represented the bastion of slavery in the Kansas Territory.[71]

Paschal Fish, Jr., the chief of the Shawnee Tribe, was the son of a white man. His father, William Jackson, had been captured as a small boy and was raised by the Shawnee who renamed him Paschal Fish. Paschal had risen to the level of chief of his tribe before his death. He had sought education and spiritual guidance for his tribe through the Quakers in the Friend's Mission in Ohio where the tribe lived for many years. He was forced to relocate his tribe to the Kansas Territory because of the poorly written U.S. Government treaties which had resulted in the settlers' constant encroachment on Indian land. The Fish Tribe brought with them to the Kansas Territory a philosophy that embraced Christianity and appreciated the benefits of education. The

---

69   Trowbridge, *Andrew Taylor Still*, 36.
70   Ibid., 37.
71   Ibid.

elder chief had requested, *"the establishment of a mission among them for the education of their children."*[72]

Following Paschal Sr.'s death, their mission school was taken over by the Methodist Episcopal Church South. The onus was on Paschal Jr. to decide what his tribe should do and if they would maintain a relationship with the church school. Paschal Jr. was sure that his father, who had been an abolitionist, would have been mortified by the Tallequal Conference vote of 1844. That vote resulted in his father's Methodist Mission School being placed under the southern leadership of the Reverend Thomas Johnson. He knew what his father's desires would have been when it came to the slavery issue. His father would not have supported slavery or tolerated the southern influence now in authority over his mission. Paschal Jr., like his father, also abhorred slavery. He chose to leave the mission school established by his father and hoped to return his people to a northern slave-free church. He believed, *"in the assertion of the Declaration of Independence, that all men are born free and equal."*[73] This decision resulted in his tribe having no mission facilities available to them. However, under the leadership of Abram Still, with funding provided by the Methodist Church North, the new Wakarusa Mission School was built to serve the Fish tribe.

In 1851, Abram had traveled ahead of the family, and with the help of the Fish tribe, had spent months constructing a new school building and a house for his family. The mission home was made out of hewn logs with a clapboard roof. There were two rooms on the first level and two rooms on the second. During the construction process Abram learned firsthand that he would be working with Indian people who possessed a sense of humor. This introduction to the Indian mischievousness began with the young Indian he employed to help erect the mission house. His name was Cephas Fish.[74]

Rovia, one of Abram Still's daughters, recounted one example of this mischievousness: *"Cephas pretended he did not understand a word of English, so my father talked to him by signs and tried to teach him his letters and to talk. It went on this way for about two months and one day they were doing some work and there was something about it that Cephas was very anxious my father should understand...out of patience he spoke it in English just as plain as anyone could speak."*[75]

---

72   J. J. Lutz, Methodist Missions Among the Indians in Kansas., 166-167.
73   Sara T. L. Robinson, Kansas: Its Interior and Exterior Life, 77.
74   Marovia Still Clark, Reminiscences, 1.
75   Ibid., 1.

Wakarusa Mission

"So Father said, 'Now, Cephas, you can talk English as good as I can and if there is anymore of your nonsense you can take your duds and get out of here.' He said, 'What made you do this anyway, Cephas?' He laughed and said, 'Oh, just for fun,' but Father said, 'Don't you know it was not much fun for me for I have been trying for two months to learn to talk and read and here you can do better than I can.' When he questioned him, he had been to one of the missions four or five years and had the best education they could give him at the missions. He was a good reader and often read to Father of evenings and could write a beautiful hand, and Father said you could not beat him in arithmetic."[76]

The Indian antics went all the way to the top of the tribe. Even their chief, Paschal Jr., *"while fairly well educated…appears that he was unable to write his name…signed as follows: "Paschal Fish. His X mark."*[77]

He always enjoyed telling humorous stories about himself. One of his favorite tales was when he was asked to attend a prayer meeting at the home of a minister. Several important clergy were in attendance and Paschal was very proud he had been included in such a religious group. He demonstrated this honor by presenting himself with an air of superiority and authority of such recognition. He walked in their midst and threw his head back with his nose stuck high in the air. This was all going very well until he went to

---

76   Clark, Reminiscences, 1.
77   Lutz, Methodist Missions, 186.

sit down. With his head held in this Saintly position he could not look down and in the process of being seated, he missed the chair entirely and landed on the back of his head. His feet ended sticking straight up above him in the air. Paschal Fish would always finish telling this story with his roaring laughter at his own foolery. *"[S]urely if anyone ever enjoyed a hearty laugh, he did."*[78]

The mission structures were completed in early March 1852, and Abram returned home to help the family load their wagons. The wagon train would head for the Indian Territory in mid-March for another new beginning. They must have prayed they were going to a place where their views on slavery would not be such an inflammatory issue. Abram Still and his family and the Methodist Church North had begun the process of developing a foothold in the Kansas Indian Territory. The church commissioned Abram to lead the way, and they knew this unwavering man would establish their philosophic presence in their newly completed Wakarusa Church Mission School. The endeavor demonstrated that the Indian Territory was not just a land used for passage anymore, but a land worthy of vision and full of possibilities for future homes and development. The Methodist Church North and the Still family were in the Indian Territory to stay. Together, they would oppose the Manual Mission Labor School and the Reverend Thomas Johnson's views on slavery.

The Still family, however, had their own personal dreams for the future. They wanted to reestablish a new home, put their lives back together, and not live in fear as they had been forced to do in their last years in northern Missouri.

After arriving at the mission, *"we were cordially received and kindly treated by our mission helpers, the Reverends Charles and Paschal Fish, and their families."*[79] Abram, Martha, and their children began developing friendships with their new neighbors who were all Shawnee Indians. Their closest neighbors were Paschal Fish, Jr., and his wife. Their house was *"only a few hundred yards from their mission* [school]."[80] The proximity of their homes helped Martha recover from her feelings of loneliness after she arrived at the mission. She needed a friend and had welcomed this relationship.[81]

---

78   Clark, Reminiscences, 9.
79   Adams, In God We Trust, 33.
80   Trowbridge, Andrew Taylor Still, 45.
81   Adams, In God We Trust, 33.

This was the first time the entire Still family had ever been separated and Martha suffered because of the absent family members who had remained behind in Missouri to farm the land. Andrew and Mary stayed in Missouri until their new son reached the age to travel. There were also many other friends she missed in Missouri. Her children occasionally saw her flee from the house for a quiet walk to a hidden knoll and observed her looking in the direction of her Missouri home. *"Sometimes, I would see her take up the corner of her apron and brush a tear away."*[82]

The friendship with the Fish family involved both the women and the men. Abram and Paschal Jr. spent leisure time together. Abram utilized Paschal's brother, Charles, to help him deliver his sermons to the Indians every Sunday. It was not uncommon for more than one tribe to attend the services. When the Wyandot and the Delaware Indians attended the same worship service, Abram had to allow time for his sermons to be interpreted in several different Indian languages. He would speak a passage from the sermon, and pause to give the interpreters time to translate the messages into their native languages. He must have wondered as he gazed out over the colorful and brightly dressed congregation, what messages the interpreters were actually delivering to the crowd.[83]

Abram's daughter, Mary Still, would later write, *"To hear these Indians sing the songs of Zion in their native tongue constituted one of the sweetest memories of my life."* She also said she had *"never heard anything like it before or since."*[84]

The Stills were in the Kansas Indian Territory, Abram was preaching the Methodist faith to the Indians, and Martha was teaching about thirty Indian children in the mission school. The fact that the services were being translated and the hymns sounded different was secondary. What was always important to Abram was doing the church's work, preaching the gospel, with the congregation not required to embrace slavery.

Fourteen months had gone by since Abram and his family had arrived at the Wakarusa Mission. It was 1853, and the time had come for Andrew and Mary Still to leave Missouri and join his mother, father, and the other children at the Wakarusa Mission. There would be four of them making the trip because their family had expanded when a son, named Abraham, was born. They had waited until their son reached six months of age before

---

82   Clark, Reminiscences, 20.
83   Clark, Reminiscences, 9 / Adams, In God We Trust, 39.
84   Adams, In God We Trust, 39.

47

beginning this journey. The family loaded their wagon with the possessions they would take and left for the Wakarusa Mission. Andrew's older brother, Edward, and his sister, Barbara, would be the only family members continuing to remain in Missouri.[85]

Andrew and his family arrived at the mission in May of 1853. Their adjustment to the mission and the new surroundings went well because the Still families were used to working and living closely together as they had done in Missouri. The main change they encountered were the people they served. Their neighbors were Indians with only one white trader residing in the immediate area. He was called Dutch Billy. The Still families all seemed to look forward to his frequent visits on the weekends when he closed his store on the Wakarusa at Blue Jacket Ford. The children especially enjoyed his visit, because he always brought them candy. Andrew's sisters, Rovia, and Mary, four years old, would run out to greet him, each taking hold of his hands to walk with him, as he approached the mission. Dutch Billy apparently had been exiled from his home in Germany and had left his family and a four-year-old sister. When he talked about home, his eyes would fill with tears and he would suddenly change the subject and begin teasing the two sisters in an effort to regain his composure. He gave each girl a summer dress on one occasion and when it was worn out, Rovia's sister kept a piece of the dress wrapped in tissue paper as a reminder of him. Everyone in the Still family thought he was a fine man.[86]

Andrew's work at the Wakarusa Mission was very similar to his efforts in Missouri. He continued to develop his skills as a physician as he worked with his father and his brother, Jim, providing medical care for the Indians. Occasionally, they would also administer medical care to white men passing through the area. They were usually soldiers, trappers or settlers. While patients frequently came to the mission for treatment, the Stills were often required to ride out on horseback to administer medical care.[87]

The cause of the deadliest diseases they treated remained a mystery with invisible germs waiting to be identified. These illnesses included malaria, typhoid fever and cholera. Outbreaks would occur suddenly and could wipe out entire Indian villages. Microscopes were unavailable and in the process of being developed. The tiny organisms, which were eventually discovered, would later provide the answers for the disease process. But for the Stills, the major treatments were palliative.

---

85   Still, Autobiography, 56.
86   Clark, Reminiscences, 5-6.
87   Still, Autobiography, 56-57.

After arriving at the mission in the summer of 1853, Andrew was challenged to provide medical care later that fall when a cholera epidemic broke out among the Indians. Andrew, his father, and his brother, Jim, treated the Indians with the medication available to them. Regardless of the treatments they used, hundreds continued to die. During that time period and without knowing the cause of cholera, people continued to become ill through drinking and ingesting the bacteria primarily found in their contaminated drinking water. The wells, rivers and streams they used for drinking water were frequently the source of the contamination. Furthermore, the contamination was primarily created by their poor sanitary conditions, such as having their outhouses on higher ground than the water supply used for drinking.[88]

The death toll that occurred from the cholera epidemic resulted in hundreds of Indians being buried in the Indian Territory. Andrew requested permission from the Indians to exhume some of the bodies. He wanted to study the effects of cholera that resulted in the deaths of the victims. He needed to carefully dissect the tissue to learn more about the disease and the damage it caused. He was allowed to dig up the bodies and began his study of anatomical pathology.[89] His curiosity and the study of medicine through anatomical dissections would dominate his medical interest for the rest of his life. There were unlimited numbers of Indian cadavers available to study and he used the skills he had learned dissecting the animals he had hunted during his childhood. He looked at the human anatomical details of each dissection in a comparative and analytical way. He correlated any changes found during the dissection process and attempted to explain the cause and effect of the illness. He was driven to improve medical treatment and prevent patients dying from cholera in the future. He looked at the cadavers during the dissection process like an engineer looked at a broken machine that needed repair. His interests focused on the structural integrity of the body and what enabled it to function at its best. He was convinced that the medicines he used were worthless in the treatment of cholera because of the hundreds of Indians who had died regardless of medications given.

He would later say *"The Indians' treatment for cholera was not much more ridiculous than are some of the treatments used by some of the so-called scientific doctors of medicine. The Indians dug two holes in the*

---

88   Still, Autobiography, 56-57.
89   Ibid., 86.

ground, about twenty inches apart. The patient lay stretched over the two, vomiting in one hole and purging in the other, and died stretched out in this manner with a blanket thrown over him. Here I witnessed the cramps which go with cholera and which dislocated hips and turned legs out from the body. I sometimes had to force the hips back to get the corpse into the coffin. As curatives they gave teas made of black-root, ladirs' thumb, saga-tee, muckquaw, chenee olachee. Thus they doctored and died, and went to Illinoywa Tapamalaqua, 'the house of God.' "[90]

Like the other settlers, Andrew didn't have the luxury of focusing on only one type of work. When he wasn't practicing medicine, he was in the field plowing and breaking out the virgin prairie ground for planting.[91]

Andrew's description regarding this segment of his life was summarized later in his writings. *"In May 1853, my wife and I moved to the Wakarusa Mission, Kansas, which was occupied by the Shawnee trible. (sic) It was all Indian there. English was not spoken much outside the mission school. My wife taught the papooses that summer, while I with six yoke of oxen in a string, fastened to a twenty-inch plow, turned ninety acres of land, closing the job the last of July. Some days I broke four acres of sod. Then during the fall with my father I doctored the Indians. Erysipelas, fever, flux, pneu-monia, and cholera prevailed among them.*[92]

"I soon learned to speak their tongue, and gave them such drugs as white men used, cured most of the cases that I met, and was well received by the Shawnees."[93]

The family all seemed to be adjusting to their surroundings at the Wakarusa Mission. Martha had learned to live comfortably among the Shawnee. Although she was relieved to find most of the Indians pleasant, there were two occasions that frightened her.

The worst event occurred when one of the Shawnee Indians, called Big Knife, tried to break into the house. Big Knife had killed several Indians ac-cording to the Indian children and they were afraid of him. On that particu-lar day he was drunk after finishing a half-pail of whiskey. He approached the Still home *"with a dirk knife in his right hand"* and was hollering a war whoop as he fought to open the front door. There were no men at home and Martha and the children struggled to keep him out by holding a table against the front door. Mary Still, one of Andrew's younger sisters, grabbed

---

90   Still, Autobiography, 56-57.
91   Ibid., 56.
92   Ibid.
93   Ibid., 57.

a big soap churning stick from the fireplace and pounded Big Knife's hands as he wrestled to open the door. He gave up on the door and went to one of the windows and began forcing it open. When he stuck his head through the window, Mary Still gave him a severe blow to the head with a gun-barrel which caused him to fall backwards away from the window. One of the older girls in the family quickly dressed in her brother's clothing and pulled a hat down over her face attempting to deceive Big Knife into thinking a man was in the house, but he was not fooled. Big Knife again charged the door and this time was successful in opening it wide enough to stick his head and right arm with the knife in his hand inside the house. Martha and the children continued to push the door against him while Mary beat him *"with all my might."* One of her blows knocked the knife from Big Knife's hand. The drunken Indian retreated once more and picked up his whiskey-pail and *"took a double header of his firewater."* During the fracas, the Indian passed out from the amount of whiskey he had drunk and this afforded one of the girls the opportunity to run outside and empty the remaining whiskey from the pail. When Big Knife woke up from the stupor he was in, his anger only increased when he saw his whiskey poured on the ground. He once again attempted to break down the door. Mary's account of the Big Knife attack ended when a party of trappers happened to wander by the mission in search of a campsite. One of the trappers, a big Scotchman, intervened and beat Big Knife with a stick and chased him off. Rovia Still recalled that Big Knife went to their neighbor's house, Paschal Fish, to get a gun. Paschal was able to quiet him down and get him on his pony. He then took him across the river to his home. Big Knife told Paschal Fish he was going to come back and kill the entire Still family. Paschal warned the Stills to be on guard because he would probably try to carry out the threat. The Still family was relieved to learn that not long after the incident, Big Knife was killed in another drunken brawl.[94]

On another occasion, two intoxicated Indians became combative in the Still's front yard. This time there were men at home. Abram and his son, Thomas, had to chase them away with oxen whips. During the battle with the Indians, the whips, attached to long poles, convinced them to mount their ponies and leave. One of the Indians named Locust later promised Abram he would never return to the mission if he were drunk because of the painful beating he received.[95]

---

94   Clark, Reminiscences, 10-12 / Adams, In God We Trust, 36-38.
95   Ibid., Clark, 13.

Other than these incidents, Martha had learned to be comfortable with the Shawnee, making many of them her closest friends. Abram was satisfied with the new mission church and was expanding the Methodist religion. The younger Still children had adjusted and learned to speak the Shawnee Indian language as they played with the Indian children who had become their friends. Andrew's medical practice had been well received by the Indians and he had an endless supply of Indian cadavers to further his medical studies in the diagnosis and treatment of disease. Mary was teaching the Indian children at the mission school, and most of the Still family had been reunited and were living together in close surroundings.

The relative calm they had experienced for more than two years at the Wakarusa Mission and the good fortune they had found in the Indian Territory was about to come to an end. Soon, they would again be undermined by pro-slavery sentiments. Opposing political movements were becoming aggressive. Each side desired to dominate the new Territory government that would be formed before the anticipated passage of the Kansas-Nebraska Bill. The first of the power plays came from Missouri Senator David Atchison, who orchestrated the appointment of Reverend Thomas Johnson as the Kansas Territory delegate to Congress. When Johnson arrived in Washington, D.C. in December 1853, he was denied a seat because Kansas had not officially been declared a Territory.[96] Not discouraged, the next political move the pro-slavery forces made was in March 1854, when Atchison and Johnson took active roles in negotiations with the Indians regarding the government's purchase of their land in the Kansas Indian Territory.

"It was in April 1854," while Martha and Abram Still were in Kansas City buying supplies for the Wakarusa Mission School, that they saw the Indian treaty party, *"get on to the boat and start for Washington to write the treaty that gave us Kansas. Several of them were our neighbors. Among the number were Paschal and Charles Fish, Pechalker and the Blue Jacket brothers, Charles and Henry."* It can only be imagined how they felt when they saw their friend, Chief Paschal Fish, Jr., with the notorious slavery politician, Senator Atchison, and their mission rival, Reverend Johnson. The Stills must have suspected this was not a good sign to have their close friends in the company of arch enemies regarding the slavery issue. They must have wondered the impact this might have on their small mission school on the Wakarusa River.[97]

---

96   Trowbridge, Andrew Taylor Still, 46.
97   Still, 57 / Trowbridge, 46 / Clark, Reminiscences, 21-22.

The new treaty with the federal government, to begin the purchase of the Indian lands, however, moved rapidly through Congress gaining the necessary signatures for approval on May 10, 1854. As part of this agreement, Reverend Johnson made sure that his mission school in the Indian Territory would be the only one receiving Federal grant money for Indian mission education in the future.[98]

But the worst blow would follow twenty days later when President Pierce, as expected, signed the Kansas-Nebraska Bill into law on May 30, 1854. The bill offered both Kansas and Nebraska up as prizes to be won by either the northern abolitionists or the southern slavery politicians. This act set off a chain of events that would affect the Still family and end the tranquility the family had enjoyed for almost three years. For Andrew and his wife, who had only been at the Mission for one year, the turmoil came all too soon after their arrival.[99]

The slavery storm had reached a critical mass and was at the door of the Still's Wakarusa Mission. The turmoil would rapidly gain momentum and eventually involve the entire country which was heading for a Civil War.

98   Still, Autobiography, 57. / Trowbridge, 47.
99   Arnold, A History of Kansas, 53.

CHAPTER FIVE
The Kansas-Nebraska Bill

The Still family found themselves once again living in an area where their abolitionist beliefs were going to be threatened and their resolve to fight against those ideals would be tested to the limit. This time there would be more than unhappy church members to deal with. The dilemma now would be even greater involving new federal statutes and the entire country focused on the area they now called home. Proslavery people from just across the Missouri border would soon become their neighbors. New Englanders, over a thousand miles away, would also enter their lives as they packed up for the migration to the Territory. A battle was shaping up and they would be right in the middle of the conflict. There was no escape for them, and the Still family, like their ancestors from Abb's Valley, did not run from a fight.

The Indians, as well, could not escape the changes written in the bill that would affect them. Some of Paschal Fish's daily visits at Abram's smokehouse probably were no longer church related activities. They must have discussed the future of the prairie. Paschal's concerns about the increase in the numbers of white settlers coming to the prairie had to have been a worry since the land belonged to the Indians. His tribe had experienced this same encroachment in the past. It had resulted in their moving from Ohio because of the white man's invasion of their land and the government's inability or unwillingness to stand by the treaties they had made with the Indians in the past. Now this invasion was starting to occur in the Kansas Territory because the land given to the Indians was some of the richest farm land in the Territory. More than likely, he agreed to sell the Shawnee Indian land to the government rather than have it stolen from them as had been done in the past.

Abram and Paschal both faced the same recurring problems. The invasion of the white man looking for rich farm ground was bearing down on the Indians, and the slavery issue was resurfacing with the passage of the new Kansas-Nebraska Bill. This bill had been skillfully drafted to deal with a number of problems concerning the development of potential new territories and states in the west. Since the anticipated expansion of slavery was part of the bill's language, the politicians had to carefully select the ingredients and flavor to try to make it palatable for everyone. In some areas, the Missourians had not even waited for the bill to be passed and began crossing into the Indian Territory to stake out their claims. They resolved, *"We recognize slavery as always existing in this Territory,"* and, *"We will afford protection to no abolitionists as settlers of Kansas Territory."*[100]

On the abolitionists' front, there had been a northern immigration initiative underway to go to the Kansas Territory if Congress passed the bill. Abram and Paschal were unable to avoid the old nemesis of the past and neither one could predict the battles that would lie ahead. All they could do was pray for guidance and trust in the Lord to lead the way.

Not all of Abram's time, however, was spent worrying about the slavery issue. He had daily work to do at the mission, including patient care and ministerial duties. His work there had progressed well enough that the main body of the Methodist Church North had recently commissioned Reverend William H. Goode to go and help the further development of the Methodist church in the area. On his arrival, Reverend Goode stayed with Abram Still at the Wakarusa Mission while he worked to organize a plan to establish the church in the Kansas Territory. On July 9, 1854, Reverend Goode rode in a wagon with Abram and a Quaker missionary and several others to witness the Lord's servants in action.[101]

The sojourn that day was through fifteen miles of beautiful prairie grass, expanding as far as the eye could see, to a place known as Hickory Point. During the journey, the wagon, loaded with the men, traveled through expanses of undisturbed prairie which often had been described as appearing as an ocean caused by the movement of the waving grass as the wind blew and rippled the tops of the blades. They believed they were bringing Christianity to these isolated families and spiritually starved people in the wilderness.

The Reverend Goode and Abram needed to appoint someone at Hickory Point to assume a position to help organize and provide spiritual leadership in the small village. Their own pastoral care would seldom be available. The person chosen would have to be extremely important because he would be the church's official representative. The church could not afford to make a mistake in choosing the correct leader. On July 9th, at Hickory Point, the Reverend Goode gave the first sermon in the Territory to the white

---

100   D. W. Wilder, Annals of Kansas, 41.
101   Goode, Outposts of Zion, 254.

settlers. It was taken from The Gospel according to Matthew, Chapter XIV. Following the service, Abram and Reverend Goode chose Lucius Kibbee, a strong immigrant from Indiana to be their leader. He was the kind of man any church would be proud to have as its representative.[102]

He stood just over six feet in height, muscular, athletic, and handsome, with dark eyes. He was strong-jawed and his skin had been tanned golden brown from the sun while working in the fields. He met men with a strong handshake—the kind of man needed nearby if falling into a swift moving stream or off a cliff. Lucius would not let go. They desperately needed a man of his character and with the qualities he possessed. As Reverend Goode summed it up, Kibbee was a sober, resolute, fearless man.[103]

The influx of people to the Kansas Indian Territory as a result of the Kansas-Nebraska Bill having been signed into law by President Pierce had begun. Both the northern and southern politicians were faced with the challenge of exerting their interests and philosophies in the race to politically control the new Federal Territories named in the bill. Officially declared a Federal Territory, an election would be required to vote for a legislature and to select a delegate for representation in Congress. The immediate goal for both sides of the slavery issue was to ensure there were enough votes in their Territory to win the contest.

The election date was set for November 29, 1854. It was President Pierce's responsibility to appoint high ranking officials, such as the Territorial Governor, Secretary, Judges and other officers required to make the Territory functional. President Pierce appointed Andrew H. Reeder as the first Territorial Governor of Kansas, and he was known to be sympathetic to the southern cause. He was scheduled to arrive in the Kansas Territory to accept his new position in October 1854.[104]

There would be many other new faces coming to the Territory and many would bring their own influences, beliefs, and agendas with them and their hopes for the future. The overwhelming forces driving the invasion of the new comers, however, were people who were politically motivated and whose ambitions were to make the Kansas Territory theirs. The slavery issue dominated a critical part of their equation that they saw for the future. The 1854 Kansas-Nebraska Bill had reopened the possibility of extending slavery through federal law and the people living in the Territories would have to decide for themselves by voting for or against the slavery issue.

---

102   Goode, Outposts of Zion, 254.
103   Ibid., 315.
104   Arnold, A History of Kansas, 66.

This method of decision-making through the voting process was known as "popular sovereignty," or "squatter's sovereignty" as many called it.[105]

Since the winners in the first election would write the formal constitution and have their delegate represent their views in Washington, both sides knew they had to win the election scheduled in November.

The southern influence, whose agricultural needs had been dependent upon slavery, supported the continuation of slavery in America. The northern politicians felt hired workers could provide the labor needed for agriculture and fought against the promulgation of slavery. It had been a calculated gamble by Congress to write a bill that would allow people in each new state or Territory to decide the outcome. The southerners in Congress expected that the Kansas Territory would vote for slavery because of the strong Missouri ties that influenced the eastern part of Kansas. They were willing to give up Nebraska to become "Free Soil" because of the strong abolition influence that already existed in that area. The politicians seemed satisfied with this legislation that had divided the country and Congress regarding slavery and many other issues. Both sides felt that this compromise kept the playing field even. A moral victory had been scored for Congress. Now the responsibility for the decisions about whether slavery should be expanded was shifted onto the backs of the Territorial voters. One thing seemed certain: if Kansas voted for slavery as expected, slavery would have successfully and legally crossed the Missouri border and would be heading West with no outlook of ever being stopped. In their view, slavery would prevail and supply the labor force needed as America expanded to the west. The South was willing to give up Nebraska to make this country a slave nation forever. The dam that had kept the slaves penned up at the 30'36' line was ready to burst.

The abolitionists had a different vision and an opposite formula for the Kansas Territory.

The political conditions existing in the Kansas Territory at the time the Kansas-Nebraska Bill was signed could not stop the expansion of slavery. There were simply not enough abolitionists like the Still family living in the Territory to support their views and win through the voting process.

Slavery was an old problem. It was one that was ignored and avoided in the original draft of the Constitution and had continued to divide the country. There was no end in sight for a solution that would solve the problem or satisfy everyone. The abolitionists in America realized the implications

---

105   Arnold, A History of Kansas, 53.

of slavery expansion allowed in the new Kansas-Nebraska Bill and they began to coordinate their efforts with a counteroffensive plan in retaliation of the law. In New England, Eli Thayer and Amos Lawrence, who were strong abolitionists, were developing their own methods for the Kansas Territory to thwart the new legislation and the ability to legally expand slavery.

They were fortunate to find a leader to carry out their plans—a man named Charles Robinson. He was the one who was chosen to provide the leadership for the abolitionists. Charles Robinson was commissioned to go to the Kansas Territory and search for land that would be suitable for development of a community to serve the needs of the abolitionists upon their arrival. This community would have to house and provide support for the hundreds of New Englanders who were being recruited and who would bring their votes and a clear and resounding message. No more slavery would be allowed in America through the expansion process of new territories and states in the future. Abolitionist immigrant voters would provide the votes against slavery. Charles Robinson left for the Kansas Territory in the summer of 1854 to begin a search for land to begin the development of the abolitionist community. The initial effort by Thayer and his Emigrant Aid Society had been put into motion.

To wage this fight, Eli Thayer dreamed of developing a town and eventually an empire. He envisioned sending thousands of people and building entire communities, schools and churches. To make his plan a reality he would need strong men who could work together as a team. This plan would also require men with a lot of money for financial backing and men who were entrepreneurs, dreamers and risk takers—men like Amos Lawrence of Boston.[106]

Amos Lawrence was a man who shared Thayer's vision of an America without slavery. He was willing to underwrite the vision by reaching into his own wallet to finance this effort. This willingness to provide funding is what separated Amos Lawrence from most of the others; he was willing to accept the gamble of success or failure with his own money. He morally felt that the expense of men's souls were worth buying regardless of the price. *To this work Mr. Thayer devoted himself with tireless energy and unceasing effort.*[107]

Together, Thayer and Lawrence began the process of trying to shift the voting population by recruiting men to go to the Prairie and build homes

---

106   Charles Robinson, The Kansas Conflict, 67-68.
107   Ibid., 68.

and a new life. They would rush new families to this frontier as soon as the facilities were established and populate the Kansas Territory with abolitionists who shared their philosophy. They would send Charles Robinson to forge the trail with never-ending wagon loads of people following his footsteps, and when it came time to vote, the Northern influence hoped to vote down slavery. The men who would cast the votes would also provide the labor that was necessary to make the farms function, thus making slavery unnecessary. There would be no slavery in Kansas.

"The present crisis was to decide whether freedom or slavery should rule our country for centuries to come. That slavery was a great national curse; that it practically ruined one-half of the nation and greatly impeded the progress of the other half...[I]t was a curse to the Negro, but a much greater curse to the white man. It made the slaveholders petty tyrants...It made the poor whites of the South more abject and degraded than the slaves themselves...[I]t was an insurmountable obstacle in the way of the nation's progress and the prosperity. That it must be overcome and extirpated. That the way to do this was to go to the prairies of Kansas and show the superiority of free-labor civilization; to go with all our free-labor trophies; churches and schools, printing presses, steam engines, and mills; and in a peaceful contest convince every poor man from the South of the superiority of free labor. That it was much better to go and do something for free labor than to stay at home and talk of manacles and auction-blocks and blood-hounds, while deploring the never-ending aggressions of slavery. That our work was not to make women and children cry in anti-slavery conventions, by sentimental appeals, BUT TO GO AND PUT AN END TO SLAVERY."[108]

The route to the Kansas Territory from Boston would be via Chicago and St. Louis and taking a steamer to Kansas City. Horses and wagons would be required for overland passage. There were multiple stops along the way requiring advanced accommodations, resupplying of staples, and provisions of food whenever possible. Hotels and inns and even individual lodging would eventually be needed to house the Emigrant Aid Company travelers in the future.[109]

Thayer and Lawrence had faith in the capable leadership of Charles Robinson. He would be responsible for establishing the supporting facilities for the men, women and children who would soon follow.

---

108   Robinson, The Kansas Conflict, 95.
109   Ibid., 69.

This was not the first time he had been challenged to establish a legal foothold in unknown territory. Robinson had proven himself and his leadership ability during the Sacramento gold rush. He was mature and experienced. He would take the immigrants and families to this prairie, and teach them how to survive in the wilderness. He had the special qualities of being fearless, intelligent, rough, but with civilized thinking. He would stand firm against any unrest or challenge he might face in accepting the monumental task. Yet he was someone who would embrace compromise whenever possible. Charles Robinson stood alone as the one man who possessed all of the necessary attributes required in Thayer's plans for the Kansas Territory. *"A wiser and more sagacious man for this work could not have been found within the borders of the nation,"* praised Eli Thayer.[110]

"Robinson was cool-headed and thought to be cautious and calculative. Robinson looks ahead, counts the cost of everything, weighs every consideration, no matter how trifling, and comes to an unchangeable conclusion...Robinson is a great thinker, and we should judge, writes better than he speaks."[111] He was a man who would work to bring peace and freedom to Kansas.

Robinson seemed destined for his role. He had been well-educated and was a physician who had grown tired of his busy practice in New England. There, he suffered from unending demands of his medical practice. Charles decided to leave this mountain of responsibilities in 1849, and headed for the California gold rush.

On the trip to California Robinson received an education quite different from what he had experienced in New England. He learned the hard lessons of *"devices, shifts and turns, deeds of daring, honor, integrity, perfidy, rascality, and deviltry than all the educational institutions of the land could have shown."*[112] He would be exposed to diseases he had not seen before in his practice, and would learn how to diagnose and treat cholera with only a limited supply of medicines.[113]

He had observed the lawlessness of the West. There he saw a man being cheated at gambling and eventually killed aboard a steamboat on his way to the gold fields in Sacramento. The perpetrators had gotten away with this

---

110   Thomas Goodrich, War to the Knife, 11.
111   Ibid., 50-51.
112   Robinson, The Kansas Conflict, 28.
113   Ibid., 29.

murder because of a lack of law enforcement and the availability of a judge when the boat reached the port at the end of their journey.[114]

During his time in California, he would later lead the "squatters-rights" movement in Sacramento which ended in a showdown and gunfight with the sheriff, mayor and townsmen of that city. Many people lost their lives in the confrontation in the streets of Sacramento and ended with Robinson being struck in the chest by a bullet and falling from his horse and taken prisoner. He was confined for months and eventually was freed, and later exonerated. He was able to leave San Francisco knowing he was the man who had provided the leadership for the establishment of squatter's rights for the gold miners in the city.[115]

This was the depth of character of the man chosen by Eli Thayer to lead his effort and take New Englanders to the Kansan Territory. Robinson would be charged with establishing an abolitionist city, take enough New Englanders there and, when the time came, legitimately vote slavery out. All of this politically charged activity would have a direct impact on the prairie of Kansas. The center of the town would be within a few miles of where Abram and his family had only three years previously unloaded their wagons at the Wakarusa River Mission. This was the spot on earth they had migrated to in an effort to escape the slavery conflict when they left northern Missouri. Instead of leaving the conflict behind, it was coming to them.

Hundreds of people, with all of their ideals and zeal, would soon end up within a forty mile radius of the Still family on the prairie of the Kansas Territory. The time had come, and the brew had thickened as the Kansas-Nebraska legislative efforts worked their way through Washington. Its effects soon began to be felt by the people in the Territory. The boiling point of the new law had created the energy to drive the slavery storm into motion. It was on its way west.

The storm had coalesced. People on both sides were being forced to choose either freedom or slavery. And, as the emotions grew, the air began to turn dark and violent. The storm would begin to blow from every direction. Lives soon would be turned and driven by a force from which they could not hide.

As the intensity increased, the hail stones turned to lead bullets, while the gorges would run with blood rather than water—and once started

---

114   Robinson, The Kansas Conflict, 31.
115   Ibid., 51-52.

flowing—there would be no way to stop the hemorrhage. The time had come for the wind to get lost in the Prairie.

CHAPTER SIX
The Birth of Lawrence
Fall 1854

Charles Robinson was summoned to Boston in June 1854. He would help plan the immigration strategy and development of a town on the open prairie of the Kansas Territory. He had experience in providing leadership under extremely hostile conditions and had survived difficult living in the past. He had learned to recognize when a fight was unavoidable and how to win a battle once conflict was engaged. He had fought a major gun battle in the streets of Sacramento and seen blood spilled and men wounded and killed on both sides as he led his men in the war against the city. His credentials and experience were exactly what Eli Thayer was looking for. Charles Robinson was commissioned as the leader in charge of the New England Emigrant Aid Society. He would be responsible for the development of a new community that would serve as a fortress to support the immigrants as they arrived. These New Englanders would be entering a hostile environment that would not support or welcome their arrival because they were outsiders and intruders who brought with them a philosophy that was in opposition to the proslavery sentiments. It was Robinson's responsibility to stand against adversity and build a town that would provide protection for the new immigrants when they arrived. This town would be a centerpiece of power for the abolitionists and demonstrate that civilization was present there. In the future it would also serve as a welcoming spot for others when they arrived. There would be new houses waiting to protect, warm and comfort those who suffered the long trek. There would be hardware and food supplies to make beginning a new life easier. This community would also provide the essential moral support to the immigrants and give them the courage to stay. The establishment of this town was thought to be the best way for the abolitionist immigrants to coalesce and survive in the Territory. Charles Robinson accepted this challenge and probably prayed he would be wise enough to accomplish what others took for granted.

In Boston, the trip westward was finalized and the details for commissioning the Emigrant Aid Company had been accomplished. Robinson was given carte blanche backing by Eli Thayer and his board of trustees *"to visit the Territory and arrange for its settlement."*[116]

Charles Robinson and representatives of the Emigrant Aid Company left Boston for the Kansas Territory to look for the land that would become their new settlement. They took a route through Chicago on their way to St. Louis. In St. Louis, they boarded a steamer which stopped on July 4, 1854, at Jefferson City on their way to Kansas City. During the stop at Jefferson City, several new passengers came on board the steamer who were legislative politicians adjourned for the July holiday. Robinson and his company encountered a lot of attention from the new Missouri passengers. The legislators threatened to drive any northern men from the Kansas Territory and swore that no abolitionist would be permitted to settle there. The Missouri politicians also touted a large reward which had been placed on Eli Thayer's head if he were captured. Robinson's cunning leadership resulted in his company being listeners, not the talkers, and thereby avoiding any physical confrontation. When his party disembarked the steamer at Kansas City, he noted the city had substantially grown in population since his visit in 1849 and many additional buildings had been erected.[117]

In anticipation of the complicated legal entanglements in purchasing the necessary land for the new town, arrangements had been made for Robinson to meet with a young lawyer in Springfield. The attorney would travel with him and provide legal counsel in the procurement of facilities for the Emigrant Aid Society and help with the purchase of the property to build the town in the Territory.[118]

The Gillis House in Kansas City was purchased for the hotel to be used by the emigrants when traveling through that area. The next project dealt with the purchase of land for the proposed town. This was a complicated issue. Almost all the land where the proposed town was to be built belonged to the Indians. Unfortunately, a large amount of reservation lands were tied up by treaties with the United States Government which disallowed that Indian land to be sold. Such were the circumstances of the Delaware tribe. However, the Shawnee Indian land was open to pre-emption and sale since the Treaty had not yet been signed by the Shawnee with the government. This Shawnee land extended thirty miles west of the Missouri state line and had not been surveyed. It was this tract of land that Robinson headed

---

116   Robinson, The Kansas Conflict, 69.
117   Ibid.
118   Ibid., 70.

out to explore. The proposed site was located on the Kansas River. When he returned to Kansas City from this expedition, a letter was waiting with instructions for him to go to St. Louis and meet the first party of twenty-nine emigrants who had just arrived. He was to accompany them to the Territory. He met these new arrivals and took them to the Kansas Territory. Upon completing this order he was then summoned to immediately return to Boston for further consultation. Robinson followed his instructions and returned to Boston.[119] When Robinson returned to Massachusetts, Amos Lawrence informed him that he had employed a man named Colonel Blood, from Wisconsin, to help him deal with the Indians and to aid in the purchase of the new building site. Colonel Blood had experience in dealing with Indian affairs, and knew the intricacies of pre-emption laws.[120]

Colonel Blood gave an account regarding the details of the purchase of the land for the new town that would eventually be named Lawrence:

"I obtained information that the Shawnee Indians had ceded their reservation south of the Kansas River...and that a portion was suitable for settlement, and the most available, the party decided to come here...I also came along on horseback, in company with a gentleman by the name of Cobb. The night before arriving here the party went into camp at the Blue Jacket crossing of the Wakarusa. Mr. Cobb and I stopped for the night at Dr. Still's, a short distance east of the crossing. The next morning I rode to the top of Blue Mound, from there crossed the Wakarusa at Blanton's Ford, arrived some time in the afternoon on the hill where the University now stands, finding the party there pitching their tents and unloading their wagons. I met Mr. Branscomb there that day. He informed me that he had bought a claim of a Mr. Stearns, and had agreed to pay him $500.00 for it..."[121]

At this point, the necessary land for the town had been purchased and the first emigrants had arrived from Boston on August 1, 1854, and were led by Robinson to the site. Charles Robinson headed back to Boston and prepared to leave on August 29, 1854, with the second contingency headed for the Kansas Territory. He was also busy with plans for the development of the community. The new immigration movement was clearly underway. Thayer's dream of settling the Territory with abolitionists from the north

---

119   Robinson, The Kansas Conflict, 71.
120   Ibid.
121   Ibid., 72.

to vote against slavery and stop it from spreading into the Territory was no longer just a dream.[122]

The second group of New England immigrants left for the Territory and were sent off on their journey with a hero's farewell. This group of the Emigration Aid Society was charged to go to the Territory and provide the labor to construct the new settlement. Charles Robinson now had enough people to lay out the town on the newly purchased land.

For the immigrants who made this trip, traveling across the wilderness was difficult. Many travelers reported hardships during their journey. The steamships used for the river passages were frequently overcrowded. Often blankets were placed parallel on the deck for sleeping because there weren't enough beds. Those that were lucky enough to get a cabin found themselves in the poorest part of the ship with little ventilation and were either cold without adequate heat or overheated in a space adjacent to the engine room. Food was meager, and only the aggressive managed to fill their stomachs while many left the galley still hungry. As one passenger put it, *"We were 4 days making the trip…a distance of 450 miles…The water is always very muddy. It was the most unpleasant 4 days I ever journeyed. I do not remember hearing a man speak on the boat whose conversation I watched at all who did not swear. The cabin presented a continual scene of card playing from beginning to end."*[123]

Once off the ship, the lodging that was thought to have been prepared in Kansas City was often not available. The few who obtained rooms did so with greater expense than expected. Often, the rooms that were available were dirty and ill-equipped compared to Boston standards. Sickness abounded in the cities and people dying from disease were commonplace. For everyone who died while in a hotel, there would be another anxious new boarder waiting to scurry in. The smell of death still lingered in the air as the new bags were unpacked. One traveler offered his own version of the city.

Kansas City was loaded with *"gamblers, pickpockets and 'jackals' of all descriptions, sights witnessed by the ladies seemed perfectly designed to offend eastern sensibilities…*

Our first impressions of this city were extremely unfavorable; and boarding in this hotel as we have for weeks past, confirms us in the belief, that…the inhabitants and the morals, are of an indescribably repulsive and

---

122   Robinson, The Kansas Conflict, 74.
123   Letters of John and Sarah Everett, 1854-1864, 1.

undesirable character...There is but one Church edifice in the city, and this unpainted, uncarpeted, and as filthy as any incorrigible tobacco chewier would wish to have it; stove, benches, and other 'fixtures' bearing unmistakable evidence that the delicious weed, had been thoroughly masticated."[124]

"During our stay...hundreds were almost constantly thronging the house, bringing various diseases with them, and seldom a boat load without more or less sick, until the very air in the rooms seemed impregnated with the disease and death. Within a few feet of our own room, lay at one time four men, sick with lung fever. A little further on, in the passage that led to our room, within a short time lay two dead bodies."[125]

Despite the unpleasant journey, and the conditions of the city, Charles Robinson and his fellow travelers would eventually leave behind the squalid conditions and push on toward the west. Where these men were going, there were no hotels, gambling houses, or saloons to deal with. There would be, however, an entirely new set of problems to face and they were about to be introduced to these hardships.

What Charles Robinson saw when he and his second contingency arrived at the town site between the rivers instantly reminded him of the Sacramento land squabbles and the tremendous task ahead. The first group of men who had arrived was still huddled up on a windswept hill with no protection, encamped in the mud and dirt. They had accomplished little progress toward starting a town. The best they had been able to do was dig in and put up their tents. They were disorganized, weary, and in need of leadership.

Robinson realized immediately that he was going to be dealing with a repeat of the California squatters' land experience. Despite the fact that a tract of land had been purchased, its ownership was still in dispute. Men claimed land without deeds and often claimed more land than they were entitled to. These men were ready to use whatever laws they could muster to show authority to enforce their sovereignty over every square foot of soil. The rule of ownership depended on the power of each individual since no law enforcement governed the surrounding Territory. This often meant that whoever was the toughest and did not blink while looking down the barrel of a revolver was the winner. [126]

---

124   Goodrich, War to the Knife, 18.
125   Ibid., 19.
126   Robinson, The Kansas Conflict, 77.

Robinson had to be extremely cautious and must have remembered what had occurred in his last battle over claim issues and the critical wound he suffered. It would have been hard for him not to think about the scar just below his heart and the bullet that had barely missed the intended target. He must have thought about his imprisonment while recovering in the brig of an old ship.

Undoubtedly, as the second group of immigrants approached the camp with Charles Robinson in their midst, the men who had arrived one month ahead of them must have had a sense of relief that help had finally arrived.

The ill feeling toward the New England Aid Society had already grown rapidly since the arrival of the first group. They represented only a small number of abolitionists in the Kansas Territory while the majority of the inhabitants in the area looked upon them with scorn. The newspapers and speeches of the day were clearly against the establishment of any Yankee community, with many proclaiming, *"Every man north of Mason and Dixon's line is an abolitionist."*[127]

Meetings were called by the proslavery sympathizers to discuss these new arrivals and the stance to be taken toward them.

The Platte Argus, a newspaper in Missouri, admonished in part, *"Citizens of the West, of the South, and Illinois! stake out your claims, and woe be to the abolitionist or Mormon who shall intrude upon it, or come within reach of your long and true rifles, or within point-blank shot of your revolvers. Keep a sharp lookout lest some dark night you shall see the flames curling from your house or the midnight philanthropist hurrying off your faithful servant."*[128]

The New England Aid Society felt justified in the migration to the Kansas Territory with a clear purpose and legal design. *"There was no employment of mercenaries, no defraying of expenses even, and no discrimination on account of political or other views the emigrants might entertain. A proslavery man had the same facilities as a Free-State man. The same was true of the settlements in the Territory."*[129]

The town, named Lawrence after its benefactor, was started despite the land ownership being claimed by several other men. The greed exhibited reminded Robinson of the Sacramento speculators when they began showing up asserting ownership of the land where Lawrence was to be built.

---

127 Robinson, The Kansas Conflict, 76.
128 Ibid., 76-77.
129 Ibid., 77.

They demanded the site be vacated. Charles Robinson described one of the encroachment attempts that he encountered:

"[T]he most belligerent of the claimants was John Baldwin. He established himself within five or ten rods of the Stears cabin bought for the town, and asserted his right to one hundred and sixty acres of land... the lands had not yet been surveyed, it was impossible to tell where the section lines would run, and the town company were [sic] disposed to act strictly on the defensive. The managers were satisfied to leave the question of title to the Land Office or the courts...Not so with Baldwin and company... they determined to remove all occupants and all improvements from their claims, which covered, or would cover if heeded, nearly the whole Territory opened to settlement. While the motive that actuated proslavery men to forestall the Free-State settlers and prevent them from getting a foothold in the Territory, some of the claimants at Lawrence cared nothing for the slavery question, but simply wanted to be bought off."[130]

The details of the conflict that ensued were filled with suspense. During the standoff, the men from each party were on both sides of the proposed town glaring at each other with threatening looks across a ravine that separated the two conflicting camps. Days had gone by with both sides refusing to negotiate or compromise. Suddenly a wagon raced into the Yankee side of the ravine. A woman jumped out and began to throw all of the contents of one of the tents out through the flaps. She then tore down the poles and canvas while four armed guards surrounded to protect her activity. The woman took her rage and anger out against the immigrants by tearing down the tent. The tent and the contents were then flung into the wagon and all involved tried to make a getaway. [131]

When the immigrants saw what was going on, two of the Yankees rushed over to apprehend the culprits. The wagon was stopped and the woman and men were forced to replace the tent and restore the contents. The tensions were now heightened as emotions soared awaiting the next move of the other.[132]

Robinson, in his usual, organized manner, began to form military-style platoons to deal with the opposition. These men were paraded on horseback in a show of military force just as he had done in the Sacramento conflict. He knew the effect that armed men had on the psyche of the enemy. Men

---

130   Robinson, The Kansas Conflict, 79.
131   Ibid., 80.
132   Ibid.

drilling on horseback with their rifles in hand sent a clear and undaunted message—challenge me if you dare to stand in harm's way—people were going to be hurt and probably killed.

This plan had the desired effect on Baldwin and his men. The confrontation turned into a war of words with notes shuttled back and forth with threats and resolves written by both sides. First, the armed men huddled around the author of the messages and later formed in tight circles when the other's response was read.

A note was sent from Baldwin's tent which read: *"Kansas Territory, October 6th. ' Dr. Robinson: Yourself and friends are notified that you will have one-half hour to move the tent which you have on my undisputed claim, and from this date to desist from surveying on said claim. If the tent is not moved within one-half hour, we shall take the trouble to move the same. (Signed,) " 'JOHN BALDWIN AND FRIENDS.' "* Robinson replied immediately sending a note that read " *'To John Baldwin and Friends. " 'If you molest our property, you do it at your peril. " 'C. ROBINSON AND FRIENDS.' "*[133]

The conflict that had been a stand-off between Baldwin and Robinson, now came down to the single tent that the woman, Baldwin's sister, had tried to remove from the contested property. Baldwin was determined to back up the action taken by his sister. He would defend her honor and had eighteen armed men on horseback only ten rods away from the tent who were waiting to charge and retake the spot in dispute. They knew they were outnumbered by the enemy but used the psychological advantage of their location to try to scare Robinson and his men. They told Robinson that it really didn't matter if they failed to win with only eighteen men in the camp because, if they failed, three thousand more would be raised to wipe them out for resisting their effort. Baldwin suggested Robinson's fate had been sealed regarding the tent property regardless of the outcome of the pending battle.

Robinson and his thirty armed men waited on the other side. Robinson heard their arguments and threats without flinching. He was as he had been in the streets of Sacramento, standing against armed attempts to run men off their land. Like the speculators in Sacramento, Baldwin would not wait for the court to decide the dispute or wait for reasonable arbitration. The guns were drawn to decide who owned the property. Robinson made it clear that they were going to fight. When one of the men asked him if they

---

133   Robinson, The Kansas Conflict, 81.

were to shoot over the charging men's heads to scare them if they charged, his answer left no doubt of his sincerity to defend their property. He said that he *"would be ashamed to fire at a man and not hit him."*[134]

John Baldwin had no way of knowing about Sacramento and what Charles Robinson had done there. He didn't know that Robinson was not going to be bluffed into submission. Even if Robinson's men were new at military strategy and uncomfortable with the armed conflict in front of them, Charles Robinson made his stand and demonstrated his willingness to fight for what he believed to be a just cause. Baldwin and his men finally realized that their efforts to drive Robinson and the New Englanders off the land were not going to succeed and they saddled their horses and rode away.

The first battle at Lawrence had been won without firing a shot. The strong leadership of Robinson had once again prevailed. The fact that in this skirmish the immigrants outnumbered the enemy three to one played a significant role as well. Baldwin and his company begrudgingly left their defensive position and their attempts to stop the development of the new town. This triumph allowed the city of Lawrence to be laid out without further interruption from Baldwin. The destiny of an abolitionist community had been guaranteed. The direction now was to move forward toward the town's development. What had only been an encampment in the Kansas Territory would become a town named Lawrence—a fitting tribute to its benefactor, Amos Lawrence, and a place of refuge for the newly arriving abolitionists.

---

134   Robinson, The Kansas Conflict, 82.

CHAPTER SEVEN
Old Bourbon

The political winds had been blowing steadily from the north during the last several months and more settlers had begun to arrive from New England. The time had come for the proslavery politicians to try to change the intensity and speed of these winds and redirect it from the south. Nature accomplishes these dramatic changes through high and low pressure systems that invisibly create the dynamics that turn the winds around spontaneously. The natural events can be so rapid and silent that the only noticeable change was the shifting of a hat from one side of the head to the other to prevent it from blowing off. The dynamics of political change are almost never painless or silent. The political system uses high and low pressure systems in a much different way. The head is adjusted and not the hat.

While the North had Charles Robinson, Eli Thayer, Amos Lawrence, and many other leaders to champion their cause in the new Territory, the South had their own powerful leader who was equally experienced and capable. His name was David Atchison. He was despised by the North because of his commitment to slavery and criticized for his whiskey-drinking behavior. David Atchison, however, was a man whom the South could count on to hold the line against the immigrant invasion that had begun.

He was exciting, a politically aggressive leader, and because of his drinking habits had been nicknamed "Old Bourbon." The Kansas Territory was located in his part of the United States, and he believed it was his duty to attack the abolitionist's emigrants and halt the potential problems they were going to cause. David Atchison accepted the struggles that lay ahead to achieve the proslavery goals of the South; and the hard-drinking, clever politician would never think of giving in to the abolitionists and would fight to the end to preserve slavery.

He had earned his reputation through dealing with politics and the use of government power. He had been a former vice president of the United States and was serving as a Senator from Missouri. In addition, he probably could have cared less what the New Englanders thought or called him. He would, however, be the one expected to provide leadership for the South. His legacy as a proslavery leader was being made while the eyes in

Washington were on him. His every move was analyzed. The expectation was that he would stop the immigration nightmare and turn the invaders around—sending all of them back to the North. If he could accomplish this undertaking, Atchison knew he would undoubtedly seal his moment in history and would be revered and honored by the South forever. In addition, he must also have known if he failed to champion the southern cause, he would run the risk of being labeled a failure. David Atchison was committed to do his best to represent his countrymen, the interests of slavery and, most importantly, win support to promulgate slavery through the rest of the country. He could not fail!

The complicated issues surrounding the continuation of slavery had fallen at David Atchison's feet. The Missouri Compromise, which had drawn the slavery tolerance line, ran along the border of his state. The new Federal Kansas-Nebraska Bill passed in May 1854, had erased that line and would start by allowing the voting process by the residents in the territories to decide whether slavery would be legalized or stopped. It was his job to make sure that the Kansas Territory had enough proslavery votes to win the contest. However, the Missourians were only a few miles away from the territorial border and could easily cross the line when the time came to vote for slavery. His job was to ensure success by preventing the invasion of people from the North who were abolitionists. That would require him to stop Robinson and the Emigration Aid Society who were arriving in the Kansas Territory in increasing numbers and beginning to cause concerns for the South.

While almost everyone expected Nebraska to vote against slavery in their new Territory and side with the North, it would make it an absolute necessity for the people in the Kansas Territory to vote with the South to keep the political playing field even and to protect the southern interests and the continued expansion of slavery.[135]

Senator Atchison had not forgotten the lack of cooperation he had experienced from his supporters in Congress. He had recently attempted to appoint his political colleague, Thomas Johnson, as a delegate from the Kansas Territory; Congress had refused the appointment.

Atchison had helped organize the men who were supposed to support Reverend Thomas Johnson, a minister, and a proslavery advocate, for this position. Instead, Congress had rebuked Johnson when he arrived in Washington. They questioned the legality of the appointment and had

---

135   Robinson, The Kansas Conflict, 93-94.

embarrassed him by denying Johnson a seat in Congress on the technicality that Kansas had not yet been officially declared a Territory.[136]

Atchison must have wondered where his southern allies were when he needed support. They had allowed Johnson to be sent back to the Kansas Territory without achieving the political appointment that would have helped strengthen the proslavery movement immediately. David Atchison had been dealt a political slap in the face by Congress when they denied his delegate's appointment to stand. He had done his job to strengthen the southern influence in the Kansas Territory, but his fellow sympathizers had not been able to capitalize on this advantage.[137]

By now, most of his southern colleagues would have heard about the northern immigrant arrival in the Kansas Territory. This migration only heightened his role as a dominate player in the slavery issue. The onus was on him to block any wavering regarding the Kansas Territory and the slavery issue. For slavery to succeed and expand, first, the Kansas Territory would have to be designated a slave territory, and then a constitution written and adopted. David Atchison and the South knew that once the slaves were legally allowed to cross the Missouri border, every new state formed in the future would have the opportunity to follow suit. He was challenged to provide the organizational support for southern power and influence to make sure that Kansas and succeeding states would be added to the Union under the proslavery flag. To accomplish this goal, the South was willing to give up Nebraska to the abolitionists and the northern states in exchange for ensuring that the Kansas Territory and other remaining territorial lands would be proslavery states when they came into the Union.[138]

However, the North threw in an unexpected tactic. It took for granted that the Nebraska Territory would be a free, uncontested Territory. They continued to send New Englanders into the Kansas Territory in an effort to vote down slavery and claim both Kansas and Nebraska in the new Bill. The North had cut the pie in half, was given the first piece; and now, began nibbling on the other half. This was an intolerable insult to Atchison and his southern colleagues. The South fought back and they counted on Atchison to lead the way. It would be up to him and his ability as an orator to rally the South and the residents of Missouri to counteract what the North had done and to organize the resistance against the Yankee Immigrants. David Atchison accepted his role, and when he spoke it was with conviction and

136   Trowbridge, Andrew Taylor Still, 46.
137   Ibid.
138   Robinson, The Kansas Conflict, 4, 19.

thunder: *"We are playing for a mighty stake,"*... *"[and] the game must be played boldly."*[139]

Atchison predicted, *"We will before six months rolls round, have the Devil to play in Kansas and in this State."* He vowed he would sooner see Kansas *"sunk in the bottom of Hell than come in a free state."*[140]

He spelled out what the other side was doing and what response would be necessary to win the battle for the Kansas Territory. He made it clear that hundreds, maybe even thousands of Yankees would be coming to the Territory to vote the northern anti-slavery mandate. He reminded his supporters that the Yankees had to travel over a thousand miles to reach the ballot box and that the North was willing to overcome every hardship to make the journey for its interests to prevail.[141]

He challenged his supporters and the southern interest to respond to this invasion. He reminded them that they lived next door to the Territory and only a few miles away from the ballot boxes. He asked them to compare their resolve to the Yankee response and commit to win the slavery issue. He challenged his allies to respond en masse and overshadow the enemy by having tens of thousands cross the border to stake a claim in the Territory. He rallied them to mount up and ride when it came time and exercise their rights across the border and cast a vote for the South.[142]

He pleaded his case regarding the Kansas Territory in a speech saying, *"The organic law of the Territory vests in the people who reside in it the power to form all its municipal regulations. They can either admit or exclude slavery, and this is the only question that materially affects our interest."*[143]

"The people of Kansas in their first election would decide the question whether or not the slave-holder was to be excluded, and it depended upon a majority of the votes cast at the polls. ...[I am] for meeting these philanthropic knaves peaceably at the ballot box and out-voting them."[144]

David Atchison continued to politically maneuver with the help of Reverend Johnson. When he and Johnson met with the Shawnee Indians, including Chief Paschal Fish, Jr., and his representatives on the *Polar Star* steamer in April 1854, they took part in negotiating a treaty that transferred

---

139   Goodrich, War to the Knife, 39.
140   Ibid., 27.
141   Robinson, The Kansas Conflict, 93-94.
142   Ibid.
143   Ibid.
144   Ibid..

control of the Indian lands to the federal government. This new treaty allowed legal access to the Kansas Territory land, and it meant that the Kansas Territory would be open for any settler to occupy and to file legal claims.[145]

Senator Atchison's plan was to make absolutely sure that the majority of the settlers would be from Missouri and represent the South. As Atchison pointed out to these settlers, they only had to travel a few miles to establish a residence in the new Territory. As he saw it, they wouldn't even have to actually stay there. All they had to do was ride across the Missouri border and stake out a claim. The requirements for making a land claim could be as simple as laying down a few stones or putting up a lean-to. No one could stop them from returning home to Missouri where they actually resided. Their lives would not be changed or hindered in any way. It would be a simple but effective strategy. When the Kansas Territory voted on any issue, the Missourians who had legally staked claims could ride back across the border and vote for the southern cause. This tactic would be used every time an issue concerning slavery or a situation that was sensitive to the South appeared on any ballot in the Kansas Territory. David Atchison formulated this plan for the South. By controlling the vote, the South would be saved.[146]

His leadership also took on a personal note. He helped organize several secret lodges to defend the position of the South and vowed to take up arms if necessary and lead his proslavery forces into battle. They formed the secret organizations to further their cause. He and his southern allies were proud of the men and the organizations they belonged to, such as, *"Sons of the South, Blue Lodges,"* and the *"Self-Defensives."* Secret coded phrases were given to the members for identification. *"All right on the hemp,"* and *"sound on the goose"* would identify members immediately. By knowing these code words, a stranger's political viewpoint would be known. Eventually, if the conflict became bloody, those words could make a difference between whether a man lived or died.[147]

Senator Atchison also found allies in the newspapers. They began spreading the word that "outsiders" coming from the North were unwelcome. Warnings were published. *"We have no sympathy for Abolitionism,"* seethed the editor of the Kickapoo Kansas Pioneer, *"and the sooner they are made to believe that the squatters of Kansas Territory have no sympathy for their blacks, nefarious, contemptible dogmas the better. We want no*

---

145   Trowbridge, Andrew Taylor Still, 46 / Clark, Reminiscences, 22.
146   Robinson, The Kansas Conflict, 94.
147   Goodrich, War to the Knife, 27-28.

Negro-sympathizing thieves among us; they will be running off our slaves whenever a chance offers. Their hearts are as black as the darkest deeds of hell. Away with them; send them back where they belong."[148]

Atchison and his allies made clear that abolitionists were not welcome in the Kansas Territory. There would be no passive attitude or tolerance. People sympathizing with the North would have to be out-maneuvered. Anyone who took the abolitionist defense would no longer be tolerated. Closing the door on new arrivals from the North would take place.

Senator Atchison openly acknowledged the new hard-line attitude that his Southern allies were forced to develop. This included the Shawnee Indians educational needs which would be centralized at the Shawnee Mission Manual Labor School run by Reverend Johnson. Johnson's school would be the only institution developing education and training for the Shawnee. It would eliminate Abram Still's small mission school located on the Wakarusa River. The abolitionists, like Abram Still, would have to go elsewhere.[149]

At this point, David Atchison and Reverend Johnson were well on their way toward getting rid of the abolitionists. They would undermine them. As far as Atchison and Johnson were concerned, the Wakarusa Mission, Abram Still, and his family were gone.[150]

In the spring of 1854, President Pierce signed the new Shawnee Treaty into federal law. Senator Atchison rallied his Missouri men, and they began the run across the border to put into motion the land-claiming process and the methods to dominate the upcoming election that he had helped formulate. Much of the choice land was quickly taken as eager riders crossed the borders on their way to stake their claims. The Missourians also established two early towns to be used by the southerners, naming one of them after Atchison himself. The other town was called Leavenworth.[151]

The plan had been implemented and pieces began to fall in place. The eastern border of the Kansas Territory was Atchison's, which meant that southern rights were going to be protected. He had done his job. All he had to do was wait for the upcoming November 1854 election. He and his allies could then formally establish Kansas as a slave territory.

---

148 Goodrich, War to the Knife, 28.
149 Trowbridge, Andrew Taylor Still, 46-47.
150 Ibid. / Robinson, The Kansas Conflict, 93.
151 Trowbridge, Andrew Taylor Still, 47.

There still were some abolitionist matters to deal with. He was aware of Charles Robinson and the Emigrant Aid Society's stand and that they had run people off of their claims to establish a "Yankee Town" to be named Lawrence. Atchison's aim was to eliminate this small number of northern men who had the audacity to force men off their legal claims. He was also aware that more men were still on the way from Boston. This company was well organized and financed by the Free-Soil movement. However, with the Indian Treaty signed and the Kansas-Nebraska Bill in place, his attention could now be turned toward eliminating this Lawrence foothold of resistance and the prevention of other towns from being established. He must have wondered how it was going to be received by the North when he ran these intruders scurrying back to Boston.

CHAPTER EIGHT
The Loss and Hope
May 1854

The Still family continued to provide Indian education, medical care, and farm the ground at the Wakarusa Mission. Whether Abram ever asked Paschal Jr. about what had occurred during his meeting between Paschal Jr., Senator Atchison, and Reverend Johnson on the ship, *Polar Star*, remains unknown. Regardless, the Stills and the other mission schools would eventually learn that their federal funding had been lost. An exception was made in the new treaty to continue and expand the funding for Reverend Johnson's proslavery school. As a result, all of the Shawnee Indian children had to have their education transferred to Reverend Johnson's Shawnee Mission School under the proslavery banner.[152]

Everything the Stills' Northern Methodist's Wakarusa Mission School had accomplished during the previous three years would end. The Still families would also be required to relocate again because even the land that the mission school had been built upon was deeded over to Paschal Fish, Jr.

The new Federal Treaties signed in 1854 regained control of the Indian land. These were the Indian lands promised forever. Despite the fact that the grass was abundant and water gushed into the rivers, the lands had been taken away from them. Instead, the vast Indian Prairie had been exchanged for two-hundred acres deeded individually to every qualified Shawnee Indian. The Shawnee Indians could only hope that this agreement would be respected in the future by a government who did not honor promises even when based on the language of nature. Chief Paschal Jr., must have realized the invasion of the white man could not be stopped from either North or South because the formers desired some of the most fertile farm ground in the country. Rather than risking having his tribe be forced to move en masse to another "promised land," he probably knew his tribe would be better off settling for what white men seemed only to respect—a registered deed. Even if it were for only two-hundred acres for each Indian, it gave

---

152   Trowbridge, Andrew Taylor Still, 46.

them an equal position with the white man and a federal legal system in place to protect their property rights in the future.

The Still family continued to suffer the political consequences for their abolitionist beliefs in an area of the country that embraced slavery, and the Shawnee tribe suffered the loss of an entire Prairie to the federal government in exchange for a few thousand acres that they would call their own. Both men had lost their individual battles and their lives would never be the same.

It remained speculation, but many believed that Chief Paschal Jr. refused to take the land away from Abram and the mission school. Instead, he insisted on buying the land and mission house from Abram Still, even though he had already been deeded the property under the new federal treaty. Their friendship in the past had probably been so profound that he could not take the land away other than through a purchase agreement between people who were friends.[153]

With the abolitionist losses and the political maneuvering taking place, the new village in Lawrence would now represent even greater importance to the abolitionists in the Kansas Territory. The northern immigrants heading to the Territory represented at least some hope for the Stills if they were going to survive and remain in the area. They could only pray that the reports were true that hundreds of other New England immigrants were planning to head their way and would eventually expand the abolitionist's numbers.[154]

Everyone also began to understand that the upcoming Territorial election in November of 1854 would be crucial regarding who would control the political outcome and future of the Territory. Whoever succeeded and elected the men who would write the new constitution would create the environment and dominate the future for the Kansas Territory. The political wars would be won or lost at the ballot box. Eli Thayer's vision could only be realized by financing enough immigrants to make it possible for northern families to come to the area and to win the majority vote. Without the Emigration Society representing the majority, any slavery issues would receive a favorable vote and the country would embrace the expansion of slavery.

The immigrants overall political strength would also be improved if the abolitionists were able to choose the delegate who would represent their

153   Trowbridge, Andrew Taylor Still, 47.
154   Ibid., 49.

views in Washington. However, it was also understood that if a proslavery candidate were to win the nomination for Congress, the Kansas Territory would write a proslavery constitution and set the political tone for the country and guarantee slavery expansion in the future. The major hope for the abolitionists was represented by the proposed town of Lawrence and its political efforts to resist slavery.

How Abram, Martha, and the rest of the Still family reacted to the Wakarusa Mission failure was summed up years later by Andrew Still's sister, Rovia, when she wrote about the experience. *"The Babtist (sic), the Quakers and the mission of the old M.E. Church were left out in the cold, but the Southern M.E. Mission in charge of Rev. Johnson was the only one not thrown out of business."*[155] It would have been very difficult for the Still family to understand and accept what had happed to them and to defend what had occurred without feeling disgust and bitterness toward the undermining participants.

The Stills and their mission had been devastated by the lack of provision for their school in the new Shawnee Treaty. They were forced to search for land to rebuild homes and new lives. This was not going to be easy on Abram Still who now was almost sixty years old. He was being forced to change his life once more because of his abolitionist beliefs.

The Stills had to overcome adversity as they had done so many times in the past. They accepted their fate and banded together. Abram's sons took the offensive and found new land. They filed claims for land along the Kansas River bottoms located approximately two miles from the Wakarusa Mission and began constructing a home for Abram, Martha, and the remaining younger siblings who were living with their parents at the mission while his sons worked on the log cabin.[156]

As if the family needed another conflict to face, another situation was thrust upon Abram when he saw a man and his horse and buggy circling in the prairie apparently out of control. Abram never missed an opportunity to help his fellowman and he went to the rescue. He *"found a man in the buggy and he was sick and delirious so Father brought him to the house and we gave him the best room and bed in the house."*[157]

Abram's commitment to the stranger began another episode that would profoundly affect his family and many of the Indian orphans who were in

---

155   Clark, Reminiscences, 19.
156   Clark 17. / Trowbridge, Andrew Taylor Still, 57.
157   Clark, 15.

their charge. Abram's ministry knew no bounds, and as a result, his entire family frequently had to pay the price for his evangelism. Once again the price would prove to be both physically and financially severe.

Rovia gave an account of what occurred when Abram brought the man into their home. *"Our accommodations were poor at best, but we gave him our best. He was in bed six weeks. My father doctored him and Mother took the best care of him she could with her other burdens and to add to the rest, he had the most malignant form of contagious inflammatory sore eyes we had ever seen. In a few days every one in the house had those horrible sore eyes and there were none of us that ever fully got over it."*[158]

Whatever the cause of the eye infection, it was extremely contagious, and infected almost the entire family. Martha Still suffered a severe complication, never completely regained her vision. However, one of the orphaned Indian children staying with the Stills paid the highest price. The infection caused her to go completely blind.

Rovia Still documented this incident in her reminiscences. *"There were still five or six Indian children that stayed at the mission during the vacation season because they were orphans and had no place to go. Two of the little girls had weak eyes and one went blind. We suffered so terribly. The blood would run out of our eyes. Father said in all his practice he had never seen anything to equal it for sore eyes. Poor mother had suffered so with her eyes. She had walked the floor for days and nights till one night about one o'clock a thought came to her that perhaps if she would go out into the cow lot and milk some fresh warm milk into her eyes it might soothe the pain, so she went and she sat there a long time milking the warm milk into her eyes. Then came into the house and sat down on the floor and leaned her head on a chair and she was so exhausted from pain and loss of sleep that she fell asleep and slept till morning. Her eyes had gotten easy, but like the other members of the family, her eyes never got well. It left us with dim vision, weak eyes, granulated lids."*[159]

In addition to the suffering caused by the stranger, it was accompanied by an unappreciative attitude as he recovered. He also used the children as his personal servants as he recovered. Rovia continued with her vivid memories of him. *"After the stranger got well enough to talk, he told us that he was from Pennsylvania, that he was a Baptist preacher and that his name was Clark, that he had come out to look at the country and take*

---

158   Clark, Reminiscences, 15-16.
159   Ibid., 16.

claims for himself and sons and sons-in-law. While he was convalescing, he kept us children waiting on him and he would order us around like so many galley slaves. If the other members of the family happened to be out, he would send us to the spring for water. He would drink a few swallows, then call for his little servants to bring him more fresh water."[160]

"He kept his buggy whip on the bed by his side and he never failed to remind us that if we didn't hurry back with the water, he would wear it out on us. So we didn't tarry long by the way...My sister Cassie and myself and the five Indian children all came in for our share of his self made authority and looked upon his buggy whip with terror. We usually spent the brief moments of intermission between our trips back and forth to the spring out back of the house redressing his pedigree and, I must say, it was not done in a very Christian manner. We had to stay in calling distance and we did not dare to make any noise in the house, for if we did, the buggy whip would loom up in sight."[161]

Apparently this Baptist preacher finally got well enough to move about and the children won back their freedom. Rovia Still, when describing this event years later, failed to offer any explanation why the children didn't complain to the rest of the family about the treatment they were receiving. Perhaps the children were raised not to question adult authority and this led to the abuse in their own home.

Despite the illness that the visitor had brought upon the family and unaware of his treatment of the children, Abram continued to help the Baptist minister beyond reasonable expectations. The results of the care and attention were astonishing.

"After he got well enough to ride out, my father hitched his old Bonaparte to the buggy and took him out to see the country and among the other places he took him up to see our claims that we had taken on the Kansas River bottom about 3 miles east of where Lawrence now is."[162]

"Father had taken claim and built a cabin on it. My two brothers and two young men from Mo. had also taken claims there and had staked them off but had not done any work on them. Father hired two men to work for him. After Father had driven all day with him and shown him every important place, they came home. Father didn't charge him a cent for his doctor bill, his board, or his horse pasture and he didn't seem to be very lavish

---

160   Clark, Reminiscences, 16
161   Ibid., 17.
162   Ibid.

83

with his thanks either. We were not sorry to see him go. The men folks were very busy putting up the hay, cutting corn, and doing other work on the farm and did not go to do any work on the claims for a couple of weeks. So one morning they got up early and went to the claims and whom do you suppose they found occupying our cabin? It was none other than the above named Bro. Clark. They had their bedding, cooking utensils, and everything packed snugly away in the cabin. Father said, 'Bro. Clark, what does this mean?' He said, 'It means that I wrote to my sons and sons-in-law and they are here on the ground, (ten in number) and we intend to have these claims and we will shoot every man that dares interfere with us or be shot ourselves.' Father said, 'This is poor pay for our kindness to you for if I had not taken you in and cared for you, you would have been in your grave two months ago.' He said, 'I can't help that.' He said, 'I will start back to Pennsylvania in a few days and bring out the rest of my family and we intend to have these claims or fight it to the bitter end.'[163]

Abram's kindness had been repaid in such an unbelievable way that even his family decided it was time to intervene.

"This enraged my two brothers and the two young men from Mo. so they picked the old fellow up and started to the river and they declared they would tie a stone around his neck and toss him in head long into the river, but Father begged them to let the old rascal go as they were not armed, only with the physical strengths of young manhood."

"His sons and sons-in-laws happened to be off in another quarter cutting timber and putting up their cabins, so if they had been present I do not know what the consequences might have been. Father and the boys came home that evening and we talked the matter over carefully and Father said, 'Well, that is a low down trick, but I guess we will have to give up our claims and look some other place for I know it will mean death to some of my family and death to some kin,' and he said, 'I would rather never have a (sic) fool of land than to get it that way. There is too much vacant land to fight over it.' "[164]

It must have been a long and quiet ride home that night after Abram's sons packed up their tools and loaded the family's personal possessions into the wagons for the slow trek back to the mission. Abram must have forced himself to dwell on positive thoughts that tomorrow would be a new day as the wagons lumbered along. He was relieved and found peace in knowing

163   Clark, Reminiscences, 17-18.
164   Ibid.

that both he and Brother Clark's sons would be alive to see the sunrise. The disappointment this event would cause the family and the words he would have to use to explain the forsaken trust to the children must have been extremely difficult. It seemed Abram was always caught in some dilemma regarding moral issues, and his family always seemed to suffer the consequences. Another calamity had fallen upon the Stills, and as always, Abram, with his never-shaken Christian principles, turned the other cheek.

The Wakarusa Mission would soon be gone because the proslavery political system closed the doors; the new claim and cabin were gone because of greed and treachery. The family had once again experienced another catastrophe at the hands of a man who called himself a minister.

As painful as it must have been to face the ambivalence surrounding men who claimed to be of faith and professed to represent Christianity, it must have made the long ride home seem even further in the wagon that night.

CHAPTER NINE
The Elections
November 1854/March 1855

The fall months during 1854 resulted in a flurry of political activity in the Kansas Territory, including the arrival of Andrew H. Reeder in October to assume his position as the first Territorial Governor. Abolitionists also continued to arrive in the Territory with their numbers growing close to 800, but they still represented only a small minority of the people when compared to the thousands of proslavery inhabitants coming across the border from Missouri. The southerners were attempting to establish a land claim which they believed would give them voting rights.[165]

The election to choose a representative to Congress had been set for November 29, 1854, and this day would be disheartening for the new arrivals from New England. As the election days approached, the hard work of Senator David Atchison began to pay off. He had ridden throughout the state and had given fiery speeches blasting the New Englanders for being "hired paupers" who had only come to vote against the slavery delegates. His verbal attacks made Missourians feel even more justified and entitled to vote in the election than the transplanted New Englanders and they continued pouring across the border. The abolitionists were shocked to see the number of proslavery men arriving. *"For days before the election they crowded by the hundreds the roads leading to the various districts, ...always carrying with them a liberal supply of bad whiskey. Maddened by its influence, they were ready for any dishonorable or violent course."*[166]

The day the voting began, several of the small districts were overrun with fraud. In Douglas, which was located only a few miles west of Lawrence, the story was reported that *"On the morning of the election* [the proslavery men]*...gathered around the house where the election was to be held. Two of the judges...did not appear, and other judges were selected by the crowd; all then voted. In order to make a pretense of* [the] *right to vote, some persons of the company kept a pretended register of squatter claims,*

---

165   Trowbridge, Andrew Taylor Still, 55.
166   Goodrich, War to the Knife, 28.

on which any one could enter his name, and the assert that he had a claim in the Territory. A citizen of the District, who was himself a candidate for Delegate to Congress was told by one of the strangers, that he would be abused, and probably killed if he challenged a vote. He was seized by the collar, called a damned abolitionist, and was compelled to seek protection in the room of the judges. About the time the polls were closed, the strangers mounted their horses and got into their wagons and cried out, 'All aboard for Westport and Kansas City...' Like frauds, only varying in particulars and persons were reported in seven other districts, the most shameless of which was the precinct designated as '110', where 584 bogus votes were thrown in a total vote of 604.[167]

"When the ballots were tallied, the proslavery candidate, John Whitfield, had defeated his closest rival by a count of 2258 to 305." Clearly, he would have won easily without any of the fraudulent votes being cast from the Missouri side.[168]

To make matters worse, late in the afternoon following the voting in Lawrence, a tragic incident occurred and was witnessed by Thomas and James Still. They were on their way home riding in the back of a wagon driven by Lucius Kibbee. He was the man who had recently been chosen by Reverend Goode and Abram Still to be the Methodist church leader at Hickory Point.[169]

Kibbee was the *"rough, strong, kind Indianan...* [and a man who was]... *sober, resolute, [and] fearless."*[170] His wagon had unfortunately caught up with some of the *"boisterous fellows from Missouri...* [who were]... *in a state of intoxication"* and on their way home from the election. As *"he passed the drunken company,"* one of the men was in the process of burning down a home owned by an abolitionist. Kibbee challenged the man named Henry Davis, and ordered him to stop. Davis, *"enraged, flew at him with a knife, making furious passes at him as he sat in the wagon, which was moving at a slow gate."*[171] Davis threatened Kibbee telling him he would cut out his heart and carve him up like a beef. Kibbee feared for his life and warned Davis to stop or otherwise *"I'll shoot you sure."*[172] Despite the warning, Davis continued to attack Kibbee with his large knife, known

---

167   Goodrich, War to the Knife, 28.
168   Ibid., 29.
169   Clark, Reminiscences, 22.
170   Goode, Outposts of Zion, 315.
171   Ibid., 316.
172   W. E. Connelley, Standard History of Kansas, 1918, Vol.1, 435. (6-7).

as an Arkansas toothpick, and Kibbee finally *"discharged his pistol, killing him on the spot."*[173]

Kibbee hid out the night of the killing and the next day went to the Wakarusa Mission to see Abram Still and Reverend Goode and admitted he was the one who had killed Davis. He stated, *"I did it—I killed him with this,"* exhibiting a long rough single-barreled pistol.[174] He then sought advice from his friends regarding the killing and which authorities he should turn himself into since the Douglas sheriff was considered to be a bogus lawman. None of them believed Kibbee would get a fair trial under the present circumstances and would undoubtedly be hung. Kibbee *"said he was ready to surrender himself into the hands of the law but that he would not be taken alive by a mob."*[175] Reverend Goode went to see the Territorial Governor on behalf of Kibbee and pleaded his case to ensure his safety. Kibbee was later arrested. The case went *"before Judge Elmore, who committed him to trial for the murder in the first degree. On the 27th day of December he was brought before Chief Justice LeCompte on a Writ of Habeas Corpus, and admitted to bail."*[176]

Kibbee *"was kept in constant fear of assassination. He had to be on guard at all times. Once a small party approached his house and he came near firing upon them thinking they were coming to do him harm, when they really had no such intentions. He was much in doubt as to being able to secure a fair trial. He determined to leave the country.... Kibbee came to the mission...and asked my father* [Abram Still] *to help him as the border ruffians were scouring the country in search of him. He had been hiding out. My father and my brothers took him to a secluded spot a quarter of a mile west of the mission where they hid him in a place where the water had washed out a deep rut and it was overgrown with bamboo and grape vines. They took some provisions and bedding and he stayed in his hiding place for two days. About midnight the second night he was there, my brother Thomas took a horse and took him as far as Cedar Creek as he was trying to get back to his old home in Indiana ...Mr. (sic) Kibbee regretted the killing of Mr. Davis. Although he killed him in self defense, he said he would always feel in his heart that he was a murderer. We never heard whether he reached his old home or not."*[177]

---

173 Goode, Outposts of Zion, 317.
174 Ibid., 316.
175 Connelley, 8.
176 Ibid., 9.
177 Clark, Reminiscences, 22-23.

Charles Robinson and the New Englanders were angry about the results of the election but saw the invasion of the proslavery votes as a serious strategic mistake. Charles Robinson was convinced *"this inexcusable blunder served to expose the game the proslavery men proposed to play, and increased the agitation and the determination in the North...[T]he antislavery sentiment of the country, had received a serious shock in the repeal of the Missouri Compromise, and was in no mood for foul play in the game set by the slave interest...[T]his invasion [also] showed conclusively that...the Free-State men were rated as inferiors and to be despised, trodden upon and crushed without ceremony."*[178]

The outcome of the first Kansas Territorial election on November 29, 1854, was shameful with flagrant and fraudulent disregard for the voting process. It went beyond being a Territorial issue. It was an absolute disgrace to the American Constitution. Charles Robinson and the abolitionists officially submitted documents and protested the results of the election. They also requested relief from the illegitimately elected officials. Further, they petitioned the government to provide protection and guarantees that the next election for choosing the Territorial Legislature in March 1855 would escape such outrages. They could only hope there would not be any more killings or blood spilled on Kansas soil.

The March 1855 election would choose the men who would write the laws to govern the Territory and the rules to live by. The community of Lawrence and the people who shared their abolitionist views would have to wait a few months for the outcome. They were now facing the uncertainty of winter weather approaching with only one guarantee—there would be winter snow.

When the snow finally arrived, it crunched noisily under the wagon wheels as people moved about the countryside. Immigrants continued to arrive and their numbers continued to worry the proslavery sympathizers. The contest for control over the Kansas Territory, and ultimately the decision regarding the balance of power over slavery, were being imprinted in the snowy countryside by the wagons. The trails, traced on the landscape and woven into the ground, would prove to be an indelible and undeniable collage of the future for Atchison and Robinson. The ruts had meaning, and whether they were beautiful or ugly, depended upon the observer and from which direction they had come to make the Kansas Territory their home.

---

178   Robinson, The Kansas Conflict, 98-99.

The indentations were clear, distinct, and deeply cut in the ground. For Robinson, the tracks coming from the north were beautiful images—projecting dreams shared by himself, Thayer, and Lawrence. Atchison would have witnessed these gouged images on the countryside with fear and horror since increasingly they were trails from the North invading his bordering state. For him the picture would have been awful, showing encroachment and spoilage of the snowy countryside like a muddy footprint made by an outsider from the North. Atchison knew he had to respond again to this invasion and muster his men to cross the border for the March 1855 election.

During January and February of 1855 Atchison plotted the strategy for the spring election.[179] Newspapers printed alarms such as in the *Westport Frontier News*:

"The election which is ultimately to decide the destiny of Kansas is at hand... Let the day of the election come when it may, 'tis the result of that day's work which finally determines the institutions of the Territory, and the future of the State. It is therefore into this battle, heart and soul, that our southern friends must throw themselves...The real battle, the decisive conflict has yet to be fought."[180]

"Like the rude hordes from the North that invaded Rome in older times and on being repulsed returned in ten-fold numbers, so will our Northern invaders return with new recruits to carry out their schemes...The reality is before us. It stands out in the acts of the 'Emigrant Aid Society,' who ship paupers west as if they were so many cattle."[181]

David Atchison also let his rhetoric fly to an angry Missouri audience to *"fight the devil with fire. ...If set of fanatics and demagogues a thousand miles off could advance their money and exert every nerve to abolitionize (sic) the Territory...what is your duty? When you reside within one day's journey of the Territory, and when your peace, your quiet, and your property depends upon your action, you can without an exertion send five hundred of your young men who will vote in favor of your institutions. Should each county in the State of Missouri only do its duty, the question will be decided quietly and peaceably at the ballot-box."*[182]

Benjamin Stringfellow's newspaper, the Atchison (Kan.) *Squatter Sovereign*, helped Atchison fan the fire: *"the crisis has arrived when such*

---

179   Robinson, The Kansas Conflict, 93-94.
180   Ibid., 102.
181   Goodrich, War to the Knife, 32.
182   Robinson, 93-94.

impositions must be disregarded, as your rights and property are in danger, and I advise one and all to...vote at the point of the bowie-knife and the revolver.[183]

"I tell you to mark every scoundrel among you that is in the least tainted with free-soilism or abolitionism and exterminate him. Neither give nor take quarter from the d—d rascals."[184]

The Leavenworth Herald rang a resounding sentiment when it published: *"remember the 30th day of March, AD 1855, as Texans once remembered the Alamo."*[185]

The last week of March brought a grim reality for Sara and Charles Robinson and for the abolitionist residents in Lawrence and the Kansas Territory. Thousands of men poured across the border from Missouri to vote in the election. Atchison's rhetoric hardened during this invasion. *"There are ten hundred men coming over from Platt County, and if that isn't enough we will send five thousand more. We've come to vote, and will vote, or kill every G-d d—d abolitionist in the Territory...besides being armed to the teeth with guns, bowie-knives, and revolvers, the ruffians wore hemp in the button-holes, as a pledge...All right on the hemp,"* which identified them as southern men.[186]

The evidence of the southern invasion was clearly visible to the abolitionist who witnessed the ruffians on their way to the voting precincts. A group of abolitionists who had recently arrived in Kansas City and were on their way to the Territory, *"traveled nearly all day among a large party of Missourians, numbers about 200, who were going to Lawrence to vote and a pretty rough looking set they were, some on horse back, some in covered wagons, and others of foot, all hardy, sunburnt, frontier men, and all well armed with guns, revolvers and bowie knives. We were often asked what county (in Missouri) we came from, and when they heard that we were from the East we had the pleasure of being called 'damned Yankees,' etc., but they did not succeed in frightening us or in driving us back, though they assured us that they could fire some twenty shots each, and that they had a six pounder with them.' ...The thing which I was most afraid of was a barrel of whiskey which we discovered in one of their wagons."*[187]

183   Goodrich, War to the Knife, 33.
184   George Washington Martin, Transactions: Kansas State Historical Society, Vol. 9, 141.
185   Floyd C. Shoemaker, "Missouri's Proslavery Fight for Kansas, 1854-1855." 328.
186   Sara Robinson, Kansas: Its Interior and Exterior Life, 20.
187   Thomas C. Wells: Letters of a Kansas Pioneer, 1855-1860, 149.

An article in the Lawrence newspaper described the invasion of men arriving the week before the election. *"We have had stirring times in Kansas...yesterday was a great day—great in the history of Kansas, big with shame...All the week, preceding the election, men were arriving from nearly all the slave States in the Union. They had men enough to outvote us, and they would do it peaceable if they could, if not, they had firearms and force enough to compel us to vote on their side. The whole week they were encamped all up and down the roads, like filthy plague spots, on the face of these beautiful prairies. Drunk and loathsome, a sight to make the heart sick,"* over one-thousand of them were in and about Lawrence during the week.*"*[188]

The spectacle had only just begun. On the morning of March 30th, 1855, the day of the election, the powerful and unabashed southern Missourians entered Lawrence with music blaring and banners flying. It was a parade of about one thousand men. They rode into Lawrence in 110 wagons, and to further flaunt the mightiness of their force, pulled along two cannons loaded with musket balls. Col. Samuel Young, of Boone County, Missouri, and his comrade, Claiborne F. Jackson, were in command. This mob had intercepted Mr. Napoleon Blanton, one of the judges appointed by Gov. Reeder. It was his responsibility to require all voters to take an oath that they were residents in the Territory. The self-appointed officials challenged Mr. Blanton about the oath issue. He stood firm about taking the oath of residency. After describing his fate if he failed to cooperate, Mr. Blanton scurried back home. He must have felt lucky to have escaped with his life. The slavery forces appointed *"a new judge by the name of Robert Cummins, who claimed that a man had a right to vote in the election if only in the Territory but an hour."*[189] It was plain that once again the border crossers were going to have it their way.

The small shanty that had been established as the voting place was then double lined for a hundred yards with heavily armed men, many of which reeked with whiskey, and all carrying bowie-knives, revolvers, and other weapons. All of the voters had to go through this line of men to reach the window. The Missouri men were cheering and playful as their men voted, often grabbing and hoisting them up on the voting booth roof with rowdy laughter. When it came time for the voters in the Lawrence camp to vote, the complexion changed.[190] As the Lawrence citizens walked in

188   Lawrence (Kan.) Herald of Freedom, June 2, 1855.
189   Robinson, Kansas: Its Interior and Exterior Life, 16.
190   Ibid., 17.

"between the double-file of armed men," [the crowd jeered,] *"with threats of shooting, or hanging, our citizens passed to the polls." Several citizens of Lawrence were driven from the ground during that day, with threats of fatal violence."*[191]

Many of the men who came to vote had to run for their lives. Edwin Bond *"was forcibly ejected from the grounds and pursued by an angry crowd."* In his escape he jumped down a steep river bank to get away from his pursuers. As he ran along the river someone shot at him and barely missed striking him in the head. Another voter, named Willis was also threatened and only *"through the influence of friends, who knew his danger,"* was saved from harm when they convinced him to leave the area. This kind of threatening behavior against the abolitionists who went to vote in the election was common.[192] Once the proslavery leaders had the votes necessary to carry the precinct, they mounted up and headed to Bloomington and other precincts thought to need additional votes.

Samuel J. Jones, of Westport, Claiborne F. Jackson, with his volunteers from the camp at Lawrence, and a Mr. Steely, of Independence, were the leaders of this group. Sara Robinson recalled the scene years later. *"Scarcely were the polls open, before* [Sheriff] *Jones marched up to the window, at the head of the crowd, and demanded that they be allowed to vote without being sworn as to their residence. Little bands of fifteen or twenty men were formed by Jackson. He gave to them guns from the wagons, which some of them loaded. Jackson had previously declared, amid repeated cheers, that 'they came there to vote... [and] that they would not go home without voting.' Upon the refusal of the judges to resign, the mob broke in the windows, glass, and sash, and presenting pistols and guns, threatened to shoot them. A voice from the outside cried, 'Do not shoot them; there are proslavery men in the* house!*' A pry was then put under the corner of the log cabin, letting it rise and fall....The two judges still remaining firm in their refusal to allow them to vote, Jones led on a party with bowie-knives drawn, and pistols cocked with watch in hand, he declared to the judges, 'he would give them five minutes in which to resign or die.' The five minutes passed by. Jones said he 'would give another minute, but no more.' The proslavery judge snatched up the ballot-boxes, and, crying out 'Hurrah for*

---

191   Robinson, Kansas: Its Interior and Exterior Life, 17.
192   Lawrence (Kans.) Herald of Freedom, Mar. 31, 1855.

Missouri' ran into the crowd. The other judges, persuaded by their friends, who thought them in imminent peril...passed out" [and left].[193]

"*After routing the opposition, the southerners got down to business. "Not satisfied with once voting, many changed hats and coats repeatedly voted.*"[194]

It was a common occurrence for the men who were not southerners to be threatened and harassed at the polling booths as described by J. N. Mace, an antislavery proponent, who tried to cast his ballot that day. *"Hardly a man could be met without his bowie knife, pistol or gun, and some with all three. I hastened to get near the box, when I heard them say: no Yankee should vote there to-day, and the first man who took the oath required by the law, should lose his life...I had with me...a small American flag...I felt the American flag had never been so disgraced... It now came my turn. I moved forward. There were two desperate fellows at the window; one at each side as I came up with my vote folded. One of them took me by the coat, and said, 'Open that vote, and let's have a look at it.' I said I came here under the protection of the United States to vote; it guarantees to me the right to vote by ballot, which is to vote secretly, and I will show no man my vote...An old man came up, and they asked me if I would give way for him to vote. I at once did so. Meanwhile, I was asked from what State I came. I told the questioner that it was from Massachusetts...After the old man had voted, I reached my hand inside of the window, with the ballot in it, and gave my name to the judges.—Immediately on this, at the word from one of the inquisitors, I was seized and dragged through the crowd, amidst cries of 'Kill the N— thief!' 'Cut his throat!' Around me, on all sides, were flourished bowie-knives, pistols, clubs, and guns. I struggled, and gained my feet...I am an American citizen...I seek protection under this—tearing the paper from the flag, and unfolding it over my head. As the stars and stripes floated to the breeze, their murderous cries were hushed: but one cried out, 'That flag is false! Said I, Who calls this flag false is a traitor!' One now threw off his cloak, stepped towards me...saying 'Did you call me a traitor?'* [There] *...was one bowie-knife within two inches of my heart, one revolver at my ear, and how many more drawn about me, I cannot say. One man struck at me with a club, but the blow was warded off by one of my friends, catching his arm as he struck. At this moment, something caught*

---

193   Robinson, Kansas: Its Interior and Exterior Life, 18.
194   Ibid., 19.

94

the attention of the crowd, and drew them in another direction. The flag had saved my life."[195]

According to the proslavery newspaper, *The Kansas Herald,* published at Leavenworth, reported the landslide victory. The official returns of the election recorded a total of 5961 votes cast, 4493 were for the proslavery party, and only 1068 supporting the abolitionist position.[196]

However, the *Louisville Journal,* another proslavery publication, was not complimentary in the assessment of the election. *"It is painful to speak of the occurrences in Kansas and upon the borders within the last few weeks, but they are too important in their nature, and are likely to be far too important in their consequences to be passed by in silence...The truth is, an army of Missourians, variously estimated at from three thousand to five thousand, armed with bowie-knives and pistols and rifles, and even cannon, marched into Kansas on the day before the election, distributed themselves wherever they were wanted, awed all opposition to silence, deposed and put up election judges to suit themselves, allowed the privilege of voting to whom they pleased, compelled by threats and the display of weapons the receiving of their own votes, offered personal violence to all who obnoxious to them, carried everything before them, and, the next day, returned to Missouri under streaming banners, and to the music of fife and drum and trumpet.*"[197]

The overall feeling following the election was one of southern victory and southern dominance. The northern sentiment was *"that the last election in Kansas was more outrageously conducted than the first.*"[198]

All eyes then turned to Territorial Governor Reeder for relief from the ballot atrocity. Governor Reeder had promised to *"perform the duties of the office of Governor with fidelity. We shall always be glad to see our neighbors across the river as friends and visitors among us...but must respectfully, but determinedly, decline to allow them participation in regulating our affairs.*"[199]

The stories must have quickly circulated around the Territory about the abusive and corrupt treatment that permeated the election. It was so obviously fraudulent to everyone, and the abusive conduct so flagrant, that while Atchison celebrated the victory, Robinson knew that there would be

---

195   Lawrence (Kan.) Herald of Freedom, June 2, 1855.
196   Robinson, Kansas Conflict, 113-114.
197   Ibid., 118-119.
198   Ibid., 115.
199   Ibid.,109.

95

outrage in the North. Ultimately, Atchison and the South would pay for such awful behavior. He knew that Americans both from the North and the South would not stand to have the sacred right of voting overrun by a bunch of Ruffians.[200]

Following the election, Robinson must have initially believed that Governor Reeder was going to intervene when Reeder sent word to ask him for protection. Reeder wanted to be surrounded by Robinson and his men *"when he declared the result of the election, a dozen men from Lawrence went immediately to his headquarters, ready to die with him if necessary while in the discharge of his official duty.*[201]

"But what was their disappointment and chagrin when, after guarding him for about two days, he decided to issue certificates of election to a large majority of persons chosen by the invaders. Charity would plead ignorance as his excuse, but even that plea cannot be entertained, for out of his own mouth is he condemned."[202] Even though Reeder condemned the invasion by the outsiders, he certified the election results. Although disappointed with Reeder's decision to give an air of legitimacy to the election, Charles Robinson was unwilling to give into the fraud that had been perpetrated. Robinson also knew how to play the political game, perhaps better than anyone. He would guide the residents of the Kansas Territory through the political maze by refusing to follow any of the laws enacted by what the abolitionists considered a bogusly-elected legislature. At the same time, he would try to prevent his abolitionist community from getting into any confrontations with the federal government. It would be a struggle and at times a delicate matter, but he could and would do it. In the meantime, it would be business as usual while he continued to build the city of Lawrence. He and the other Free-Soilers in the Kansas Territory would simply ignore the newly elected government. He formed committees to enact this approach when forced to deal with the bogus officials. These committees filed formal protests with acting Territorial Governor Reeder regarding the election results and the way the voting was handled. Robinson also petitioned Eli Thayer and Amos Lawrence to send him the one thing that they had not brought with them in adequate supply—guns, lots of guns and ammunition for protection. If he could get a few cannons smuggled into the city, also, he felt they could be very useful in the future.[203]

---

200   Robinson, The Kansas Conflict, 109-110.
201   Ibid.
202   Ibid.
203   Ibid., 125.

The people of Lawrence and the abolitionists surrounding the town would have to accept the fact that from that time forward, they would have to protect themselves against the violence of the border ruffians. Their motto would be protection without aggression. Robinson knew that the most critical thing was to have absolutely no confrontation with the federal government. He would lead and guide them through this complicated process of non-compliance with the Territorial Government while observing all federal laws. As long as everyone understood this fine line of defiance, he felt he would eventually win the contest against the bogus government of the Territory and restore the dignity of American principles even in this remote prairie.[204]

Charles Robinson was a gifted leader and he must have prayed for the strength and wisdom to accomplish this magnificent feat. Unfortunately for Robinson, there were two men heading for Lawrence who were not going to cooperate with him or his strategy to win the political battle. Rather, they were coming to attack and fight. Their names were James Henry Lane and John Brown. Lane was driven by opportunity while Brown professed he was on a mission from God. The future for the city of Lawrence and the abolitionists' dreams were about to take on a new meaning.

---

204   Robinson, The Kansas Conflict, 121-122.

CHAPTER TEN
Springtime 1855

Following the March election of 1855, the months slipped by for the people residing in the Territory. Springtime had finally arrived. Time had also run out for the Still family at the Wakarusa Mission school. *"Our mission life is closed; Kansas is open for settlement. The Indians have made a treaty with the United States and consequently the missions are all discontinued."*[205]

Many of the Still family members moved to the banks of Coal Creek. It was on land located only *"five miles southeast of the present town of Lawrence"* in a location closer to other abolitionists and gave them added safety.[206]

Andrew's brother, James Still, also began building on a claim on the south edge of Blue Mound. Some of the older children were allowed to leave to continue their education. Andrew's sister, Mary, left for Illinois to attend Miss Celestia Cranson's School for Young Ladies, and her brother, John Wesley, attended the McKendree College at Lebanon, Illinois.[207]

Early in the summer of 1855, Andrew Still would also refocus his energy as he, along with a group of other abolitionists, began work on a 320-acre tract of land that would eventually become the town of Palmyra.[208]

During this summer, a great day of celebration had been planned on the Fourth of July in the city of Lawrence. The main topic to be discussed in the town, however, was the lack of political response by the politicians regarding the bogus election. It had been anticipated that by July there would have been assistance available to solve their election grievances and deal with the fraud of the elected officials who ruled over the residents of the Territory. Instead, many severe laws had been enacted by these proslavery officials. These laws included either imprisonment or death to anyone who tampered with the slave system in Kansas. Even the mere censure of

205   Adams, In God We Trust, 41.
206   Clark, Reminiscences, 18.
207   Adams, 42.
208   Trowbridge, Andrew Taylor Still, 1828-1917, 57.

slavery, *"by speaking or by writing,"* was punishable by imprisonment *"at hard labor for a term not less than two years."*[209]

It must have seemed strange that the first celebration in Lawrence, during 1855, was to be Independence Day, the Fourth of July. It was an irony that the basic rights of Lawrence citizens had been denied by what they deemed a fraudulently elected territorial government. Furthermore, the federal powers continued to support the elected officials. This continued silence seemed to condone the fake elections, and by not reacting to the reported treachery at the ballot box, sanctified the results. The Territorial Governor, Andrew Reeder, however, continued to contest the results of the blatant deceitfulness at the territorial level.[210]

The abolitionists in the Kansas Territory felt abandoned by a federal government that had turned away and allowed bullies to overpower them. There were no reasonable excuses for the prolonged indifference. Even when multiple reports had been filed to document the election events, there had been no retribution for the blatant deception. Nevertheless, for the citizens of Lawrence, it was the Fourth of July, and the seventy-ninth birthday of America. Even with the sting of the injustice of the election on everyone's mind, it could not stop the celebration of freedom. The wagons were pulled by *"several teams, of oxen as well as horses, the roughness of the vehicles being hidden under garlands of green leaves and flowers."*[211] The citizens put on their best clothes and prepared to celebrate the country's anniversary despite all of the recent turmoil.

"As the Fourth of July approached it was decided to celebrate that day in a fitting manner. The question of fitness was not easily settled. Those who wanted a celebration to glorify the Government and Union desired colonel Lane for orator, but such as wanted a celebration to correspond to the condition of the people as subjects of Missouri desired Dr. Robinson. As this was the more numerous class at Lawrence, he was selected...The gathering was very large, some walking sixteen miles to attend it. The Shawnee and Delaware Indians were present and participated in the proceedings. Being the first Fourth of July celebration in Kansas, and Kansas being virtually a conquered province, the likes of it will never be seen again. The two organized military companies, armed with Sharps rifles, besides many

---

209   Robinson, The Kansas Conflict, 162.
210   Ibid., 155.
211   Robinson, Kansas: Its Interior and Exterior Life, 69.

volunteers, appeared in uniform and were presented with a beautiful silk banner by the ladies."[212]

The Still family was very excited about going to the July 4th event. The children didn't get to leave home very often, and the joy of actually seeing a developing town where children their ages lived, would have been a welcome change. However, the men in the family had to be careful on their trip to Lawrence. Threats toward them and bad feelings had escalated as the days passed following the March 30th debacle.

Finally, the Stills' wagons were underway, and the July sun took a direct bead on the land below with temperatures soaring. The girls would have been overwhelmed by parts of the prairie that had sunflowers so tall that they merely had to reach out and pull the flowers off the plants to make a bouquet for their mother. They also were able to decorate their own hair, making a crowned tiara out of the flowers.[213]

Although Lawrence was only seven miles away, it probably seemed like a long journey before they arrived. In Lawrence the Stills ate *"dinner in a sod hotel as there were very few shacks put up yet. They celebrated in the grove."* As Marovia Still remembered, *"this was the first celebration I ever attended and I ate my first ice cream that day."* The children were not disappointed by the rustic nature of the events since this was the biggest celebration they had ever attended.[214]

Andrew's daughter, Marusha, was six years old, and his son, Abraham, was two and a half. While the children scampered about the town of Lawrence, the adults were taking advantage of being together in such a large number. The main topic of conversation was unmistakably about the threat of war. Charles Robinson wasted little time in calling the men together for a discussion of an organized political front and formulated a military plan should it become necessary for the town of Lawrence and the abolitionists to defend themselves. Six weeks prior to this celebration, the first of the boxes of Sharps rifles had been smuggled into Lawrence in five boxes marked "Books." Charles Robinson's Fourth of July speech made it clear to the crowd that his plan was "self government" in defiance of the fraudulently elected officials who represented the South and the interests of slavery. He was ready to institute the plan immediately.[215]

---

212   Robinson, Kansas: Its Interior and Exterior Life, 144.
213   Clark, Reminiscences, 45.
214   Ibid.
215   Robinson, Kansas: Interior and Exterior Life, 69, 71.

Robinson stood before the crowd in Lawrence and shouted his words of freedom as loud and as clear as any American had ever done in its seventy-nine years of existence:

"What are we? Subjects, slaves of Missouri. We come to the celebration of this anniversary, with our chains clanking upon our limbs; we lift to Heaven our manacled arms in supplication; proscribed, outlawed, denounced, we cannot so much speak the name of Liberty, except with prison walls and halters looking us in the face. We must not only see black slavery...planted in our midst, and against our wishes, but we must become slaves ourselves...Fellow citizens...it is for us to choose for ourselves, and for those who shall come after us, what institutions shall bless or curse our beautiful Kansas...Let every man stand in his own place, and acquit himself like a man...Let us repudiate all laws enacted by foreign legislative bodies, or dictated by Judge Lynch over the way. Tyrants are tyrants, and tyranny is tyranny, whether under the garb of law or in opposition to it. So thought and so acted our ancestors, and so let us think and act."[216]

It was an inspirational speech. Many men in the crowd more than likely were ready to begin battle immediately, regardless of the cost of lives, even if the federal government would become involved. Some of the young abolitionists were probably against any peaceful solution in the Kansas prairie, and must have welcomed the opportunity to engage in battle against slavery. A few wanted to exploit the value of plunder for their own self gain. Most, however, were like all young men, eager to show their courage.

In this group of men was a man not so young. James Henry Lane—a man experienced in seizing an opportunity when the time was right. Lane had already fought in the Mexican War and earned himself the distinction of colonel. He had been a lieutenant governor, had served in the U.S. House for his home state of Indiana, and had voted for the Kansas-Nebraska Bill. As a seasoned, tireless, but unscrupulous politician, and as a military man, he was ready for any fight that would earn him importance. Since slavery seemed to be the issue at the moment, he would attach himself to that cause. He didn't particularly care about the Negro, or for that matter, he could support slavery if it bettered his position. He had been known to say:

"I look upon this nigger question just as I look upon the horse or the jackass question. I would as leave sell a Negro as a mule," he had said. *"It is merely a question of dollars and cents."*[217]

---

216   Robinson, The Kansas Conflict, 147-152.
217   Goodrich, War to the Knife: Bleeding Kansas, 1854-1861, 50.

"If Kansas had been a good hemp and tobacco state [I] would have favored slavery."[218]

What James Henry Lane saw on that Fourth of July was an emotional crowd of young men who were eager to fight for a cause, and slavery was the driving force at this moment in time. Luckily for him, Lane had the charisma that appealed to the young men. He was born into a family of orators. His father, Amos Lane, served in the Indiana state legislature as speaker of the house in 1817. His father was an *"ardent champion of Andrew Jackson, and won the title of "The Wheel Horse"*…[and he] *possessed a voice of remarkable force and power… [and] woe to the man who incurred his displeasure."* His eldest brothers entered the West Point Army Academy *"at the age of thirteen and graduated four years later."*[219] James had the political and military background ingrained in him from the very beginning of his childhood.

James Lane was a *"tall, gaunt, hollow-cheeked, thin lipped philanderer with a mass of unruly black hair and what had been described as the 'sad dim eyes of a harlot.'"*[220]

He was *"a spellbinding stump speaker, at times comical, at times maudlin, often ribald and obscene, Lane had, as one listener discovered, a 'magic faculty by which he controlled primitive assemblages, convincing them against their judgment and bending them against their will.'"*[221] *"Lane had an enormous gift for intrigue, devilment, and fiery rhetoric. He talked like none of the others. None of the rest had his husky rasping, blood-curdling whisper or that menacing forefinger, or could shriek 'Great God!' on the same day with him."*[222]

James Lane was just the man that a newly forming army would long to have. His charisma was so great that he could order a fatal charge of new recruits up a hopeless hill in battle with no regard for consequences. Men would obey him, and men would die for him.

He was also the kind of man who did not fit into Charles Robinson's cerebral war where the battles would only be won if the recruits stayed hidden and never fired a shot. The men in Robinson's scenario would fire only if attacked and to defend their lives. Jim Lane's thinking was exactly the opposite, and Lane was Robinson's worst nightmare in Lawrence. James

---

218   Goodrich, War To The Knife, 50.
219   Stephen Wendell Holmes, The Political Career of General James H. Lane, 14-15.
220   Edward E. Leslie, The Devil Knows How To Ride, 11.
221   Goodrich, 50.
222   Leslie, The Devil Knows How To Ride, 11.

Lane wouldn't have listened to Robinson's judgment or reason. Lane always wanted to shoot first and then ask questions. His plan was always to attack and beat the enemy into submission.

It was James Lane who glared at Robinson from the crowd during that Fourth of July speech in 1855. He knew he had come to the right place at the right time. Later, James Lane would become known as *"the Grim Chieftain of Kansas."*[223] For the time being, all he had to do was wait for the enemy to make a mistake. Unfortunately, many of them had formerly been his friends. He was sure it would be soon the way rhetoric was flying all over the Territory.

While Charles Robinson spoke to the crowd and attempted to explain his careful and methodical plan to eventually win the battle for a free Kansas Territory, he must have hoped that his ideas would be supported by those who were listening. Lane's actions would later prove he did not agree with Robinson's passive philosophy. But he would not be alone in creating internal conflicts for the abolitionists in Lawrence.

The Lawrence Fourth of July celebration finally ended after the men, who joined the newly formed militia, had attempted to parade in military style before the families who attended the festivities. Even though many of them had never drilled before, this march had been an effort to bring unity of purpose to a struggling group who had chosen to try to make Kansas a free Territory and eventually a Free State. It also cemented into their minds that in the future any protection against the proslavery forces would be up to them. This exercise had been serious and was not done to impress the others who had been watching the drills. The steps of these marching men had taken on a serious cadence following the speech by Charles Robinson. Each man, whether marching or not, must have known that his life might be determined by learning the commands that the officer in charge shouted as they moved the recently smuggled rifles to his verbal commands.[224]

The gaiety that was bubbling over in the wagons as they all headed to the celebration must have turned to serious conversation about a potential armed conflict as the Still family and the other residents left the town of Lawrence for the ride home. Everyone had to have sensed that there was a new purpose and commitment in their struggle to survive in the Kansas Territory. And it was about to begin.

---

223   Leslie, The Devil Knows How To Ride, 11.
224   Robinson, The Kansas Conflict, 144-145.

Their fears were soon justified. During the summer of 1855, the Territorial Governor, Andrew Reeder, finally removed seven of the proslavery legislators from their offices on charges of technical election violations and replaced them with abolitionists. He also declared the entire proslavery legislative body illegal. This declaration resulted in Reeder's removal from office by the Washington political powers in August of 1855. He would be replaced by Wilson Shannon, a man who was deemed in Washington to be a stronger proslavery proponent. Governor Shannon vowed to support and to enforce the laws written by the elected officials in the March 1855 election.[225]

To complicate matters, another man named John Brown was making plans to head to the Territory in the fall. His wagons would be packed with swords and sabers. Brown was a leather-skinned man of fifty-six, stiff-necked who held his head arched slightly forward, and had eyes with a *"chilling, reptilian quality,"* suggesting an inner imbalance of a mind diseased or deranged.[226] He would bring six of his sons with him, John Jr., Fred, Salmon, Owen, Watson and Oliver. The Brown family would travel in relative silence on a path that would be straight and unquestionable. He and his sons believed in their destiny, and he would later say that the trip and mission had been *"ordained by the Almighty God, ordained from eternity, that I should make examples of these men."*[227] They were heading to the Kansas Territory to lead the fight against slavery. This was the place where he planned *"to have a shot at the South"* and hopefully embroil the entire country in a Civil War.[228]

John Brown, unlike Jim Lane, would not be patient and wait for the other side to make a mistake to justify a conflict. He was on his way to the Kansas Territory to start one.

---

225 Robinson, 155 / Trowbridge, Andrew Taylor Still, 56.
226 Goodrich, War to the Knife, 125.
227 Goodrich, 123 / Nichols, Bleeding Kansas, 113.
228 Robinson, The Kansas Conflict, 264.

CHAPTER ELEVEN
Charles Dow
Fall of 1855

As Jim Lane had suspected, the day came when the proslavery men in the Territory began open warfare with the men who opposed it. The abolitionists were now commonly referred to as "free-soilers, free-booters, Yankees, and nigger thieves."[229] The rhetoric had grown more threatening as the days approached the fall of 1855, and the squabbles between many of the proslavery men and the abolitionists continued. Usually the confrontations and fights were shrugged off as either too much liquor or bad tempers on both sides.

Often arguments would creep into conversations between neighbors who had come together for dinner and the discussion drifted to the trouble they were having with one another. Thomas Breese of Hickory Point had experienced this uncomfortable situation in his home. He had invited Mr. and Mrs. Buckley and several other neighbors to join his family for dinner. Breese and his wife found themselves in a very awkward situation when Mr. Buckley *"commenced with great threats on the abolitionists and Yankees; what they would do with them; how many they would shoot down, and so forth."*[230] Breese had tolerated the threats made against many who were his friends but he felt obligated to challenge Buckley saying, *"Mr. Buckley, the way to shoot down the abolitionists and Yankees is, to use them well, and when you go to the polls, then give your vote, and let them do the same. His wife* [Mrs. Buckley] *was sitting present, and ordered me to say nothing to Mr. Buckley on that occasion whatever, and let him alone; and let him do as he pleased."*[231]

The verbal attacks continued and Breese finally reached the point where he could no longer remain seated at his table. He rose and told Buckley... *"if that was the game, just go ahead, I would say no more. After Thomas Breese had left the table he observed Mr. Buckley stating... 'that he meant to shoot*

---

229   Lawrence (Kansas) Herald of Freedom, June 2, 1855 / Goodrich, War to the Knife, 36.
230   Special Committee, 34th Congress, House of Representatives, Report 200, 1044.
231   Ibid.

the paunch of old Branson and Dow, because they were abolitionists, and would steal his niggers.' That led to our neighborly intercourse being broken up. "[232]

Another incident had recently occurred with the outspoken and fearless abolitionist and attorney, Sam Wood. This argument also didn't help settle any nerves in the Hickory Point area. Wood, in his two-horse buggy, accompanied by his wife and child, had stopped at Lewis Farley's house. Wood's first words to Farley were to *"inquire who owned niggers in that neighborhood. Mr. Farley told him of several who owned niggers. Wood remarked that if he were a nigger, he would not serve his master an hour after he came into the Territory; that it was a free country, and niggers were free the moment they were fetched there."* [233]

One of Farley's neighbors jumped into the argument. *"I told [Wood], if he was a nigger and belonged to me, and attempted to cut up any of his shines, I would whip him like hell, and make him behave himself."* [234]

Sam Wood's wife intervened. She *"begged us not to say anything more about politics, and have no disturbance. Nothing more was said then, and Wood got a bite to eat, and drove off with his family."* [235]

Up until this time, nothing had been done by either side that was unforgivable. The conflicts had been mainly between squabbling neighbors who disagreed over property lines, claim-jumping, slave ownership, and who qualified as a legal resident. Most of these arguments had been won or lost depending how many friends were present in the crowd and whose side the majority rallied behind.

On November 21, 1855, the situation dramatically changed when the squabbling ended and the consequences of violence began. A man named Charles Dow had pulled on his boots that morning to begin another hard, back-breaking work day on his land. This included a trip to Hickory Point and the blacksmith shop to have a broken wagon axle rod repaired. The blacksmith, a man named Poole, would heat the rod in his coal furnace and hammer the metal back together to mend the break. Unfortunately, the trip to the blacksmith shop required Dow to cross the front door of Franklin Coleman's cabin. Coleman had become Dow's worst enemy. The conflict between Dow and Coleman had been a longstanding "claim-jumping" disagreement over their adjoining property lines. Dow had claimed his

---

232   House of Representatives Report, 1044.
233   Ibid., 1052.
234   Ibid.
235   Ibid.

property under the Squatter Laws rules of abandonment. The property had originally been owned by a proslavery man named White who built a cabin and made some other improvements. White had disappeared from the site long enough for the property to be considered abandoned. Mysteriously, White's cabin burned to the ground and this event infuriated the proslavery men, especially since Dow had filed a claim for the property following the suspected arson.

The proslavery men appeared at the new claim the first day Dow began work on the property. Franklin Coleman and eleven other proslavery men rode out to question Dow about his involvement in the cabin burning.

Coleman and the other men *"accused Dow of being accessory to the act."* Dow *"asserted his innocence, as regarded the destruction of White's house."*

Then Coleman asked Dow *"if he was not aware of the intention of the Free-State men to destroy it." Dow answered "that was his business."* This argument ended with no admission of wrong-doing by Dow and with reluctant acceptance by Coleman of Dow's innocence of torching White's cabin. For that moment the disgruntlement between them had been put on hold but the conflict between them continued over the property lines.[236]

The property dispute had further increased in intensity when a government survey had recently laid new corner posts that favored Dow's side of the property giving him ownership of almost all of the hickory timber located between them.

Coleman had been increasingly upset with the new government boundary lines and the loss of the timbered area of the property to Dow, making the conflict even more disturbing. The dispute had become even more heated and the threats had escalated on the morning of November 21st when Dow had stumbled across Coleman and a friend working on a lime-kiln in the heavily wooded area of the disputed claim. Dow challenged the men for trespassing and ordered them to leave, but Coleman refused to concede and continued to argue with Dow over the property rights. Dow went for re-enforcement, asking his best friend and neighbor, Jacob Branson, to help him. Dow and Branson returned to the lime-kiln location, and Coleman would later swear that the returning men had been armed. He believed they had come back to kill him. Coleman abandoned the lime-kiln and ran for his life.[237]

---

236   O. N. Merrill, A True History of The Kansas Wars, 1856, 78.
237   Ibid., 75-80.

The fact that Dow was an abolitionist and was befriended by Jacob Branson even further stamped his fate as an enemy of Coleman and all the other proslavery men. Once again the hornet's nest had been stirred up over the lime-kiln location with neither man backing down. Both felt that the other had encroached on his claimed land.

Although Dow was not afraid of Coleman, he did not look forward to running into him again that day anymore than he would want to cross a property with a vicious dog lying in the front yard. However, he would not give into fears or threats that his Hickory Point neighbor had made against him. Furthermore, he refused to carry a gun for protection and continued to live his life with courage and without fear. Later that day, Dow arrived at the blacksmith shop and gave the axle skane to Poole for repairs.[238]

After the confrontation with Dow that morning, Coleman decided he'd had enough of this property line dispute. He had run away from the lime-kiln when approached by Dow and Branson with their claims of encroachment. He went home and loaded his shotgun with buckshot in both barrels. Coleman then enlisted two of his proslavery friends, Mr. Hargous and Mr. Buckley, to help him resurvey the property. They would put new stakes in the ground that favored his interpretation of the boundary lines and ignore the government's lines that favored Dow's claim. The three men went to work heavily armed when they staked Coleman's claim deep into the hickory timber. Buckley had been the man who had in the past bragged that *"he meant to shoot the paunch of old Branson and Dow,"* and now Coleman was going to give him his chance to follow up his threats.[239]

Coleman and his friends laid out the new boundary lines which gave them great satisfaction as they drove the stakes into the ground and took property away from Dow. Buckley had also heard rumors that Dow had threatened to beat his brains out. The threat had added to his enthusiasm and enjoyment as he drove the stakes into the ground which took away Dow's property foot by foot. Buckley was in the same hostile mood as Coleman, and he also had a belly full of whiskey. When Buckley left his house that morning with his loaded shotgun, he told his wife he was going to kill a beef.

After the three men finished moving the property line, Buckley headed to Hickory Point and the blacksmith shop to confront Dow. He passed by the home of Mr. McKinney, who was repairing his house. McKinney observed

238   House of Representatives Report, 1041.
239   Ibid., 80.

that Buckley was carrying a shotgun and was staggering drunk in the street. McKinney called out to him, concerned with his motives, but Buckley ignored his neighbor and entered the blacksmith shop with both barrels of his shotgun cocked. There he confronted Charles Dow. McKinney stated he *"heard some loud talking in the direction of the shop."*[240]

Later, testimony would be given in the Congressional investigation by many people who witnessed the incident. Sam Gleason was one who would testify he was also present at the blacksmith shop that day, and he heard the argument between Buckley and Dow. Gleason stated in sworn testimony *"I was present at the blacksmith shop, near Mr. McKinney's on the 21st day of November 1855. I heard hard words in his shop, and ... Poole, say he would not have such words in his shop"* ...[He told] ... *'Buckley, if you cannot behave yourself, go out of the shop'*... Poole and Dow continued to work on the wagon part and *"soon had the wagon skane and lynch-pin fixed."* After Dow left the shop to head home Poole asked Buckley *'why did you not shoot?'* Buckley answered, *'I hate to shoot a man on hearsay; ... I'll be damned if I won't shoot him yet.'* Buckley's gun was then cocked at both barrels; ...He then left the shop, and started on his horse in the direction after Dow."*[241]

McKinney would also add testimony concerning what he and his son witnessed when Dow came out of the blacksmith shop and walked toward his house. Coleman was standing at the corner of the house *"with a double-barreled shotgun... They both went off down the road together towards Coleman's house. When they got opposite his house I heard a gun fired... and saw the smoke of the gun, and Mr. Coleman throwing the gun on his shoulder. I observed to my son, 'I wonder what Coleman is shooting at.'"*[242]

It was later that day when McKinney found out about the gun shot he heard. The report came from Mr. Buckley who said *"there is a man lying dead in the road."*[243] Other witnesses later corroborated with their observations of the murder. Almina Jones testified, *"I saw the smoke of the gun, and saw the man fall. When the gun was fired, I should think those persons were some 20 or 25 yards apart. When I drove by, the man seemed to be dead; lying perfectly still."*[244] Gleason, who had been in the blacksmith shop during Buckley's verbal attack on Dow, added to his testimony re-

240   House of Representatives Report, 1040-1042.
241   Ibid., 1042-1043.
242   Ibid., 1040.
243   Ibid., 1041.
244   Ibid., 1050-1051.

garding the brutal slaying, *"I saw the murdered man, who was Dow, lying with his head in the wagon track and his feet on the side of the road, with the skane and lynch-pin still in his hand...I saw the blood running from his neck, his mouth, and nose; and saw the blood on his breast...I noticed two shot-holes in Dow's neck as I was looking at him."*[245]

Thomas Breese, who was a friend of Dow, would hear about his death from his daughter. *"[P]ap, they have killed Mr. Dow, and he is lying in the middle of the road alone, about opposite Coleman's."*

Breese said he *"ran then afoot just as fast as I could. When I got there the body had just been removed to Mr. Branson's house. I saw the puddles of blood in the road. I then turned back to home. The next morning I went to Mr. Branson's and saw the body of Dow there. I helped to dress the body, and saw the wounds. There was one slug, went into the jugular vein on the left side, and one in the jugular vein on the right side of the neck, entering in front. There were four shots went into his breast on both sides, just above the pit of his stomach, three of which went clear through his body, and lodged in the back of his coat. These slugs were scattered, two on each side, a short distance apart, some six inches below the wounds in the neck. The slugs that passed through his body were of lead, and looked as if they were made of lead beaten out and cut off; were of irregular shape, and are now in the possession of Mr. Branson. We buried him on the Saturday following...Dow was one of the finest young men I ever got acquainted with—a quiet, peaceable man, and worked for me a great deal."*[246]

Dow's body and the blood pooled on the road where he lay gave clear evidence that Coleman had a good aim. The only reported reactions by Coleman after he had shot Dow was to snap the shotgun back on his arm, then up to his shoulder, as a man might do after shooting an elk or deer. Coleman then turned and walked into his house and left Dow dying in the road.[247]

When Jacob Branson was notified about Dow's murder, he immediately headed for Hickory Point, and when he arrived, found the body of Dow lying in the roadbed with his head in a wagon wheel rut. There were gaping holes in his neck and chest. Branson was told that it was Franklin Coleman who had shot Charles Dow.[248]

---

245   House of Representatives Report, 1043.
246   Ibid., 1044-1045.
247   Ibid., 1040.
248   Ibid., 1042.

Dow's body lay in the road for hours because people were afraid to be seen as abolitionist sympathizers. They feared retribution. This fear was well founded and documented by McKinney, who had witnessed the confrontation from the side of his house. He stated, " *'I believe I will go down there.' Chapman said, 'I would not nigh them. You know how it is here. They do not like you very well for building on this claim here, and you might be in a little danger yourself.' That was the reason I did not go to take charge of the body of Dow.* "[249]

Dow had been murdered. His head lolled in a wagon wheel rut without even the decency of allowing his body to be moved to the side of the road or covered up. The only apparent recognition Dow had received had been from people who rode by in their wagons and gawked to see if they recognized the man who had been killed. The men who had been involved in the killing continued to come back and circle around him several times that day like a bunch of vultures looking at his body. From the moment Dow had been shot, murder had replaced reason; silence had replaced arbitration; and fear had replaced respect. And the course of events on the prairie had been changed—forever.

---

249   House of Representatives Report, 1041.

CHAPTER TWELVE
Blanton Bridge
November 27, 1855

Before his death, Charles Dow had lived with Jacob Branson for several months while he worked his new claim. They had developed a strong friendship and a bond had formed between them. His friend had been hunted down like an animal and shot in the road at Hickory Point.[250] All that remained of his friend was a cold white corpse that lay in the back of his wagon. Jacob had carefully wrapped Dow's body in a tarp in preparation for burial.[251]

On Saturday the 27th of November, Charles Dow was buried. Emotions would have been at a peak as the men who were Dow's friends watched the dirt fall from the blades of the shovels closing the hole in the ground that contained the body of their friend and neighbor. It would have been impossible for these men not to have wanted revenge for the loss of their ally. The murderer, Franklin Coleman, had already escaped from Hickory Point going to the proslavery authorities for protection. Several of Dow's friends talked about burning down Coleman's home. This emotional appeal came pouring from the depths of the men who were in the process of burying their friend. While this punishment must have momentarily seemed appropriate and provided the men with an emotional release against Coleman, Salem Gleason had the wisdom to speak up against the proposal. *"At the grave, just after it was filled up, a motion was made by a man named Farley to burn the house of Coleman who had left his house and family. I told them, saying, here is this man murdered, and for us to go to doing such a thing as that, it will operate against us. It will be better to fetch the offender to justice than to destroy property. The persons there fell in with me, and argued not to do it."*[252]

Franklin Coleman had escaped and had already planned his next move. He knew that if he turned himself in to his friends, rather than waiting for

---

250   Merrill, History of the Kansas Wars, 78.
251   Special Committee, 34th Congress, House of Representatives, Report 200, 1042.
252   Ibid., 1043.

the news to get to Lawrence and the other free-soilers, that his outcome would likely be a better one. He would, in all likelihood, be protected from the abolitionists at Hickory Point and the wrath of the Lawrence crowd if he could reach the Shawnee Mission where Reverend Johnson was entertaining Wilson Shannon, the new governor who had replaced Reeder. Reverend Johnson and Governor Shannon were well-known proslavery proponents and they had the political power to back them up. [253]

Franklin Coleman later gave this testimony about what happened after the murder: *"For the alleged charge of killing Dow I came to the Shawnee Mission and surrendered myself into the custody of Sheriff Jones, of the county in which I resided, the governor directing that I should be taken before a magistrate of my county. I was carried by the Sheriff to Bull Creek, and there met an express warning me of the danger of going back into the neighborhood to appear before the justice, there being a large armed force there greatly excited. I returned back to the governor, and he then ordered the sheriff to take me to Lecompton, before Judge Lecompton. The sheriff took me to Lecompton, and I was there in the custody of the sheriff some eight days. Judge Lecompton did not arrive there. My witnesses did not appear on account of the excitement existing in the country, and I requested to be let go to the Wakarusa camp, where Squire Saunders and some of my witnesses were. Being unable to get witnesses to appear, to fully investigate the matter, I gave my recognizance before Squire Saunders to appear before the circuit court of Douglas County, and so far as I know that recognizance is in force against me yet."* [254]

The friends of Charles Dow were convinced that Franklin Coleman was going to be allowed to run free after he killed Dow. Even if Franklin Coleman had turned himself in to the Territorial Governor and Sheriff Jones, they knew neither of these bulwarks of slavery was going to grieve about the loss of an abolitionist. They also suspected that the laws of the county were going to be used to protect Coleman and he was going to get away with the murder of Dow. The sequence of events was also more than they could bear so soon after burying their friend. *"Coleman's house was burned some few days after Dow was buried."* [255]

Nicholas McKinney recounted what occurred at this abolitionist gathering which took place on November 26, five days after the murder. He

---

253   Merrill, History of The Kansas Wars, 1856, 82.
254   House of Representatives Report, 1054.
255   Ibid., 1044.

testified *"I was at the public meeting held at Hickory Point, in the relation to the murder of Dow. I think there were about 100 persons there, and it was held at the place where the murder was committed; the men standing in a circle around the spot where Dow was found."*[256]

The pool of blood had dried where his body had been, but the dark spot did not erase the memory of the hideous crime. The events had been staggering. They feared that the judge would determine the killing justifiable, and the sheriff would turn Coleman loose. Then everyone would pretend that no crime had been committed. It was as if Charles Dow never existed at all. A crime had been committed and the evidence could not be ground away and hidden no matter how many wagon wheels rolled over the murder site. Jacob and the other men vowed to avenge his death and to do all they could to bring Franklin Coleman to justice. The men must have stood looking at one another trying to decide how to make Coleman and the others pay for spitting in the face of justice. Soon, several of the men could no longer control their anger. They headed for Franklin Coleman's home.

"Three or four men broke down the door, rushed in, emptied a straw bed upon the floor, and fired it. S.C. Smith and S.N. Wood, and others rushed into the house, smothered the flames, clearing the house, and amid the greatest excitement, some crying, 'Burn the house,' and others interceding to save the property.[257]

It would have burned to the ground if it weren't for Sam Wood. He and several other men put out the fire and chastised the men. *"S.N. Wood jumped upon a fence and said murder, pillage, and arson were the peculiar avocation of our enemies, that houses were too scarce to be burned, and that this meeting must not be disgraced in this way."*[258]

The angry men simply retreated and waited until Sam Wood left for the ride back to Lawrence. They emerged into the night with their lanterns glowing and headed back in the direction of Coleman's cabin. The cabin was torched. In the early morning darkness, on the morning of the 27th, Buckley's house and its contents were also burned to the ground.[259]

Many frightened proslavery families who had lived in Hickory Point and witnessed the meetings and the burning of Coleman's cabin, scurried to the county sheriff. Some went back across the Missouri border for protection. Those that ran for help in Douglas County went directly to Sheriff

---

256   House of Representatives Report 1046.
257   Robinson, The Kansas Conflict, 184.
258   Ibid., 184-185.
259   House of Representatives Report, 1051.

Jones. On the other side of the border, they appealed to the only elected officials they had, whether bogusly elected or not, for retribution. These officials reassured them that they had already enacted laws to deal with people like the Hickory Point crowd. They had a man whom they could count on to enforce their laws, Sheriff Samuel Jones.

Sam Jones, Sheriff of Douglas County, was a man who looked like a sheriff. He was tall, muscular, and had a coarse yet overall handsome face. A heavy black shock of hair was symmetrically set off with a full set of sideburns, beard and thick mustache. He stared out at the world through deeply set eyes that were draped with coarse, thick eyebrows. A large, broad, flat nose gave clear evidence that he did not shy away from any fight and could take a punch. His coarse features gave Jones the overall feeling of sturdiness.[260]

Undoubtedly, as expected of all lawmen, he wore his star with pride and backed up his authority with action or a posse when necessary. Sam Jones would have been confident that he had the full support of the state of Missouri, as well as the federal marshal who represented the Country. He enforced laws as he was required or ordered to do by the judge of Douglas County and other authorized officials. His past performance suggested he thought he was invincible, unbeatable and unafraid. One thing he believed unquestionably, he worked for, and was supported by the South. Men like Senator Atchison, Territorial Governor Wilson Shannon, and even the President of the United States supported the slavery government. The power behind him was overwhelming, and the proslavery men of the Kansas Territory were well entrenched, with reinforcements waiting at the Missouri border if the need arose.[261]

The abolitionists were his problem now. He must have known when he accepted the recent appointment as Sheriff of Douglas County and had given up his safe, secure job as postmaster of Westport Missouri that he would be expected to deal with the newly-arrived abolitionists if they got out of order. He must have anticipated that sooner or later, one of them would step out of line and break the law. When that happened he would be ready to respond swiftly and with the powerful authority that went along with being the sheriff. Within hours of Coleman's and Buckley's cabins

260   Goodrich, War to the Knife, 111.
261   Robinson, The Kansas Conflict, 194-195.

being torched and burned to the ground, he responded to the lawlessness and was prepared to go after those responsible.[262]

Jones must have wondered who these outsiders thought they were when they took the law into their own hands and dealt out punishment against Coleman and Buckley. He had done his job when Coleman turned himself in voluntarily by taking him to Lecompton. The judge had turned Coleman loose on his own recognizance at the cost of five-hundred dollars.[263] The case was pending. It had not been open for interpretation by anyone, including the free-booters. These abolitionists had made a big mistake when they decided to revenge the death of Dow. He would soon teach them a lesson that they would not forget. Sheriff Jones had been told by the proslavery men at Hickory Point that Jacob Branson had been the instigator behind the reaction of the Hickory Point crowd and that the old man was the one who led the revengeful mob to torch the cabins.[264]

Earlier, Sheriff Jones had personally dealt with these abolitionists during the March 1855 election. He was the leader of the men who stormed the election booth and broke out all the windows and sent the appointed officials running for their lives.[265]

He and his men had shown the newcomers in the Kansas Territory who ran things in this part of the country, and it appeared that they needed a firm reminder. What was worse than questioning the law, these abolitionists had taken their revenge out on the proslavery men in the area. In his mind, Coleman and Dow's fight had been about property lines and had nothing to do with slavery. These facts had not escaped Sheriff Jones, Governor Wilson Shannon or any of the other proslavery people of the surrounding area. In their view, the abolitionists had shown that they had no intention of obeying Territorial laws.

Sheriff Jones gathered his posse to go after the reported leader of this mob. Jones intended to nip this challenge of the law quickly. He wanted to do so while it was fresh in people's minds and he was determined to punish the offenders severely. According to his plan, Jacob Branson would be arrested and punished and that would put an end to this kind of behavior once and for all.[266]

262   Robinson, The Kansas Conflict, 183-184.
263   Merrill, True History of the Kansas Wars, 82.
264   Robinson, The Kansas Conflict, 183-184. / House of Representatives Report, 1059.
265   Robinson, Kansas: Its Interior and Exterior Life, 18.
266   Goodrich, War To The Knife, 74.

The Douglas County Sheriff's posse rode out toward Hickory Point on Monday night and headed after Jacob Branson. The posse was fully armed and ready for any encounter when the horses were reined to a stop in front of Jacob Branson's cabin. The Sheriff walked up to the door of the cabin and he and several of the posse, *"in a violent and insulting manner took him away."*[267] It can only be imagined what Branson and his wife must have feared as the door burst open inside their home.

Sam Wood, who had tried to prevent the cabin burning, had been on his way home to Lawrence from the meeting site of Charles Dow's murder with his companion, J. B. Abbott. As Wood explained, *"It was very dark... but finally, about ten or eleven o'clock, found our way to Blanton, where... we were told that a large party of armed men had just passed towards Hickory Point."*[268]

Wood realized that this was probably a posse that had come to take in Jacob Branson. Wood began to rally his men to meet in a location not far from Branson's cabin. He and his travel companion, Major Abbott, rode to the cabin to intervene in the capture of Jacob Branson. Along the way Wood asked Abbott *"what we should do if we found the rascals at Branson's. Abbott replied, 'You are the leader; just what you say.' With tightened rein, revolvers in our hands, we galloped into the thicket, and in a moment were at the door of Branson. His wife, an old lady, in choking accents replied, 'Twenty armed men have got him and gone.' 'Where?' I asked. 'Towards Lawrence,' she replied and at the same moment said they would 'murder him,' which I believed true, and sprang into the saddle, and into the inquiry, 'Where are you going?' replied, 'To save your husband or die.'"*[269]

Wood and Abbott spent the next two hours in search of Sheriff Jones and the posse that had arrested Branson but they were unable to locate the party. They finally split up. Abbott headed out to recall the men sent earlier to the Hickory Point rendezvous point. Wood went to Abbott's home where men were also to report. Wood found twelve men at Abbott's house. He reported to them that he feared Jones and his posse had already escaped with Branson. The militia had arrived at Major Abbott's that night, excited, and carrying their squirrel guns and pistols. Some of the men came with no weapons at all.[270]

---

267   Robinson, The Kansas Conflict, 183-184.
268   Ibid., 185.
269   Ibid.
270   Goodrich, War to the Knife, 74.

Those who arrived at Abbott's were probably relieved to see Colonel Sam Wood among those who were gathered. He was one of the few experienced leaders of the local militia and he had a reputation of being fearless in battle. With the impending conflict between the free-booters and the proslavery posse led by Sheriff Jones, the settlers needed more than raw recruits with squirrel guns. They needed seasoned leadership with men like Wood.

When Abbott arrived at Hickory Point, he stayed only long enough to update the men about his failure to locate the posse and the sheriff. Then he rode back to join Wood and the others. They appeared *"discouraged and dispirited, fearing they had escaped altogether."*[271]

Wood and Abbott, fearing they had failed, were in the process of sending a message to the proslavery town of Franklin to get information regarding Branson when *"all at once someone announced, 'They are coming.' Pell-mell we rushed out of the house and got into the road ahead of them, they halting within two rods of us. A moment passed in silence."*[272]

During that moment Wood and Abbott must have realized the differences between the two groups confronting each other. The men who rushed outside the cabin were the ones who had responded to the call. Most of these men were not militarily trained and had never been in a gun battle before. Their weapons and the ammunition that was stuffed into their pockets were for killing squirrels and rabbits. Besides Sam Wood and Major Abbott, there was only one other among them who had been a soldier, Capt. Hutchinson, who also had the reputation as an old fighter. The other brave men who had come to help save Jacob Branson that night had never been tested in battle.

Wood and Abbott now found themselves in a terrible and awkward situation. They would be responsible for the first armed conflict defying the authority of the bogus government and the laws they represented. Until now, all the confrontations had been verbal. This one, however, meant organized resistance with guns. They were standing in the way of the sheriff and his posse, with their prisoner, Jacob Branson, who was attempting to cross Blanton Bridge. There would be no further questions regarding whether the anti-slavery residents of the Kansas Territory intended to obey the laws, and there would be no going back after this confrontation. They decided to

---

271   Robinson, The Kansas Conflict, 185.
272   Ibid.

fight Sheriff Jones and his twenty-man posse at the bridge in an attempt to free Jacob Branson.[273]

Major Abbott and Sam Wood must have known that potentially many men could be killed that night when they made their stand against Sheriff Jones and his posse. They also did not know if they were going to be looked at as heroes or outlaws by the rest of the Kansas Territory and there was no time to ask their fellow citizens about this or put the decision to a vote.[274]

As Major Abbott, Sam Wood, and their men lined the road in front of Blanton Bridge, the sheriff stopped the posse a few yards away from the armed men.[275] Sheriff Jones surveyed the men in front of him

"He shouted out, 'What's up?' Major James Abbott responded for his group:... 'That is what we want to know.' "[276]

Major Abbott had positioned himself in front of his men and stood holding his revolver pointed at the ground. As he hollered back his response, the large revolver suddenly let out a loud roar sending the lead ball into the roadbed. No one knew for sure if the major had accidentally fired his gun or if he had pulled the trigger to get the respect and attention of the sheriff and posse that he faced. Undoubtedly, the sheriff and the horses must have jerked nervously at the unexpected explosion. It must have taken a few seconds for the sheriff and his men to regain their composure. Major Abbott's men, on the other hand, had just witnessed the first shot of the battle and it had come from their side. The adrenaline must have soared through their veins, with quickened heartbeats responding to the instinct of danger. There were no doubts that Major Abbott meant to stop the sheriff and to rescue Branson, regardless of the consequences. The standoff had begun.

The startled sheriff could only repeat his previous question, *"What's up...?"* Major Abbott responded this time without firing his weapon, *"Is Branson there?"* From the middle of the posse came the response from Jacob Branson himself, *"Yes, I am here and a prisoner."* When the men heard Jacob holler back his response, several of the men could no longer remain quiet and let Major Abbott talk for them. Three or four of them screamed at once as if almost cheering, *"Come over to your friends..."* Branson answered back with concern and desperation in his voice. He

---

273   Robinson, The Kansas Conflict, 185-186.
274   Ibid.
275   Ibid.
276   Goodrich, War to the Knife, 75.

knew he would be killed if he stayed with the posse, yet he had just been threatened by the men around him. *"They say they will shoot me if I do."*[277]

Sam Wood now entered the discussion. He walked to the side of Major Abbott and quickly responded, *"Let them shoot and be damned; we can shoot too."* Branson then said, *"I will come [even] if they do shoot,"* and he started his mule forward.[278]

The tension must have been tangible as Jacob Branson slowly rode forward, looking directly into the guns of his friends. Their guns were cocked and lowered to defend or revenge him if he were killed. At the same instant, he could hear the weapons at his back being cocked to prevent him from escaping custody.

Instead of the roar of the shotguns, Jacob heard a voice behind him ring out loud and clear, *"I ain't going to shoot."* The same man in the posse who uttered the words was the first to lower his shotgun. When the other nineteen men in the posse saw their comrade lower his gun, it must have caused a split second of doubt in the unity of their purpose and, almost involuntarily, the others also lowered their weapons.[279]

Sheriff Jones realized immediately that he had lost control of the situation. He gouged his spurs into the side of his horse and rode forward to face the men who had confronted him. He told them, *"he was Sheriff of Douglas County, Kansas, that he had a warrant to arrest the old man Branson, and he must serve it."*[280]

The response from the men lining the road was unmistakable and without compromise. The sheriff was told by Sam Wood, *"that they knew of no Sheriff Jones; that they knew of a postmaster at Westport, Missouri, by that name, but knew of no Sheriff Jones."* Wood continued to challenge Jones' authority by saying *"that they had no Douglas County in Kansas, and what was better, they never intended to have."*[281] Another man responded that *"they knew no laws but their guns!"*[282]

The men of the posse heard the degrading remarks coming from the other side and joined in the word battle. One of the posse recognized Sam Wood as the spokesman for the group obstructing the bridge. *"Why, Sam*

---

277 Goodrich, War to the Knife, 75.
278 Ibid.
279 Ibid.
280 Robinson, The Kansas Conflict, 186.
281 Ibid.
282 Goodrich, War to the Knife, 75.

120

Wood, you are very brave to-night; you must want to fight." Colonel Wood replied *"that he was always ready for a fight."*[283]

The men in both groups began to argue with one another. Jones made one last attempt to regain authority by saying, *"There is no use to shed blood in this affair; but it will be settled soon in a way not very pleasant to abolitionists,"* and started to ride through those standing in his way in the road.[284]

No sooner had he started forward, when one of the old men, named Phillip [Hupp], *"set the trigger and cocked his old squirrel rifle quicker than he or any other man ever did it before and said to Sheriff Jones, "Halt or I will blow your damned brains out..."*[285]

The Sheriff stopped *"and stayed right there, saying gently to Mr. Hupp, "Don't shoot."*[286]

The men who had blocked the bridge had clearly won the battle. They had Jacob Branson with them after forcing his release by the posse. They had been the only ones to fire a shot even if Major Abbott had done it accidentally into the roadbed. They had the sheriff sitting on his horse with a twenty-man posse behind him begging not to shoot. They had stood up to the fraudulent government and Sheriff Jones and they had won the contest.

Major Abbott and Colonel Wood calmed their men, including Mr. Hupp, and allowed the sheriff and his posse to pass Blanton Bridge on their way back home.[287]

"After Jones left, and Mr. Branson realized he was safe...the brave old man...broke down and cried like a child. The reaction after the terrible nervous strain through which he had passed had come. The tears rolled down his cheeks and his huge body shook with the sobs."[288]

The abolitionists had stood firm and had acted against the unlawful government with armed resistance. Sam Wood, however, would have to face Robinson and tell him what had happened that night at Blanton Bridge. The event had not been peaceful. The men at the bridge, however, could take pride in what they had done to rescue the old man. At the same time they had to have been worried about the revenge that was sure to be swift when Sheriff Jones told the proslavery men what had occurred. It was

283   Goodrich, War to the Knife, 75.
284   Ibid.
285   Ibid., 76.
286   Ibid.
287   Ibid.
288   Ibid.

too late to ask Charles Robinson what they should have done back at the bridge. All they could do now would be to fight for their lives in the defense of Lawrence when the retribution poured across the border in response. Lawrence and the abolitionists had to begin preparing for an attack that was sure to come. It was only a matter of time.

CHAPTER THIRTEEN
The Wakarusa War
December 1855

As Sheriff Jones rode back to Douglas County, the intensity and humiliation must have been painful. He had been forced to look like something that he wasn't, a coward. As he rode along with the posse in the darkness that night, he must have struggled to live with the ugly image portrayed back at the bridge. He had been disgraced in front of his posse and had given up his prisoner without a fight. Furthermore, he begged for his life—quietly asking a crazy old man pointing a squirrel gun at his head not to shoot. Jones' reputation as a fearless lawman had been tarnished. He reacted like most men do when embarrassed and their courage is compromised; he searched for excuses to justify the incident. Jones chose a defensive strategy. He would say that he had been hopelessly outnumbered. According to the exaggerated written report he submitted to his authorities, the dozen men who challenged him at the bridge had become forty armed to the teeth. He undoubtedly convinced himself he had ridden into a hopeless trap and only his trained eye would have seen rifles and guns of every description aiming at him. His story would support the notion that if he had challenged this mob, it would have meant certain death to all the men in the posse. He probably fantasized that he would have gladly given his life for duty, but it was his responsibility to protect the lives of the men in the posse. With the mental fabrication in place, it would have been easier for him to turn his head and look back at the posse without feeling shame.[289]

He probably felt profound anger when he looked at the man in the posse who had been the first one to lower his shotgun and mutter, "I ain't going to shoot." Not only had that man spoken out of place, but when he lowered his weapon, he confused the others in the posse regarding their willingness to fight it out. It was this man and not Sheriff Jones who had been responsible for the failure to bring in Jacob Branson—it was his fault. Undoubtedly, Sam Jones continued to work on the rest of the story he would tell when he

---

289   G. Douglas Brewerton, The War in Kansas, 159-160.

reached home. The details at the bridge were probably hashed and rehashed over and over in his mind and the common thread to his alibi was the men had not followed his lead.[290]

The rationalization of the events that occurred at Blanton Bridge were documented in Jones' letter to Wilson Shannon, the Territorial Governor, on November 28, 1855, and captured the magnitude of the distortion when he asked for an army of 3000 men to retaliate and carry out the law.

"To His Excellency

Wilson Shannon

Governor of Kansas Territory

Last night I, with a posse of ten men, arrested one Jacob Branson by virtue of a peace-warrant regularly issued, who, on our return was rescued by a party of forty armed men, who rushed upon us suddenly from behind a house upon the road-side, all armed to the teeth with Sharpes [sic] rifles.

You may consider an open rebellion as having already commenced, and I call upon you for three thousand men to carry out the laws. Mr. Hargis (the bearer of the letter) will give you more particularly the circumstances.

Most Respectfully,

Samuel J. Jones

Sheriff of Douglas County" [291]

As Jones dealt with his defeat, a deep fire of revenge began to burn internally and he started the legal steps toward retribution when individual arrest warrants were issued for the men who had confronted him at the bridge.[292]

The effects of the confrontation at Wakarusa were not limited to Douglas County. When Sheriff Jones and his posse reached home following Branson's rescue, another firestorm was set off as the news spread rapidly in the surrounding communities of Leavenworth, Atchison, and Lecompton and other proslavery strongholds. There were wild stories of eye-witnessed terror, cabin burning, women and children screaming in fear, and open rebellion by the fanatical abolitionists of Lawrence who now had taken armed control of the Kansas Territory.[293]

During the period between November 27th, and the beginning of December, newspapers headlined–*"TO ARMS! TO ARMS! It is expected that every lover of Law and Order will rally at Leavenworth on Saturday,*

---

290   Robinson, The Kansas Conflict, 186.
291   Brewerton, The War in Kansas, 1856, 159-160.
292   Trowbridge, Andrew Taylor Still, 60.
293   Robinson, 200.

December 1, 1855, prepared to march at once to the scene of the rebellion, to put down the outlaws of Douglas County, who are committing depredation upon persons and property, burning down houses and declaring open hostilities to the laws, and have forcibly rescued a prisoner from the Sheriff. Come one, come all! The laws must be executed. The outlaws, it is said, are armed to the teeth, and number 1000 men. Every man should bring his rifle and ammunition, and it would be well to bring two or three day's provision. Every man to his post, and to his duty."[294]

The request by Sheriff Jones did not stop with the Territorial Governor. On November 28th, the same day Shannon received Jones' letter, he wrote to the President of the United States, Franklin Pierce, to inform him about the grave situation and indicated that federal troops might also be required to quell the events. *"The time has come when this armed band of men, who are seeking to subvert and render powerless the existing government, have to be met and the laws enforced against them...If the lives and property of unoffending citizens of this Territory cannot be protected by law, there is an end to practical government, and it becomes a useless formality. The excitement along the border...is running wild...This feeling and intense excitement can still be held in subordination if the laws are faithfully executed; otherwise there is no power here that can control this border excitement, and civil war is inevitable...We are standing on a volcano, the upheavings [sic] and agitation beneath we feel, and no one can tell the hour when an eruption may take place.*"[295]

Meanwhile, the agitation and confusion would grow in the Kansas Territory. The story of the rescue at Blanton Bridge continued to be embellished, and the men who took part in the incident had warrants issued for their arrests.

The army of 3000 men requested by Sheriff Jones, and supported by Governor Shannon and President Pierce, became a force of 1500 proslavery men who were organized into the Missouri Militia. This army planned to move forward to a war camp site located on the Wakarusa River.

On the other side of the border, Charles Robinson was analyzing the military information. He understood the dire circumstances the town of Lawrence would soon face and started preparation for an imminent attack. He ordered the abolitionist forces to prepare the town for a defensive strategy. Then he began the political tactics to stop the impending war. First, he

---

294   Robinson, The Kansas Conflict, 196.
295   Ibid., 213.

needed to know how many men from Lawrence had been involved in the bridge incident. It turned out only two were identified—Sam Wood and Samuel Tappan.[296]

As a result of the incident at the bridge, the political storm that had been slowly coalescing over the past months had reached the boiling point in the Kansas Territory. Both sides prepared for an all-out war. The men from Missouri, who joined their proslavery comrades at the Wakarusa River, would come with the conviction that they were stopping insurrection against the United States. Some of the men brought guns used by their grandfathers against the British to win freedom for the country. The story told by Sheriff Jones about the rescue of Branson had been one of intolerable lawlessness and defiance by the abolitionists. The proslavery men would not tolerate open rebellion against the sheriff in the performance of his duties. The sheriff had received a legal warrant for Branson's arrest and no one would be allowed to interfere with the lawful process. As these Missouri men saw it, the Lawrence abolitionists had finally proved they were insurrectionists by taking Branson away from the sheriff and his posse.

A large army of 1500 Missouri men arrived at the Wakarusa River on December 2, 1855. The men who arrived on the banks of the river were ready to fight. They were proud to respond to their country's call and perform their patriotic duty. [297]

Although fighting seemed imminent, the Wakarusa War had really started when the first shot had been fired by Major Abbott into the roadbed at Blanton Bridge. The incident had sent the undeniable message that the abolitionists in the Kansas Territory were going to fight back and refused to recognize what they perceived to be the bogus authorities in power.

When Charles Robinson learned the details of the Blanton Bridge rescue and realized the only Lawrence men involved were Wood and Tappan, he formulated a political defensive argument. It was that these men had acted independently when they challenged Sheriff Jones for his prisoner. The never-daunted Colonel Sam Wood additionally had accepted full responsibility for his and Tappan's actions and had stated *that he would willingly be arrested in order to test in the Supreme Court the right of Missouri to make laws in Kansas.*[298]

Robinson had little doubt that even though the town of Lawrence had nothing to do with organizing the rescue attempt, this incident would give

---

296   Robinson, The Kansas Conflict, 188.
297   Nichols, Bleeding Kansas, 57.
298   Robinson, 188.

the proslavery forces the justification they needed to destroy the town. That fear was verified when *"Squads and companies of armed men began to arrive at Franklin and the Wakarusa"* to attack the town of Lawrence.[299]

"Robinson was given supreme control...he was forced to prepare the town to defend itself. The town became a military camp, earthworks were thrown up and preparations for a defense made as complete as possible."[300] This threat also forced him to accept the help of the shrieking Jim Lane who had the experience and reputation as the most senior military man among them. Groups of men began arriving from all over the Kansas Territory to help defend the town from the invasion of the Missouri Militia. When the volunteers rode into Lawrence carrying their weapons they were cheered by the outnumbered abolitionists. The largest group of defenders to arrive was an army of one-hundred armed men from Topeka.[301] Earthen entrenchments were dug at both sides of Massachusetts Street. Many women refused to leave the men for a safer place. Some women made cartridges, *"their nimble fingers keeping time with each heart-beat for freedom, so enthusiastic are they in aiding defense."* Other women vowed to fight it out at the side of their men when the attack occurred.[302]

Despite the frenzy and preparation, this calamity and uproar must have been a welcome sight for Jim Lane. He had waited impatiently for a conflict to begin after arriving at Lawrence because he was the most senior military man in the community. As a result, his personal feelings regarding the Negro and his opportunistic character had to be overlooked. What could not be ignored was that he had experience and had commanded troops in war. Unquestionably, he possessed superior leadership experience in military matters. The war threat thrust him into the full importance that he savored, and he was placed second-in-command only to Charles Robinson. Lane took charge of defense and discipline, *"Lane walked beside the companies, in an easy, swinging military gait, and gave orders in his short, shrill voice...Lane would sometimes make a speech...On such occasions* [he] *was fiery and his remarks were calculated to rouse up the men to the fighting point."*[303]

Robinson needed fire, zeal and military organization, but he only wanted it to be defensive. He knew that this strategy was crucial. It was the

---

299   Robinson, The Kansas Conflict, 191.
300   Ibid.
301   Ibid.
302   Robinson, Kansas: Its Interior and Exterior Life, 143.
303   Goodrich, War To The Knife, 79.

only way that he could win the battle for Lawrence, Eli Thayer, and the abolitionist cause. Robinson spoke as commander in chief to try to take the stinging initiative out of Lane's words: *"Men of Lawrence, and free-state men, we must have courage, but with it we must have prudence! These men have come from Missouri to subjugate the free-state men, to crush the free-state movement...They...will wait at least for a plausible excuse before commencing to shed blood. This excuse must not be given them...If the Missourians, partly from fear and partly from want of a sufficient pretext, have to go back without striking a blow, it will make them a laughing-stock...This is the last struggle between freedom and slavery, and we must not flatter ourselves that it will be trivial or short...These may be dark days, but the American people and the world will justify us, and the cause of right will eventually triumph."*[304]

The Wakarusa War, however, was about to take an unexpected turn. On December 6, 1855, nine days following the bridge incident, a young man named Thomas W. Barber would pay the ultimate price. [Barber] *"was a quiet, inoffensive and amiable man, unexceptionable in his habits, and much attached to his wife."*[305]

Thomas Barber had joined the First Regiment of the Kansas Volunteers to help the abolitionists defend Lawrence should the town come under attack. Barber's young wife was extremely fearful and begged him not to enlist but *"turning a deaf ear"* he ignored her pleas.[306]

Thomas Barber had been in Lawrence on December 6, and at 1:00 p.m., had started home, riding alongside his brother, Robert Barber, and Robert's brother-in law, Thomas Peirson. They had traveled about seven miles from Lawrence when they observed a group of approximately fifteen men on horseback in the distance. This group of proslavery men had come to fight in the attack on Lawrence. Thomas Barber and his two companions were unaware that they were in danger until two of the men in the Missouri group broke away and rode on an angle to cut them off. The proslavery men ordered Barber's trio to halt and began questioning them about where they were from and *"What is going on in Lawrence?"* One of the attackers moved his horse closer to the side of Thomas Barber's mount. [307]

Thomas Barber answered the men's questions and said, " *'Nothing in particular.' Their reply back would be terse ...'Nothing in particular, hey?*

304   Robinson, Kansas: Interior and Exterior Life, 123.
305   Merrill, History of the Kansas Wars, 1856, 84.
306   Ibid.
307   Ibid., 84-85.

... we have orders from the Governor to see the laws executed in Kansas.' Thomas Barber then asked, *'What laws have we disobeyed?'* Upon hearing this, the rider of the gray horse raised his hand and pointed toward his party, at the same time exclaiming, *'Then turn your horses' heads and go with us.'* Thomas replied they would not obey the orders... This response was challenged by their attackers...*'You won't, hey'*...and the man who was closest to Thomas Barber drew his pistol and fired at him while spinning his horse's head around to ride away. The other proslavery attacker also discharged his weapon at Barber's party. Thomas Barber *"was entirely unarmed"* but the other two men were carrying guns. Robert Barber drew out his pistol and shot three times at the fleeing attackers but none of the bullets found their mark.[308]

As Robert Barber later recounted, *"The main body of horsemen was still halted, but full in sight. Thomas Barber then turned to us and said, 'Boys, let us be off!' we started accordingly, at a full gallop, on our road... After riding in this manner for about a hundred yards, [Thomas]... said to me, 'That fellow shot me;' he smiled as he said so... [Robert] then... asked him, 'Where are you shot?' He pointed to his right side. I then remarked, 'It is not possible, Thomas.' To this he replied, 'It is,' at the same time smiling again."*[309]

Robert did not think his brother *"realized how badly he was hurt. After uttering these, his last words, [Thomas] ... dropped his rein and reeled in his saddle."* When Robert saw that his brother was about to fall, he grabbed his overcoat. *"I held him thus for nearly a hundred yards; I could then hold him no longer, and he fell to the ground; as he did so I slipped from my horse, at the same time calling out, 'whoa;' both horses stopped immediately; I bent over my brother, and found that he was dead"*[310]

The news soon circulated about Thomas Barber being killed. His body was brought to Lawrence and placed at rest in the lobby of the newly finished Eldridge Hotel. The town of Lawrence had witnessed the first retribution for the Blanton Bridge rescue. If any of the Lawrence people had any doubts about the seriousness of the army waiting to attack the city, they had no further doubts as the corpse was in clear view lying in the hotel. The passersby really didn't even have to look into the hotel to see Thomas Barber's body to know about the terrible consequences of his death. Mrs.

---

308   Merrill, History of the Kansas Wars, 1856, 84-86.
309   Ibid., 86-87.
310   Ibid., 87.

Barber was with her dead husband, and the wailing of his young widow could be heard echoing in the streets.[311]

The town of Lawrence tried to deal with the young man's death and comfort Barber's distraught and hysterical wife. After this incident, Charles Robinson had a difficult time convincing his men to stay defensive only. He and his safety committee continued to order Jim Lane not to attack, but to wait and fight only if invaded. On at least one occasion Colonel Lane had to be threatened with arrest to restrain him from attacking the militia.[312]

Robinson worked tirelessly to defuse the situation and end the confrontation without any more shots being fired at Lawrence. While he carefully planned the strategy with his army, the people in Lawrence must have been afraid that they would be taken by surprise. The nights would have seemed unusually long.

Outside of Lawrence, the abolitionists in the surrounding countryside also began to feel the threats following the bridge incident. Arrest warrants had been issued for several men living outside of Lawrence, including a warrant for Andrew Still, who had been named as being at the bridge when Jacob Branson was freed.[313]

During this stressful period, the Still family was aroused one night from their sleep at two o'clock in the morning. A young neighbor boy had crawled quietly to the Still's cabin to warn the family about the invading army of 1500 men who were arriving at the Wakarusa River. Andrew answered the tap at the door because the other men in the family were away from the homestead. Abram was gone providing needs for the church, and Andrew's brother, Thomas, was already in Lawrence helping James Lane with the fortification plans. The boy told the Still family that a large group of proslavery militia men were coming in their direction. He also told them that the Missourians were killing men, women and children and burning houses. The youngster suggested they hide out at their neighbor's house hidden in the middle of a big cornfield. The Still family slipped quietly out of the house and started on the mile and a half journey to Mr. Henry Landon's home located in a cornfield.[314]

The moon was full that night and while its light made the walking easier, it also exposed the escaping family to detection. The little band of family members, who represented three generations of the Still family, hurried

311   Robinson, Kansas: Interior and Exterior Life, 145-148.
312   Robinson, The Kansas Conflict, 207.
313   Trowbridge, Andrew Taylor Still, 60.
314   Clark, Reminiscences, 25.

along the path, realizing danger was close at hand. During the escape that night, they were afraid that each step might bring them into sight of the dreaded Missouri Border Ruffians. The cornfield was finally reached and it swallowed up the frightened family between its rows. When they reached the middle of the field, they came to a clearing with a small house. They could see that the house was surrounded by their neighbors from miles around who had also escaped. The little house was only big enough for a single bed, a table and a stove, but it represented to the neighbors that huddled both inside and out, a safe haven from being discovered by the men who had come to avenge the bridge incident. There must have been a growing feeling of hope and strength as more families appeared in the clearing and caused their numbers to increase.[315]

As daylight approached, the families heard the sound of horses coming into the cornfield. It was a combination of hoof beats and the dry, parched corn stalks being snapped off as the horses came closer. The hidden families must have been worried that this might be their enemies coming. They realized they were hopelessly outnumbered.[316]

As the horses approached the clearing, there must have been relief when the families recognized the twenty-five Hickory Point Abolitionist Moonshiners riding through the cornfield. The Still family would have had an additional sense of thankfulness when they saw that Thomas Still was one of the men riding with them. The men were heavily armed with their cargo of guns and bullets. The Moonshiners were probably just as happy and relieved to find their friends and family members unharmed and alive, hiding at the cabin. They had brought enough weapons to protect themselves from the Missouri Border Ruffians, should they be attacked. The Moonshiners were able to accompany the families safely from the cornfield to their homes.[317]

According to Rovia, after the fleeing family arrived back at the Still's cabin, her mother, Martha Still, had to cook a lot of breakfast that morning. She needed to feed the entire family including the group of men who had accompanied them safely to their home. *"Mother was getting breakfast for them and stepped outside to go to the smoke house to cut some meat for all*

---

315   Clark, Reminiscences, 25-26.
316   Ibid., 26.
317   Ibid.

of them when all of a sudden a half dozen border ruffians came galloping up with their guns on their shoulders."[318]

"*One of the number said to Mother, 'Hello old woman, is your husband there?' She said, 'No, he isn't at home.' 'Are your sons there?' She said, 'Yes.' 'Well, tell them to come out here.' She stepped into the house and said, 'There are a half dozen border ruffians out here that want to see you.' Hurrying out where upon the 25 Moonshiners from Hickory Point and my three brothers poured out of the house with their Sharps rifles gristling [sic] in the sun and to use the present day slang, they 'ran some.' They ran a few hundred yards and threw up the white flag. Our men went out and talked with them. They said, 'Is Dr. Andrew Still in the crowd?' He said, 'Yes.' 'Is Major Abbott here?' 'No.' 'Is Captain Saunders here?' 'No.' 'Well, we have drawn a bead on you three fellows for helping to take Branson away from us at Blanton's bridge, but you're too many for us now, but if you will come over to Franklin tonight we'll fight it out with you.'*"[319]

"*So our boys promised to be on hand...* [and later that night] *... they had quite a little skirmish and the border ruffians retreated.*"[320]

The components were all in place for the Wakarusa War. The Missourians were now camped at the Wakarusa River. These men had been called up by the highest-ranking federal official in the area, the Territorial Governor, Wilson Shannon. The men who answered that call already hated the men whom they were asked to fight. The governor had given them a legitimate license to go into the Territory and exterminate the abolitionists and the town of Lawrence which was their stronghold.

Missouri's Senator Atchison would likewise do his part in leading the attack. He had longed to lead the South to achieve his goals in the Kansas Territory and he must have been ecstatic by the invitation provided when the abolitionists overstepped the law at the bridge. He donned the title of "General Atchison" for the charge against the northern Yankees. He was also given leadership over the militia. General Atchison was probably elated that the men who rescued Jacob Branson at the bridge had given him the excuse to attack and wipe out the antislavery forces in Lawrence.

On the other side was Charles Robinson, the consummate politician and thinker, who felt that victory in this war would only be won if no shots were fired. It was as if he had a chess board in front of him. He had studied the move made at Blanton Bridge to rescue Jacob Branson for the revenge

318   Clark, Reminiscences, 26.
319   Ibid.
320   Ibid.

of Dow's death. One pawn was set aside from the board. The sheriff was stopped and blocked at the bridge. A bishop had been moved to block the knight. Fifteen hundred men were camped on the Wakarusa River and were waiting to attack. The town had been cut off. Anyone coming or going from Lawrence would be stopped by the invading army and detained, searched, and in many cases robbed of possessions.[321]

Robinson saw the men on the other side of the chessboard attacking his side with ferociousness. The death of Thomas Barber was unmistakable evidence to the town that the militia had come to kill. With Barber's death, another pawn was moved off the board and placed into the box of lost men.[322] Charles Robinson had to make the next move. It was his turn to begin the offensive. First, he had to send a message to warn the Territorial Governor, Wilson Shannon, that he was about to make a terrible mistake by attacking the innocent people of Lawrence.

After Barber's death on December 6, Robinson wasted no time and immediately sought out men who could break through enemy lines to deliver his message to Governor Shannon at the war camp. It would not be easy because the town was surrounded by armed men. *This message was taken to the Governor by two young men through the lines of the enemy camped at Franklin and on the Wakarusa. It was a most hazardous mission, as they had to encounter drunken men as well as sentinels nearly the whole distance*"[323] but the men managed to break through the lines to deliver a succinct message to the governor.

"*To his Excellency, Wilson Shannon,*

"*Governor of Kansas Territory:*

"*Sir: As citizens of Kansas Territory, we desire to call your attention to the fact that a large force of armed men from a foreign State have assembled in the vicinity of Lawrence, and are now committing depredations upon our citizens, stopping wagons, opening and appropriating their loads, arresting, detaining, and threatening travelers upon the public road, and that they claim to do this by your authority. We desire to know if they do appear by your authority, and if you will secure the peace and quiet of the community by ordering their instant removal, or compel us to resort to some other means and to higher authority.*"[324]

---

321   Robinson, The Kansas Conflict, 199.
322   Ibid., 203.
323   Ibid., 199.
324   Ibid..

Governor Shannon read the message and asked for time to respond to the request. When the messengers returned an hour later for his reply, he engaged them in a long conversation accusing the abolitionists of burning sixteen houses with women and children driven out of doors. *"We told him we were sorry that he had not taken pains to inquire into the truth of the matter before he brought this large force into the country...that this information was wholly and entirely false."*[325]

For the first time since the Blanton Bridge incident, the governor had heard the abolitionists' side of the matter. *"This must have been a revelation to the Governor, as it was intended to be."*[326] Wilson Shannon would soon realize he had gotten himself into a dilemma. After *"he got his eyes opened by the message and interview...hastened to the encampment of his army of invasion or occupation. After conferring with the high officials in command, he sent to Lawrence, as previously arranged, for an escort to visit that town."*[327]

Governor Wilson Shannon found himself in the middle of a battlefield against an innocent town. The sheriff had made him look like a fool. Shannon had unknowingly called for a war against a community that had done nothing wrong.

The next day, Wilson Shannon was escorted to Lawrence, and when the two sides initially met on December 7, 1855, the meeting was held in the Eldridge Hotel. Wilson Shannon and his delegation, which included the grandson of Daniel Boone, had to go upstairs in the hotel to meet with Robinson and his council. This entrance required them to pass by the body of Thomas Barber and his wife, who was still grieving with agonizing sobs.

"Words can never convey the mingling emotions which moved the crowd, or the heart-crushing agony of the young wife. There were no children in the household, and all the affections had twined around this one idol. All of life, all of happiness, were centered in him...It seemed as though her heart must break, and in her distress and shrieks, the brave, strong hearted men mingled tears and muttered imprecations of vengeance upon the murderers.[328]

Even the strong men who came from the enemy's militia to meet with Robinson at the hotel could not ignore the pathetic suffering of the grieving wife as they passed the pale corpse of the youth who had been sacrificed.

---

325   Robinson, The Kansas Conflict, 200.
326   Ibid., 199.
327   Ibid., 201.
328   Ibid., 203 / Robinson, Kansas: Interior and Exterior Life, 145-146.

Colonel Boone, who was a seasoned and fearless fighter, felt compelled to express his feelings at the pitiful sight. *"I did not expect such a thing as this!"*[329]

"Governor Shannon was visibly affected when, on going up-stairs to the council-room, he saw the dead body of Barber stretched upon a bench, dressed as he had fallen from his horse, and with eyes apparently staring at the stairway, and the moans of the widow, as they were heard from another room, were not consoling to his feelings.[330]

When the Missouri delegation, led by Wilson Shannon, found Robinson and Lane in the upstairs room, *"Governor Shannon needed no new facts or arguments, but at once confessed his mistake. He had misunderstood the situation, admitted there was no cause to attack Lawrence, and that no crime or violation of law had been committed in the town. His only solicitude was to get his army to their homes without bloodshed. He did not claim that he had a right to disarm the people, although his army would demand the Sharps rifles."*[331]

This request to confiscate the Sharps rifles was challenged by Charles Robinson. He would not allow his men to give up their weapons. He would later tell his men that if the enemy continued to insist on giving up the Sharps rifles, that they should *"keep the rifles and give them the contents."*[332]

Governor Shannon knew he now had to face Sheriff Jones and the Missouri militia who had been promised that when they came to Lawrence they would be able to wipe out the town. His peace effort would disappoint the men who had come for blood. Shannon had decided that this peace agreement would probably best be announced with federal troops present to prevent any mutiny from occurring in the southern ranks. He had chosen to use the federal troops promised by President Pierce. What Governor Shannon had not counted on when he sent for these Fort Leavenworth forces under the command of Colonel Sumner, was a delay. Colonel Sumner, on the other hand, had decided to request written orders from the War Department before he proceeded.[333]

Jefferson Davis' political actions might have been anticipated when he refused to issue orders for the federal troops to intervene and assist Wilson Shannon in Lawrence. *"As Jeff Davis was the head of this department, and*

329   Robinson, Kansas: Interior and Exterior Life, 146.
330   Robinson, The Kansas Conflict, 203.
331   Ibid., 201.
332   Robinson, Kansas: Interior and Exterior Life, 155.
333   Robinson, The Kansas Conflict, 204.

as he probably desired a conflict of the militia or posse with the citizens, and knew the presence of United States troops would prevent it, he declined to send the order, as authorized by the President. "[334]

Governor Shannon had lost his federal backup and was left to resolve the issues between the militia and Robinson on his own. This meant he would have to bring Robinson and Lane together with the militia officers and referee the meeting between the two sides. On December 8th, the delegation left Lawrence for the meeting with the militia that was encamped at Franklin.[335]

"Accordingly he desired a delegation from Lawrence to accompany him to Franklin and meet with the captains of the militia. Lane and Robinson complied with his request. At the meeting...Governor Shannon led off with an explanation of the settlement, giving the position occupied by the citizens of Lawrence. After him, Colonel Lane attempted to speak, but his opening so offended the thirteen militia captains that they started to leave the room, saying they did not come there to be insulted. Governor Shannon begged of them to remain and hear Dr. Robinson. Lane did not proceed, and Robinson in a few words, explained the action of the people of Lawrence, saying that no attempt had ever been made to serve any process in the town, legal or otherwise, by any officer, real or pretended. Jones was appealed to by a militia officer to know if Robinson told the truth. Jones replied that he did. Then, the response about the room was, 'We have been damnably deceived.' As to the Sharps rifles, Robinson appealed to them to say if they would, as American citizens, submit to be deprived of the constitutional right to bear arms, or if they would respect any people who would thus submit? The leading men saw their predicament, and said, 'Boys, it is no use, they have got us; we can do nothing at this time, and the conference ended.' "[336]

The Volunteer Militia had hopelessly been trapped without a justifiable cause for this war. Now Robinson would send them all back home looking like a bunch of fools for coming in the first place.[337] He had made a masterful, reasoned and astute move against the enemy. Check mate.

Even General Atchison had to submit reluctantly and was forced to accept the argument of Charles Robinson. He supported Wilson Shannon's decision to call off the war.

---

334   Robinson, The Kansas Conflict, 204.
335   Ibid.
336   Ibid., 204-205.
337   Ibid., 209.

Following this meeting, there was speculation about assassination attempts on both Robinson and Lane on their journey back to Lawrence. There was reasonable evidence which backed up the claim.

After the dinner at the camp ended, a solitary soldier was to escort Robinson and Lane that night back to Lawrence and to see them safely through enemy lines. He rode no farther than one-hundred yards with them when *"he said good-night and left his charge to get by the guards as best they could. At this Lane said to Robinson, 'Hurry up, this means assassination; they mean to kill us,' and started his horse upon the run."*[338]

Another incident occurred that contributed to the suspicion of a planned assassination. Three heavily armed men took over a cabin east of Lawrence and were apparently waiting for Robinson and Lane in case they made it that far. Their plan was foiled when they were arrested by the men of Lawrence. *"It is not doubted but these men were out for the purpose of killing the guests of the Governor and the captains of the militia."*[339]

Despite the planned assassination attempts, Robinson and Lane were able to find their own way home through the lines and returned safely to Lawrence. Robinson would later tell a story about his horse falling while galloping to safety. James Lane rode on without coming back to help him. Robinson, as always, managed to survive on his own.[340] Robinson had accomplished what he desired—the conflict had ended without the use of arms. Lawrence had been spared.

On the other side, Governor Shannon had been politically embarrassed. Wilson Shannon had come to the Kansas Territory to enforce the proslavery position. He was expected to be tough when dealing with the abolitionists. When the bridge incident occurred, he thought that it would be his chance to show the Washington politicians that he was capable of carrying out a crushing blow against the antislavery forces. It was fortunate for the abolitionists that the issue which he chose turned out to be a weak one. He had supported a massive armed response and had overreacted to the incident. His support of Sheriff Jones' position resulted in an avalanche of power being unnecessarily unleashed.

When Shannon discovered his error and needed help at the federal level to minimize his mistake, he was left without backup. The federal troops were necessary to guarantee that no mutiny occurred in Jones' posse or in

338   Robinson, The Kansas Conflict, 205.
339   Ibid., 206.
340   Ibid., 205.

the ranks of the militia volunteers. It became apparent that some men in Washington actually hoped that the confrontation would escalate and that it could not be stopped. They evidently wanted confrontation in order to stop the abolitionists' movement and destroy their town once and for all.

Not only had Wilson Shannon not been supported by Washington, he had also been made to look weak by Robinson and the men in the Kansas Territory. Shannon had to admit that he was the one who had made the mistake to call for a war. He was also the one who was forced to accept the uncompromising attitude of Robinson and Lane regarding the Sharps rifle confiscation. He was then required to sign an agreement to pay for any damages caused by his militia while in Lawrence.[341] And finally, he was the one who was forced to look into the dead staring eyes of Thomas Barber when he walked up the stairs to negotiate with Robinson. It was his ears that heard the screams and moans of the grieving wife, and it was his heart that experienced the pangs of guilt for the unnecessary murder. Shannon had suffered defeat and humiliation in almost every way.

Peace had been achieved at great personal cost, but not everyone was satisfied with the outcome.

One of the most outspoken critics was the man who would eventually fulfill his need to embroil the proslavery men in battle—John Brown and his sons had arrived at Lawrence to take part in the conflict. Midday, on December 7, a strange, solemn wagonload of men entered the town. *"To each of their persons was strapped a short heavy broad sword,"* remembered George Washington Brown of the *Herald of Freedom. "Each was supplied with a goodly number of fire arms, and navy revolvers, and poles were standing endwise around the wagon box with fixed bayonets pointing upwards."*

Although the group was received with "great eclat," as were all arrivals, it soon became clear that the old man in charge had come not merely to defend Lawrence from attack, but "to draw a little blood."[342]

The problems that John Brown caused were immediately recognized and dealt with by Robinson. *"From the moment he commenced fomenting difficulties in camp, disregarding the command of superior officers, and trying to induce the men to go down to Franklin, and make an attack upon the proslavery forces encamped there. The Committee of Public Safety was*

---

341   Robinson, The Kansas Conflict, 202-203.
342   Goodrich, War to the Knife, 84 / Nichols, Bleeding Kansas, 70 /
       Stephen B. Oates, To Purge This Land With Blood, 107.

called upon several times to head off his wild adventure...and Old Brown retired in disgust."[343]

The other side also had their zealots who resisted leaving without a battle. Some of the 1500 men refused to retreat or to follow orders. The angry men would not leave without an attack and retribution. On the night of December 8th, Robinson had a mysterious and unexpected miracle appear on the scene to cast a blow against the would-be attackers at the Wakarusa River. It was Mother Nature herself that arrived with the most bitter, numbing, ice-chilling cold that could be imagined. The arctic cold front that hit that night was the worst freezing weather that anyone had ever remembered experiencing in the Territory. Not only did the temperature drop to the bottom of the thermometer, but the wind *"blew almost a hurricane, as it knows how to blow in Kansas."*[344] The tents were blown to the ground and the fires had to be put out at the campsite. Sheets of ice froze the skin of anyone exposed, and caked hair, beards, and mustaches with frozen water. Even the toughest man was forced to crawl away from the Wakarusa River and head for home.[345]

The final event of the Wakarusa War was a peace jubilee celebration that was held in Lawrence on December 10, 1855. Governor Shannon, although invited, understandably declined to attend the event. Sheriff Sam Jones, however, had the courage to accept the invitation.[346] It can only be speculated why the sheriff attended the jubilee. Perhaps he wanted to immediately test the sincerity of the abolitionists about cooperating with him as the sheriff. Maybe he wanted to show Robinson and the town that he wasn't afraid of them and wanted to immediately establish his authority there. Perhaps he went to begin a more friendly relationship with the town, feeling that the sooner this was accomplished the better. Regardless of what the sheriff's intentions were, he was treated rudely. Many of the group of men who supported Jim Lane became so abusive that assassination of the sheriff was entertained that night. Only Charles Robinson, rushing in to quell the riotous behavior, stopped the mob from attacking the sheriff.[347]

There would have been little doubt that the peace jubilee at Lawrence was not held with the intention of making friends out of enemies. Sheriff Jones must have known that all the promises of cooperating with the

343   Robinson, The Kansas Conflict, 264.
344   Nichols, Bleeding Kansas, 75.
345   Ibid.
346   Robinson, The Kansas Conflict, 208.
347   Ibid..

law made during the peace agreement had been talk without substance. Furthermore, after the treatment he had received from Lane and his men at the jubilee, he must have had little doubt about whether or not the people of Lawrence respected him as their sheriff. The disrespect shown to him that night was an omen of the future. The Wakarusa War had ended but the conflict was not over.

CHAPTER FOURTEEN
The Obsession
Spring 1856

Sheriff Sam Jones must have been consumed with feelings of bitterness as the army loaded their weapons into the wagons for the trip back to Missouri following the abrupt end of the Wakarusa War. What would have made it even more painful for Jones was that the war was called to a halt by Shannon and Atchison who were his political allies. The army had already left when Sheriff Jones was invited to attend the Lawrence peace jubilee. There, he was again forced to endure threats, insults, and rough encounters with the abolitionists. With each incident, he continued to be humiliated and was denied any satisfaction of being able to punish the men who had taken away his prisoner at Blanton Bridge. He had developed a greater level of hatred for the Lawrence citizens who had mocked his dignity and authority as the Douglas County Sheriff.

What made the embarrassment event worse, Sheriff Jones had requested the militia, and they had come. Fifteen hundred armed men had responded to restore his authority and honor to the badge he wore. Many of the men had traveled a long distance to reestablish law and order and to put an end to his embarrassment. This mighty crusade had been stopped. The offenders had not been wiped out or punished. Not a shot had been fired at Lawrence except for the killing of Barber. Jones had not even been in the group of men who chased Barber's brother and brother-in-law across the prairie. He had not fired his gun. The men who had taken his prisoner at Blanton Bridge were openly laughing at him and remained free and unpunished in Lawrence. They continued to brag about how they had taken Jacob Branson without a fight and how "Old Phillip Rupp" had drawn a bead on him with his squirrel gun and made Jones beg for his life like a coward. If that were not humiliating enough, the abolitionists were allowed to keep their smuggled weapons. None of the Sharps rifles were confiscated despite the demand that all weapons be seized. Sheriff Jones was not happy with the outcome of the Wakarusa War nor was he going to accept the disgrace the Lawrence crowd reveled in at the jubilee at his expense.

It was ridiculous to call the confrontation at the Wakarusa River a war when no shots had been fired or enemies killed in battle. Instead it had become a disgusting political mess. It had been reported that a Missourian had been accidentally shot by his own sentry, and another proslavery man had been killed by a falling tree, and a third killed in a drunken row. Some people might count these deaths as war casualties but not Jones.[348]

He must have wanted blood spilled. He demanded the men responsible for the assault at Blanton Bridge be apprehended and turned over to him for punishment. He more than likely wanted Jacob Branson led back to him on a mule and turned over to him as a prisoner. But most of all, he wanted his pride and dignity back, and his honor restored as the Sheriff of Douglas County.

Even if Sheriff Jones had tried to forgive the Lawrence crowd for the bridge incident, his reception at the Lawrence jubilee reaffirmed what was in store for him when he returned with arrest warrants for the men who had stopped him at the bridge.[349] He had heard the assassination threats being made by Lane and his men because *"Lane's voice could be heard in different rooms, detailing to the eager listeners the most painful circumstances of poor Barbour's [sic] death, and, with wonderful ingeniousness, keeping up the wicked spirit of vengeance among those whom he exercised any power."*[350]

In addition, Sheriff Jones had counted on the new Territorial Governor, Wilson Shannon, to act like a true southerner and to support the mighty force that had been congregated on the Wakarusa River to destroy the abolitionists, and their town of Lawrence. Instead, Shannon had failed the South and the message had been smeared in the newspaper headlines. Dr. Stringfellow, the editor of the Lecompton paper had printed in bold face type *"Shannon has played us false!" The Yankees have tricked us. The Governor of the Kansas Territory has disgraced himself and the whole pro-slavery party...When this difficulty comes up again, we should leave our chicken-hearted commanders at home."*[351]

Despite the continued danger, Sheriff Jones decided to keep up the pressure on Lawrence and the abolitionists, in anticipation of another mistake like the one they made at Blanton Bridge. The next time he would finish

348   Goodrich, War To The Knife, 86.
349   Robinson, The Kansas Conflict, 207-208.
350   Ibid.
351   Goodrich, War to the Knife, 86 / Atchison Squatter Sovereign, Jan. 1, 1856.

what had been left undone by the army of men who had camped on the Wakarusa River.

The year 1855 came to an end and, although difficult for both sides, it had been *"less bloody than its successor."* The final tally had been two proslavery men killed with three abolitionists meeting the same fate. The count had not included an abolitionist, *"brutally mobbed...severely beaten...tarred and feathered,*[and] *sent down the Missouri on a raft."*[352]

Although the physical confrontations between proslavery and free-state forces were at a stalemate, the political maneuvering continued. Charles Robinson later recounted this time period as follows: *"Two elections for delegate to Congress had been held, one on the 1st of October, when General Whitfield was voted for by the Slave-State men, and one on the 9th of the same month, when Reeder was voted for by the Free-State men."*[353]

"On the 15th of December, a few days after the close of the Wakarusa war, the election on the adoption of the Topeka Constitution was held...1731 votes for, and 46 votes against the Constitution; and 1287 against and 453 for free negroes. This vote to free the negroes was to be construed as instructions to the Legislature to exclude them from Kansas by Law. If not so excluded the constitutional provision would be inoperative."[354]

"On the 22d of December came the convention for the nomination of State Officers...Lane himself was a candidate with all the appliances of which he was master...those who were aware of Lane's career in Kansas, including his attempt to take the offensive at the late war, did not dare trust him at the head of the State movement, a new man was agreed upon, namely, Dr. Robinson."[355]

In other words, those on both sides of the slavery issue continued to search for political solutions to avoid further bloodshed; but despite their efforts, a majority vote could not be reached and a legislative solution obtained to solve the conflict.

Meanwhile, the year 1856 brought little relief with Sheriff Jones' obsession to impose his authority on Lawrence. His anger continued to boil and his legal status continued to be challenged in Lawrence. As part of the agreement to stop the Wakarusa War, Robinson pledged to recognize and support the law in the Territory. Sheriff Jones and the proslavery forces

---

352   Robinson, The Kansas Conflict, 219.
353   Ibid.
354   Ibid.
355   Ibid., 220.

143

interpreted this commitment to mean that they would recognize the Douglas County Sheriff as a legal law enforcement officer. In fact, Robinson and the town continued to challenge any laws enacted or officials appointed by the Missouri invaders as bogus.

Following the end of the Wakarusa War, this uncompromising attitude had been demonstrated once again against Sam Jones when he entered Lawrence to arrest a man for a "breaking and entering" charge. A witness to the attempted arrest gave the following account when the sheriff ran into the wife of the man he had come to apprehend.

"The little lady, with true Yankee grit" informed the sheriff that *"he would not be permitted to arrest her husband,"* and was armed with two colt pistols. She stuck one of the revolvers in the sheriff's face to back up her resistance while a crowd of Lawrence residents surrounded Jones. The mob taunted the sheriff and pointed out that she was only a woman *"resisting the laws, and not the people of Lawrence."* The sheriff waited for someone to stop the man's wife from interfering and eventually she was grabbed by the wrist. The sheriff forced her husband into a wagon to escort him to jail but his wife had not given up the battle and as soon as she had been released *"drew a revolver and...fired at him, just grazing his temple and cutting off a large lock of his hair. She fired four times, but without effect."*[356]

Once again, Sheriff Jones had suffered at the hands of the Lawrence residents with blatant disrespect shown against him and open refusal to obey him and his authority as the sheriff.

Senator Atchison also continued to be dissatisfied with the people of Lawrence because he had been politically outmaneuvered and said, *"I was a peace maker in the difficulty lately settled by Governor Wilson Shannon... But, I will never again counsel peace."*[357]

The feeling that persisted among the proslavery men following the Wakarusa War was summed up in the *Squatter Sovereign* newspaper, which said: *"As it is, base cowardly, sneaking scoundrels will go unpunished, and be left free to perpetrate their infamous outrages wherever they may find an unprotected proslavery family."*[358]

During the winter of 1856, both sides of the slavery issue continued to strengthen their positions and resolve to emerge as the winner of the contest. Eventually, the face-to-face encounters were quieted by the cold, nasty weather and the need to stay home by the fire. During this time, the conflict

356   Goodrich, War to the Knife, 90-91.
357   Ibid., 87.
358   Robinson, The Kansas Conflict, 223.

remained relatively quiet. The lull ended on January 17th, when a group of abolitionists were en route to vote for Free-State officers and establish a new government in lieu of the "bogus" government. The election in their precinct had been moved to Easton since the mayor of Leavenworth had forbidden the election to be held in that city which was dominated by pro-slavery sentiments. The Kickapoo Rangers, an organized band of southern sympathizers, had responded to the persistence of the would-be-voters in that area and rode out to seize the ballot box. The voters, however, were not about to give up the ballot box and gunfire broke out with one of the Kickapoo Rangers falling dead in the gunfight.[359]

The following day, Reese Brown and seven other free-soil men who had been at the election, left Easton in a wagon to head home. [They] *"had proceeded about half way when they were met by the Kickapoo Rangers, consisting of thirty mounted men."*[360] The Rangers ordered them to surrender and they only did so when their situation seemed hopeless and *"under a promise that their persons should be safe. The terms were violated."*[361]

A correspondent for the *New York Tribune* related the story. *"The prisoners were taken back to Easton: but Brown was separated from them, and put in an adjoining building. A rope was purchased at the store, and was shown to the prisoners."* [The Rangers began to drink liquor heavily and] "unwilling that all of *these men should be murdered, the Captain allowed the other prisoners to escape."* [Then the Kickapoo Rangers anger was taken out on Brown as they] ... *"began to strike him."* [He begged for his life and offered to fight them one at a time or for them to] ... *"pit him against their best man-he would fight for his life; but not one of the cowards dared thus to give the prisoner a chance."* He ... *"volunteered to fight two, and then three; but it was in vain...These men, or rather demons, rushed around Brown, and literally hacked him to death with their hatchets."* [The final blow was inflicted by a]..."*coarse-looking wretch*...[with a large hatchet striking Reese Brown along the]...*side of the head, which penetrated the skull and brain many inches..."* [As Brown fell to the floor]..."*his remorseless enemies jumped on him,* [while] *one of the...rudest savages, spit tobacco juice in his eyes."*[362]

359   Goodrich, War to the Knife, 91-92.
360   Ibid., 91.
361   James Redpath, Capt. John Brown, 95-96.
362   Ibid.

At this point in the attack even some of the Kickapoo Rangers *"took pity and tried to bind the victim's wounds. With brains oozing from his skull, however, Brown's case was hopeless, and the belated rescuers opted to carry the dying man home to his wife."* [He told his family] ... *"I have been murdered by a gang of cowards, in cold blood, without any cause. And as the poor wife stooped over the body of her gallant husband, he expired."* [363]

According to Charles Robinson, Brown had been steadfast in his commitment to defend Lawrence. He *"was one of the noblest men ever in Kansas. He was true as steel and brave as a lion, and hence was feared and hated by his opponents. Everyone agreed including... Captain Martin, of the Kickapoo Rangers...*[that the]*...murder was most cowardly.* Martin had tried to save him, *but the mob was too drunken and desperate to heed him or any one else. Nothing would answer but his death, and he fell a hero and martyr in a noble cause."* [364]

It was events like these that showed the depth of the hatred that had taken over the emotions of the men who were becoming involved in these outrages. As the news and shock of this attack was spread through the Lawrence community and the surrounding homes of the free-soil neighbors, another incident was also reported of a proslavery man being beaten and his leg nearly hacked off at the hands of free-soil men. Each new event fortified the competing side to prepare for a bloody future as open hostilities began to escalate with cruelty demonstrated beyond reason. [365]

Despite the continued confrontation with the proslavery forces, in March 1856, Robinson and the town of Lawrence pushed forward to legitimatize their newly formed independent government. They organized their own State Legislature and called for an assembly on March 4, 1856, as demanded by the provisions in their new Constitution. They organized both houses, and Reeder and Lane were elected as United States Senators. They adopted *"a memorial to Congress asking for admission into the Union as a State."* [366]

Senator Lane took the constitution and memorial to Washington, *"which passed the house July 3, 1856, by a vote of 99 to 97, but it failed to pass the Senate."* [367]

---

363 James Redpath, Capt. John Brown, 96.
364 Robinson, The Kansas Conflict, 222.
365 Goodrich, War to the Knife, 92.
366 Robinson, The Kansas Conflict, 228.
367 Ibid.

A moral victory was won in Washington, however, when on March 19, 1856, a Congressional Committee was appointed to visit the Kansas Territory to begin the investigation of the voting fraud, which included the invasion of voters from the state of Missouri. The committee arrived in the Territory on April 18, 1856, and began taking a large volume of testimony. The Majority Report given to Congress supported the abolitionists' position that the ballot box had included fraudulent votes and that the proslavery candidate for delegate, John W. Whitfield, had been illegally elected. Furthermore, the laws that had been enacted under him had been used to punish persons in an unlawful way.

The Minority Report used a different argument and found a different interpretation of the election results. It held that even if the ballot box had been stuffed by the invaders from Missouri, the legal voting residents had carried the majority with enough votes to have elected Whitfield anyway. Since Whitfield had won the election, discounting the bogus votes, any laws enacted under his authority should be valid and upheld.

When the House of Representatives voted in Washington, after considering both reports, a vote to remove John W. Whitfield from his delegate seat was 110 yeas, and 92 nays. The delegate seat was vacated by Congress.[368]

Spring of 1856 arrived in the Territory and the hard winter and the skirmishes somehow had passed. However, not forgotten by Sheriff Jones were the men who were still free and unpunished for their part in the assault at Blanton Bridge. When the weather allowed, and traveling in the countryside became a little easier, the sheriff returned to Lawrence on April 19, to arrest Sam Wood as one of the Branson rescuers. Sheriff Jones found Wood chatting with friends in an open street. *"He said to Wood, 'You are my prisoner.' 'By what authority?' was the very natural reply. 'As Sheriff of Douglas County.' 'I do not recognize such authority,' said Wood, adding, however, that he would go with him if he would allow him to go to his house, only a few steps distant, first. This the sheriff refused, and Wood declared, 'Then I'll not go with you at all!' and coolly walked away."* [369]

Sheriff Jones, unwilling to give in to Wood, *"tried to follow, [but]… a jeering mob rushed in, stole his pistol, then 'jostled' him until Wood escaped. The whole affair only lasted two or three minutes."* Jones, once again, had not been respected as the sheriff and realized he would need

---

368 Robinson, The Kansas Conflict, 230.
369 Robinson, Kansas: Its Interior and Exterior Life, 197.

adequate manpower to carry out his mandate. He returned the following day with a posse of four men and tried to arrest another of Branson's rescuers. He encountered resistance from a mob of residents who rushed in to interfere. At the end of the *"scuffle Jones was struck in the face. As the posse left town once more empty-handed, the free-soilers, according to a witness, 'Threw their hats in the air, and clapped their hands.'"*[370]

To make matters worse, the man who had struck Sam Jones in the face was S. F. Tappan, another one of the Branson rescuers at the Bridge.[371]

This incident was the final and ultimate insult. Sheriff Jones and his four-man posse had been run out of town by some of the men from Lawrence who had embarrassed him at Blanton Bridge. The sting of being struck in the face must have smarted even more with the hat throwing and jeers echoing in his ears as he scurried out of town.

The next move the sheriff made was the one strategy that Charles Robinson had feared the most and would have avoided at any expense. Sheriff Jones went to the U.S. Cavalry and requested federal troops to intervene in the affair. For the first time, the United States Government became involved in supporting the arrest of the men accused in Jacob Branson's escape at the bridge. The sheriff rode into Lawrence again, but this time he was accompanied by Lieutenant James McIntosh and a file of U.S. Dragoons.[372] The hearts of everyone in Lawrence must have sunk when men in dark blue uniforms rode into town with the sheriff and were led by an officer with gold bars on his shoulders. The message was clear. This dispute was no longer a Territorial confrontation with the local postmaster-turned-sheriff—this was an action supported by the United States Army. The residents of Lawrence, for the first time in their lives, were faced with being accused of open sedition, as well as being classified as traitors. The abolitionists must have felt tremendous fear as the sheriff, the lieutenant, and the dragoons arrested six of the Blanton Bridge offenders. Lieutenant McIntosh would later write in his report of the event:

"From that time until sundown [Sheriff Jones]...*succeeded in arresting six of the offending individuals. While making these arrests a large crowd was assembled in the street; and, although no resistance was made or violence resorted to, public excitement was great."*[373] At sundown the prisoners were locked up in a room for the night and Lieutenant McIntosh and his

---

370   Goodrich, War to the Knife, 109.
371   Robinson, The Kansas Conflict, 232.
372   Goodrich, War to the Knife, 109.
373   Ibid.

men set up their tents behind the building. He placed two of his men in the room with the prisoners to prevent escape.

McIntosh tried to encourage Sheriff Jones to sleep inside the building with the prisoners and guards for protection, but the sheriff refused the request, ignoring any danger he might be facing. Later that evening Sheriff Jones accompanied McIntosh to a water barrel for a drink *"and while standing at the barrel a shot was fired from a crowd of about twenty persons. Mr. Jones immediately said, 'I believe that was intended for me;' but having heard several other shots during the evening, which I thought were fired in the air...I told him I thought he was mistaken."*[374] The two returned to their tent and Jones would confirm that he was the target. He found a bullet hole in his pants.

Lieutenant McIntosh was outraged by the assassination attempt and returned to the crowd where the bullet had come from. The lieutenant heard another shot fired and some of his men came running to find him with the report that *"the Sheriff is dead."* Lieutenant McIntosh went back to his tent *"and found Mr. Jones lying upon the floor, and [saw] that he was still alive."*[375]

The sheriff had been sitting in the tent, *"the outline of his figure being clearly revealed by the light inside, was shot in the back. The wound was between the right shoulder and spine. Notwithstanding, Gen. Whitfield's express to Missouri the next morning, with intelligence that Jones was in a dying condition."*[376]

The reaction that followed this assault on the sheriff was colossal and many newspapers across the country found editors searching for their largest bold-faced black print to headline the cowardly injustice that had occurred in Lawrence that night.

The Atchison *Squatter Sovereign*: *"THE ABOLITIONIST IN OPEN REBELLION-SHERIFF JONES MURDERED BY THE TRAITORS...SHOT DOWN BY THE THIEVING PAUPERS!"*[377]

The *Union* newspaper at Lecompton: *"Oh, murder most foul!-cold blooded assassination, blacker than hell!"*[378]

John Stringfellow roared, *"HE MUST BE AVENGED. HIS MURDER SHALL BE AVENGED, "if at the sacrifice of every abolitionist in the*

---

374   Goodrich, War to the Knife, 109-110.
375   Ibid., 110.
376   Robinson, Kansas Interior and Exterior Life, 200.
377   Malin, John Brown and the Legend of Fifty-Six, 47.
378   Goodrich, War to the Knife, 110.

Territory. We are now in favor of leveling Lawrence, and chastising the Traitors there congregated, should it result in the total destruction of the Union."[379]

Even though Sheriff Jones was not dead, he had been seriously wounded in the assassination attempt. From the proslavery viewpoint it clearly reflected the fact that law and order had been murdered. The rules of authority had been murdered. The respect for the proslavery philosophy had been murdered.

To the proslavery side, the degree of lawlessness of the abolitionists had been demonstrated. They had no limits, and they were going to achieve their goals against slavery regardless of who had to be killed, including a sheriff if necessary.

Charles Robinson and the people of Lawrence found themselves in a hopeless position. The entire country had been stirred up against the abolitionists as a result of this deplorable act. No amount of apologizing, or prayers given publicly, could now satisfy the cry for revenge against Lawrence. Robinson and the town publicly rebuked the perpetrators for this act and offered to help find the person and punish any offenders for this cowardly crime.[380]

This time the cool-headed leadership of Charles Robinson would not be able to abort the assault that was sure to come to Lawrence. He could no longer save his town and the people from the revenge that would be coming from across the border. The energy and the emotions that had been whipped up in the men on the river banks of the Wakarusa the previous December had not been released because the proslavery men had been sent home and forced to live with their pent-up hostility. There had been no relief from the climax of anticipated confrontation and the excitement that had welled up. When the news spread about Sheriff Jones being shot, it was like the clanging of bells across the land calling again for a massive show of force against the abolitionists. Pulses must have quickened as emotions awakened for another chance to finally pour out the hostility and anger that had been smoldering in these men for months.

Within days, the southern militia assembled their weapons, obtained warrants, and finalized plans to invade Lawrence. They planned to wipe out the abolitionists and the cause that had brought them to the Territory. Aware of this plan and before the impending attack could take place,

379   Malin, John Brown, 47.
380   Robinson, The Kansas Conflict, 234.

Charles and Sara Robinson were sent out of Lawrence and given the task to go to Boston and plead the case of the abolitionists before the North. Furthermore, Robinson was to carry with him testimony already taken by a Congressional Committee to save it from being seized and destroyed by the invaders from the South. He and Sara retreated without concealment or disguise, and made it only as far as Lexington, Missouri. Charles was arrested there and accused of being a fugitive from justice. He was removed under armed guard from the riverboat. Sara, however, was allowed to travel on to Boston with the Congressional documents.[381]

The men and women of Lawrence were in a terrible predicament. The vast majority had not supported the shooting and cowardly act against Sheriff Jones. The attempted assassin had not been caught or even identified as residing in Lawrence. The town had been forewarned about the response that was brewing in a correspondence to Charles Robinson prior to his departure. Colonel E. V. Sumner, the commander of the First Cavalry had written:

"Headquarters First Cavalry,

"Camp Near Lawrence, April 27, 1856.

"Sir: As there are no municipal officers in the town of Lawrence, I think proper to address you before returning to my post. The recent attempt made upon the life of Sheriff Jones will produce great excitement throughout the Territory and on the Missouri frontier, and I consider it of the utmost importance that every effort should be made by your people to ferret out and bring to justice the cowardly assassin. It is not too much to say that the peace of the country may depend on it, for, if he is not arrested, the act will be charged by the opposite party upon your whole community. This affair has been reported to Washington, and whatever orders may be received will be instantly carried into effect. The proclamation which requires obedience to the laws of the Territory as they now stand until legally abrogated, will certainly be maintained, and it is very unsafe to give heed to people at a distance who counsel resistance. If they were here to participate in the danger, they would probably take a different view of this matter.

"I am sir, very respectfully, your obedient servant,

"E. V. Sumner,

"Colonel First Cavalry Commanding.

"To Mr. Charles Robinson."[382]

---

381   Robinson, The Kansas Conflict, 236-238.

382   Ibid., 233.

The response for retaliation against the abolitionists and the town of Lawrence suggested a conspiracy in the assassination attempt. The abolitionists had never opposed the United States Government and were not traitors or seditionists, but the assassin had not been arrested. The abolitionists in Lawrence, however, would be treated as U.S. enemies.

Robinson responded to Colonel Sumner the same day he received the correspondence and acknowledged the seriousness of the problem, agreeing that the attack against Jones had been cowardly and had not been supported by the citizens of Lawrence. The guilty person, if identified, would be turned over to the authorities because that day the sheriff was *"acting with the authority of* [the federal]*... Government."*[383]

The Territorial Governor Wilson Shannon had also written to the secretary of state. He explained his belief that an organized secret military organization existed and was recognized *"by means of the signs and grips."*[384] Their plan would be to only recognize and obey legal authority when accompanied by federal officials and troops or otherwise to openly resist all Territorial officials. Shannon further warned that there was an *"arsenal* [in Lawrence], *well supplied with all the munitions of war, which have been purchased in the East and secretly introduced into that place."* He counted the inventory in detail outlining the *"ten pieces of artillery, at least one thousand stand of Sharps rifles, and a large supply of revolvers."* He gave testimony to the number of men who were believed to be present and would fight to defend the town. He estimated the number *"to be about five hundred men."*

"I have the honor to be your obedient servant,
'Wilson Shannon.'"[385]

As a result of Sheriff Jones being gunned down in Lawrence and a request from Governor Shannon to stop the lawlessness in the Territory, the United States Marshal issued a proclamation to... *"law-abiding citizens of the Territory* [to help him] *... as soon as practicable,* [enforce the] *... proper execution of the law."*

"'Given under my hand, this 11th day of May 1856
"'I. B. Donelson
"'United States Marshal for the Kansas Territory.'"[386]

---

383   Robinson, The Kansas Conflict, 234.
384   Ibid., 240.
385   Ibid., 241.
386   Ibid., 243.

An armed conflict against Lawrence would be organized and led by U.S. Marshal Donelson. The approval went all the way to the White House with President Pierce supporting the planned assault.[387]

The citizens of Lawrence knew that the posse and militia were prepared to launch an attack. Messages were sent repeatedly to the Territorial Governor, Wilson Shannon, and to I. B. Donelson, begging them to stop the impending assault and offering support in any way to avoid the conflict. A letter from each side demonstrated the peace effort and the response from the army of attackers.

A letter from Lawrence, dated May 14th, appealed to Marshal Donelson for understanding and promised unwavering support to him. They explained they had *"reliable information...that large bodies of armed men* [had] *assembled in the vicinity of Lawrence.* They asked the Marshal to tell them what charges were being made against them and what demands he would require. They pledged to assist him *"in the execution* [of] *any legal process. We declare ourselves to be order-loving and law abiding citizens, and only await an opportunity to testify our fidelity to the laws of the country, the Constitution, and the Union."*

"We are informed, also, that those men...openly declare that their intention is to destroy... [Lawrence] *...and drive off the citizens.*

Very Respectfully,
"'Robert Morrow
"'Lyman Allen
"'John Hutchinson
"'I. B. Donelson, United States Marshal for the Kansas Territory.' "[388]

Noticeably missing from the signature block of the letter written to Donelson was the chief leader of Lawrence, Charles Robinson, who was unable to sign because he was locked in a jail in the town of Lecompton.

The marshal responded the following day with a communication accusing the people of Lawrence of *" 'professed ignorance* [and he] *... must conclude that* [they were] *... strangers, and not citizens of Lawrence, ... or have been absent for some time.* [He challenged their pledge to] *... offer no opposition now, nor at any future time, to the execution of any legal process, "* [He told them that it was] *... difficult to understand* [and asked them what had] *produced this wonderful change in the minds of the people of Lawrence?* [Had] *... their eyes been suddenly opened, so that they are now*

---

387   Robinson, The Kansas Conflict, 242-243.
388   Ibid., 247.

able to see that there are laws in force in Kansas Territory which should be obeyed... [He told them he was] *...well aware that...Lawrence is armed and drilled, and the town fortified...*[that they had been] *... openly defying the laws and ... recently...attempted assassination of Sheriff Jones while in the discharge of his official duties in Lawrence?* [He asked them again if they were] *...strangers to all these things?* [He offered them reassurance that if]*...no outrages have been committed by the citizens of Lawrence against the laws of the land, they need not fear any posse of mine.*"

"*'Respectfully yours,*

"*'I. B. Donelson, United States Marshal of Kansas Territory"*[389]

The fate of Lawrence had been decided. Charles Robinson was in jail. Senator-elect Reeder was in hiding. One final plea to the Federal Marshal, I. B. Donelson, to stop the hundreds of men who were camped on the outskirts of town from invading Lawrence had been denied. All the citizens could do was to wait for the attack and pray it would not be as brutal as they feared.

Actions began to speak louder than words. As the Lawrence citizens hunkered down awaiting the wrath of an onslaught, an innocent man from Lawrence would be murdered. In a manner that mimicked the Thomas Barber killing during the last invasion from Missouri, a similar outrageous murder occurred and resulted in the loss of another fine young man. This death must have proven to Lawrence that the mounting attack was not going to be without brutality despite what Marshal Donelson had said in his communication. How long would it be before they came to burn and destroy the town must have been on the mind of everyone as the residents walked the streets of the town. They were acutely aware that the body of another young man lay dead in the Eldridge Hotel, resurrecting the aura of death and tragedy only recently portrayed by the body of Barber. The people of Lawrence could only wait! " *'We are in a bad fix,' said Sam Walker. 'Things look bad, very bad, at present.'* "[390]

The abolitionists must have felt abandoned and alone. Most were trapped in the town of Lawrence with only a few sympathizers like the Stills scattered around the countryside. The eyes of the South must have watched as the authorized federal army of volunteers marched toward Lawrence to exterminate the town. At this moment the proslavery forces held every key to victory. Their abolitionist enemy had made the final mistake

---

389   Robinson, The Kansas Conflict, 247-248.
390   Goodrich, War to the Knife, 113.

by committing acts so damnable that the entire nation from Washington down to the Douglas County Sheriff had been turned against them. The First Cavalry Federal Troops under Colonel Sumner could only stand by and watch the destruction, and if ordered, would have to participate in the invasion. Certainly Colonel Sumner could not provide intervention to stop the assault.

For Charles Robinson and the abolitionists in Lawrence, their nightmare was about to begin. The pent-up rage that had been building against their cause over the past two years was about to be released like a break in a dam, sending a flood of hatred down upon them without any way to stop the destruction once it had begun.

CHAPTER FIFTEEN
The Sacking of Lawrence

On May 21, 1856, the wait was over.[391] The proslavery army rode into Lawrence flying a white flag with black stripes and a single white star. According to Charles Robinson's wife Sara, the only consolation was *"the United States flag was not desecrated by waving* [it] *over their pollution."*[392] The people of Lawrence must have felt betrayed by the U.S. Government. They saw many invaders carrying U.S. muskets supplied from the federal arsenal and led by Marshal Donelson. The size of the force was overwhelming. The number of men and guns and the amount of ammunition they brought resulted in the town surrendering without any resistance.

To reinforce the hopeless feeling of the abolitionists, Charles Robinson's home was one of the first to be surrounded by the militia and designated the proslavery command center. Next, the invaders positioned their cannons on the brow of Mount Oread, demonstrating their overwhelming artillery that they would use to stop any resistance against their mission.[393]

While this military activity took place, the proslavery greeting party, led by United States Deputy Marshal W. P. Fain, and his posse of eight representatives, rode their horses to the front of the Emigrant Aid Company's recently completed Eldridge Hotel. Mr. Eldridge, the proprietor of the hotel, met the Marshal and his posse on the front steps and invited them inside for dinner. The dinner party would be joined by Eldridge's wife and children who had only just recently arrived in Lawrence. The unwelcome militia would represent the first group to attend a public event in the newly finished hotel. After the meal was over, the Marshal left the hotel and began arresting the Lawrence citizens with the warrants he had been given by the judge in Lecompton.[394] Mr. Eldridge continued to appease the invaders and accompanied the prisoners and the Marshal's posse to the Robinson home, which would also serve as a jail at their proslavery headquarters.

---

391 Anna Arnold, A History of Kansas, 1931, 77.
392 Robinson, Kansas: Its Interior and Exterior Life, 244.
393 Ibid., 241.
394 Ibid.

The final order that was given to the posse under Marshal Donelson's control would demonstrate irresponsibility, neglect, and unimaginable dereliction of his duty. He *"dismissed his monster posse of two hundred and fifty horsemen, and five hundred infantry,* [and told them] ... *he had no further use for them, but Sheriff Jones has writs to execute, and they were at liberty to organize as his posse."*[395]

Donelson discharged the posse, which had been serving under federal orders. These men would immediately join the posse under the authority of the Douglas County Sheriff and received their orders directly from Sam Jones. The fate of Lawrence would be up to Sheriff Jones' discretion and whether he would interfere with any ransacking, plundering or looting. He immediately began the process of destroying the buildings that had been named as military targets.

Sheriff Jones' obsession had finally been achieved with his complete control over the town. In this moment of triumph, he rode forward amid *"yells of applause"* and requested the army to help him carry out the laws.[396]

At approximately one o'clock that afternoon, Sheriff Jones and his posse of about twenty-five men, carrying U.S. muskets with fixed bayonets, rode to the Eldridge Hotel and requested a meeting with a citizen named Pomeroy. General Pomeroy had become one of the leading spokesmen in Lawrence since Charles Robinson and Governor Reeder were in jail at Lecompton. Jim Lane had already escaped to Iowa to avoid capture. General Pomeroy came forward and voluntarily surrendered to Sheriff Jones. Jones then demanded General Pomeroy to surrender all of the cannons and Sharps rifles in Lawrence to him *"and, taking out his watch, he added, 'I give you five minutes to decide whether you will give them up.' "* [397]

Pomeroy stood his ground and agreed to give up the cannons but not the rifles because they were private property.[398]

Meanwhile, another large army of invaders with about five to eight hundred men marched down to the bottom of Mount Oread and formed into a large square column around General Atchison who was waiting to make a victory speech to them amidst cheers from the crowd.[399]

Old Bourbon loudly shouted out his message to them: *"Boys, this day I am a Kickapoo Ranger, by G-d. This day we have entered Lawrence with*

---

395   Robinson, Kansas: Its Interior and Exterior Life, 241-242.

396   Ibid., 242.

397   Ibid.

398   Ibid.

399   Ibid., 242-243.

Southern Rights inscribed upon our banner, and not one d--d abolitionist dared to fire a gun."[400]

"Now, boys, this is the happiest day of my life. We have entered that d–d town, and taught the d–d abolitionists a southern lesson that they will remember until the day they die. And now boys, we will go in again, with our highly honorable Jones, and test the strength of the d–d Free State Hotel, and teach the Emigrant Aid Company that Kansas shall be ours. Boys, ladies should, and I hope will, be respected by every gentleman. But, when a woman takes upon herself the garb of a soldier, by carrying a Sharps rifle, then she is no longer worthy of respect. Trample her under your feet as you would a snake! Come on, boys! Now do your duty to yourselves and your southern friends."[401]

"Your duty, I know you will do. If one man or woman dare stand before you, blow them to h–l with a chuck of cold lead."[402]

When Atchison's speech was finished, the army, now under Sheriff Jones' control, advanced toward their main target. When they reached the front of the Eldridge Hotel, the Sheriff announced aloud that the hotel, and two Lawrence newspapers, *The Herald of Freedom* and *The Kansas Free State,* had been declared nuisances and were to be destroyed by his militia. He also shouted to the crowd that he had been issued orders to carry out the destruction by the First District Court of the United States.[403]

The army carried banners and flags bearing the inscriptions, *"Southern Rights,"* *"The Superiority of the White Race,"* *"Alabama for Kansas north of 36'-30';"* *"Bibles not Rifles."* They also carried the Stars and Stripes, as well as a flag *"with white stripes with a crouched tiger in the corner."*[404]

Sheriff Jones told Colonel Eldridge that he had only two hours to vacate the hotel before the army would begin firing their cannons to destroy the building. During the two hours that Jones had given him, Eldridge was required to remove his family and all of the furnishings that had taken weeks to assemble. Eldridge knew that it would be impossible to comply with the sheriff's demands and asked only for enough time to remove his family which included one of his children who was ill.[405]

---

400   Robinson, Kansas: Its Interior and Exterior Life, 242-243.
401   Ibid. / Transactions of the Kansas State Historical Society, Vol. 9, 141.
402   Robinson, Kansas: Interior and Exterior Life, 243.
403   Ibid.
404   Nichols, Bleeding Kansas, 107.
405   Robinson, Kansas: Interior and Exterior Life, 244.

Some of the proslavery men who only hours before had finished dinner with Eldridge and his family now began throwing furniture, mirrors, and marble-top tables from the windows of the building. The hotel had been furnished with beautiful and expensive pieces of furniture. It was considered the most elegant hotel west of St. Louis.[406] After the men grew tired of throwing furniture from the windows, they turned to looting everything they desired to take back home including *"boxes of cigars, wines, oysters, sardines, and cans of fruit."*[407]

The army had become a mob and headed toward the newspaper offices as the Sheriff continued to exercise his legal authority. The editor, Josiah Miller, was looking out of the window of his newspaper office, *The Kansas Free State*, and saw the mob coming. *" 'Well, boys, we're in for it',"* he said. *A brick crashed through the window of the store below, then another came up into the shop. Then the men swarmed in, destroying…as they moved. A case of type was dumped on the floor, a press smashed. 'To the river!'*…[the mob shouted.][408] *"The type of the* Herald of Freedom*… office were also put into the Kaw* [river], *and the press broken."* The building was set on fire *"several times, but put out by the bravery of some of the young men in Lawrence, who were not deterred by the threats of the mob."*[409]

The Carolina red flag was then raised above the Eldridge Hotel with the army now focused on the total destruction of the building. In an attempt to accomplish the goal, the militia placed four cannons in position and began firing cannon balls into the walls in an attempt to bring it down…*"At the commencement of the cannonading, Jones had been asked, 'Can you feel no pity for the suffering you have caused?'*

"His reply was, 'The laws must be executed.' And turning to two of his posse, he said, 'Gentleman, this is the happiest day of my life, I assure you. I determined to make the fanatics bow before me in the dust, and kiss the territorial laws.' Then, as another round was fired, with a bitter, scornful sneer he said, 'I have done it, by G-d! I have done it!' "[410]

The men hollered in expectation of the collapse of the building as they fired thirty-two cannon balls, weighing from six to eighteen pounds, through the walls which produced little structural damage to the integrity of the hotel despite the screams of *"Now here she goes!"* With each roar

---

406 Arnold, A History of Kansas, 78.
407 Robinson, Kansas: Interior and Exterior Life, 244.
408 Nichols, Bleeding Kansas, 107.
409 Robinson, Kansas: Interior and Exterior Life, 245.
410 Ibid., 246.

of the cannons and after the smoke had cleared, the hotel remained standing showing few signs of damage. The lack of destruction by the cannons greatly disappointed the posse since they had expected the hotel walls to come tumbling down in ruin. Instead of savoring victory for their efforts, the posse became impatient and "weary."[411]

Next, the men tried to the use kegs of gunpowder to blow up the building and many kegs were carried into the cellar and ignited without much success, producing little effect other than smoke and a few broken windows. Finally, a decision was made to burn the building down and fires were started in each of the hotel rooms. This tactic resulted in the total destruction of the hotel.[412]

"When the walls of the hotel had fallen in, ... [Jones]... *turned to his posse and said, coolly, 'You are dismissed; the writs have been executed.' "*[413]

By now, the army of men had turned into a drunken mob and they broke into private homes looking for anything of value to take and they destroyed whatever they left behind. To add to the insult of the looting that day, the militia paraded through Lawrence wearing the clothing stolen from the Lawrence citizens and donned capes and sashes made out of the heavy curtains and tassels taken from the hotel.

After the personal contents had been pilfered from the Lawrence homes, many of the houses were mutilated, defaced, and wrecked beyond repair. Many stores were also entered and ransacked in the same barbaric manner.

Among the atrocities that occurred that day was a man who was shot at by ruffians believing they were firing at Senator Reeder trying to escape. Thankfully his injuries resulted only in a broken leg when he fell from his horse. A more shocking and blatant disregard for the citizens of Lawrence was demonstrated when the posse fired at a group of women who were standing only about one hundred yards away from their attackers. The gunfire was followed by taunts from the men as they celebrated and they *"threw down their guns and shouted, while swinging their hats, "Hurrah for South Carolina! Down with the abolitionist! Slavery in Kansas, by G-d!"*[414]

At around seven o'clock in the evening, the attack came to an end and the wagons filled with the spoils and booty headed back to Missouri. Two

---

411   Robinson, Kansas: Interior and Exterior Life, 245.
412   Ibid., 246.
413   Ibid.
414   Ibid., 247.

hours later, the Robinson home was engulfed in flames and burned to the ground along with all of their possessions.[415]

The attack on Lawrence May 21, 1856, had ended. There would be many accounts written later by residents who suffered through the sacking of Lawrence and witnessed firsthand their town left in ruin. The attackers rode victoriously back to their homes covered with braided ropes, silks and satins dangling from their saddlebags, and with cigars, wine, and goodies stashed in every pocket to enjoy with the people who awaited their return. The militia's biggest treasure, however, was that the town of Lawrence, which represented the protest against slavery, had been crushed. All of the important abolitionist leaders were jailed by the southern forces. The hotel, which had been called a fortress, had been destroyed. Both of the newspapers, that had printed opposing views, lay broken with all of the type in the bottom of the Kansas River. Amazingly, not a shot had been fired by the residents to stop the assault. This lack of response further suggested to the proslavery forces that there was a cowardly lack of resolve of the men who lived in Lawrence. In their view, the invaders had sent them all running for cover and demonstrated the abolitionists were no match for the South. According to the victorious militia, the Kansas Territory would now go along with the southern vote and slavery had been saved. This turn of events was clearly evident as the smoke rose from Lawrence.

There were antislavery forces outside of Lawrence, however, which had been spared during the attack. One of the families was the Stills, who watched in horror through their telescope from the mound as they observed what was occurring below. Rovia Still's memories were vivid. *"Those that were on the mound took turns looking through the telescope...and saw them burn several houses."* She also described the family's efforts to defend themselves should an attack occur. *"They were very busy at our house making cartridges. My sister-in-law...was a very fast hand at the work and while the boys molded the bullets she with two or three others, tied the papers on and filled them with powder and fastened the ends and then they were ready to put into the Sharps rifles. They worked at this all day and night and made many cartridges."*[416]

The Stills from their vantage point had observed the destruction of the town. They witnessed what would happen when Sheriff Sam Jones and Marshal Donelson were granted federal authority to enforce the Territorial

---

415   Robinson, Kansas: Interior and Exterior Life, 248.
416   Clark, Reminiscences, 31.

laws and the proslavery mandate. They also knew that the abolitionist leaders who had been jailed would have little hope of legitimate legal
representation.

Not all of the abolitionists outside of Lawrence, however, were as fortunate as the Stills. The retreating posse, while passing through the Wakarusa
area, stopped at the Fish family's home. They robbed them, stole their horses, and tore down their fences as they departed. [417]

As terrible as the consequences had been in Lawrence, with their town
burned, it had not extinguished their hope. Robinson and Reeder were still
alive; Lane was in Iowa recruiting an army; and the abolitionists outside
the town had not given up.

---

417   Robinson, Kansas: Interior and Exterior Life, 251.

CHAPTER SIXTEEN
John Brown's Revenge

Following their defeat in Lawrence, the remaining abolitionists in the Kansas Territory were forced into a defensive posture. They knew they would be vulnerable to other militia or ruffian attacks in the future. However, for John Brown, being on the defensive was not an option. Brown had a plan, and it was *"not to settle," or "speculate"—or from idle curiosity; but for one stern, solitary purpose—to have a shot at the South."*[418] He and his sons had been heading toward Lawrence to help fight Federal Marshal Donelson, the Douglas County Sheriff, Sam Jones, and the Southern Militia on May 22nd. Before they reached their destination, Brown and his men learned that the town had already been attacked and the Eldridge Hotel destroyed. As a result, the hopeless Lawrence mission was abandoned.

Brown also would hear about another southern atrocity that occurred on the day after the Lawrence attack—the brutal cane whipping of Senator Charles Sumner. Sumner was an outspoken antislavery advocate and a Senator for the state of Massachusetts.[419]

The Senator had been attacked as he wrote at his desk in the U.S. Senate chamber. The beating was in retaliation for his scathing remarks about Andrew Pickens Butler, an aging Senator from South Carolina. He had charged that Senator Butler *"... had chosen a mistress to whom he has made vows, and who, though ugly to others, is always lovely to him, though polluted in the sight of the world, is chaste in his sight, I mean the harlot slavery."*[420]

Senator Butler's nephew, Congressman Preston Brooks, and other southerners were outraged by these insensitive words. Brooks decided to personally defend his uncle's honor. Brooks would later state... *"I felt it my duty to relieve Butler and avenge the insult to my State....To punish an insulting inferior one used not pistol or sword but a cane or horsewhip.*[421]

---

418   Robinson, The Kansas Conflict, 264.
419   Goodrich, War To The Knife, 119.
420   Ibid.
421   Ibid., 120.

Massachusetts Senator Charles Sumner would later describe the incident. *"While thus intent, with my head bent over my writing, I was addressed by a person who approached the front of my desk...[He said]...I have read your speech twice over, carefully; it is a libel on South Carolina and Mr. Butler, who is a relative of mine. While these words were still passing from his lips, he commenced a succession of blows with a heavy cane on my bare head...I was stunned so as to lose my sight."*[422]

Brooks later admitted, *"Every lick went where I intended... [Sumner] ...was reeling around against the seat, backwards and forwards...I gave him about 30 first rate stripes. Toward the last he bellowed like a calf. I wore my cane out completely."*[423]

When several senators tried to step in, others interfered. *"Let them alone, God damn you, cried one of those savoring the punishment. At last, Sumner went down in a heap, as senseless as a corpse, said an onlooker, his head bleeding copiously from the frightful wounds, and the blood saturating his clothes."*[424]

As a result of the sacking of Lawrence and the beating of Sumner, John Brown decided it was time for the abolitionists to retaliate. He had chosen his own method of striking back against the proslavery South. He would act with aggression and terror immediately. He would no longer wait in a defensive posture, and he intended to lead an offensive attack against the enemy. No one was left to stop him. Charles Robinson was jailed; Lawrence destroyed; and the hostility which had been carried out shamelessly against Senator Sumner in the Capitol Building only furthered his resolve. John Brown was on the attack. He *"went crazy-crazy, when they heard the news. It seemed to be the finishing decisive touch."*[425]

John Brown had been waiting for the day to come when he could attack the southerners on a field of battle and spill blood in the name of Abolitionism. He was prepared to die and to sacrifice anyone, including members of his own family, for what he thought was his personal God-driven crusade to end slavery. He believed he had been chosen by the Almighty to lead this battle.

Brown immediately began to enlist men to fight against slavery. His message would be steadfast to anyone who would listen: *"we are going*

---

422   Goodrich, War to The Knife, 120.
423   Ibid.
424   Ibid.
425   Oates, John Brown, 129.

down to make an example, are you coming with us?"[426] *"Something must be done to show these barbarians that we, too, have rights."*[427]

One of John Brown's sons, John Brown Jr., would later explain the events following the southern attacks. His father had decided to kill as many of their enemies in as horrible and brutal manner as possible in an effort to cause terror through these revengeful acts. John Brown believed this strategy would help prevent abolitionists from being killed in the future.

In an effort to execute such a fearful attack, Brown and his sons began sharpening their navy cutlasses knowing *"that a retaliatory blow would fall."*[428]

When one man in the raiding party refused to take part in the raid, *"John Brown drew himself up to his full height. I have no choice, he said. It has been ordained by the Almighty God, ordained from eternity, that I should make an example of these men."*[429]

More information about these raids would later be provided in sworn testimony by James Townsley who had joined the Pottawatomie rifle company in May 1856. According to Townsley, when Brown halted his defense of Lawrence, he forged ahead on a new plan of attack that would involve a raid on the Pottawatomie Creek area. As Townsley later testified, Brown had convinced him to provide his wagon and horses for the trip. The group was made up of *"Old John Brown, Watson Brown, Oliver Brown, Henry Thompson (John Brown's son-in-law), and Mr. Winer, ...All the party except Winer, who rode a pony, rode with me in my wagon."* They were ... *"within two or three miles of the Pottawatomie Creek,"* when they stopped and *"camped about one mile above Dutch Henry's crossing."*[430]

Townsley said that John Brown *"wanted me to pilot the company up to the forks of the creek, some five or six miles above, into the neighborhood where I lived, and show them where all the proslavery men resided; that he proposed to sweep the creek as he came down of all the proslavery men living on it. I positively refused to do it. He insisted upon it, but when he found that I would not go, he decided to postpone the expedition until the following night. I then wanted to take my team and go home, but he would not let me do so, and said I should remain with them. We remained in camp*

---

426   Goodrich, War to The Knife: Bleeding Kansas, 123.
427   Oates, 129.
428   Goodrich, War to the Knife, 123.
429   Nichols, Bleeding Kansas, 113.
430   Robinson, The Kansas Conflict, 266.

that night and all the next day. Some time after dark we were ordered to march."[431]

The *"whole company* [headed] *... in a northerly direction, crossing Mosquito Creek."* The first cabin they came to was unoccupied. The second home they encountered was a cabin occupied by the Doyle family. John Brown, accompanied by three of his sons and his son-in-law, stepped on the front porch of the Doyle home and ordered the family to open the door. Townsley, Frederick Brown, and Winer remained close to the wagon *"a short distance from the house."* Townsley's party was suddenly attacked by a large dog, and he and Frederick Brown killed the animal with their swords. Reluctantly, Mr. Doyle opened the door of the cabin, and the raiding party entered the home. John Brown then marched Mr. Doyle and his two sons from their home and down a road toward Dutch Henry's crossing. Townsley would swear under oath that *"Old John Brown drew his revolver and shot the old man Doyle in the forehead, and Brown's two youngest sons immediately fell upon the younger Doyles with their short two-edged swords. One of the young Doyles was stricken down in an instant, but the other attempted to escape, and was pursued a short distance by his assailant and cut down."*[432]

Townsley also testified that the remaining family members struggled inside the home where Mrs. Doyle continued to beg John Brown to spare her other children. The most revealing testimony about this struggle was given by Mahala Doyle, James Doyle's wife, the mother of the two sons slain that night. She said that on Saturday night May 24, 1856, at about eleven o'clock, she and her husband and their children, four boys and one girl had already gone to bed. They were all awakened when they heard the sound of men in their yard and footsteps on their porch. Next, they heard rapping at their front door and someone calling for Mr. Doyle to come outside. Her husband got out of bed and opened the door to answer some questions about where one of their neighbors by the name of Wilkinson lived. Immediately after the door was opened, Brown and his men pushed their way into the house and told Doyle that he and his sons were prisoners and they must surrender. *"These men were armed with pistols and large knives. They first took my husband out of the house, then they took two of my sons, the two oldest ones, William and Drury, out...My son John was spared because I asked them in tears to spare him. A short time afterward I heard*

431   Robinson, The Kansas Conflict, 266.
432   Ibid., 266-267.

the report of pistols. I heard two reports, after which I heard moaning, as if a person was dying; then I heard a wild whoop. My husband and...sons did not come back any more. I went out the next morning in search of them, and found my husband and William... lying dead in the road near together, about two hundred yards from the house. My other son I did not see...until the day he was buried. I was so...overcome that I went to the house. They [all] ...were buried the next day. She signed the sworn statement of truth, Mahala "X" Doyle."[433]

Out of fear for the remaining family members, Mrs. Doyle packed up all their belongings and left their home in the Kansas Territory to return to Missouri.

James Doyle's son, who had been spared, told the same story about the massacre: *"they roused us up, and told us that if we would surrender they would not hurt us. They said they were from the army; they were armed with pistols and knives; they took off [with] my father and two of my brothers, William and Drury. We were all alarmed. They made inquires about Mr. Wilkinson, and about his horses. The next morning...I went in search of my father and two brothers. I found my father and one brother, William, lying dead in the road, about two hundred yards from the house; I saw my other brother lying dead on the ground, about one hundred fifty yards from the house, in the grass, near a ravine; his fingers were cut off; his head was cut open; there was a hole in his breast. William's head was cut open, and a hole was also in his side. My father was shot in the forehead and stabbed in the breast. 'John Doyle.'*"[434]

The vanquished and the conquered each told the situation as experienced from their own point of view. One side was teaching the other about fear and terror; the other side provided the flesh and blood for the sacrifice. It was a demonstration of the savagery of retaliation.

These deaths were only the beginning of the terror that reigned that night on the 24th of May. John Brown's revenge had not yet been satisfied as he headed down Mosquito Creek to the home of Allen Wilkinson.[435] Townsley's later testimony supplied the details of the massacre and explained what occurred after arriving at the Wilkinson home. *"Here the old man Brown, three of his sons, and son-in-law, as at the Doyle residence, went to the door and ordered Wilkinson to come out, leaving Frederick*

---

433   Robinson, The Kansas Conflict, 396.
434   Ibid., 395-396.
435   Ibid., 267.

Brown, Winer, and myself standing in the road east of the house. Wilkinson was taken and marched some distance south of his house and slain in the road, with a short sword, by one of the younger Browns. After he was killed his body was dragged to one side and left.[436]

Mr. Wilkinson's wife, Louise Jane, would later testify *"one of them said, 'You are our prisoner. Do you surrender?' He said, 'Gentlemen I do.' They said, 'Open the door.' Mr. Wilkinson told them to wait till he made a light; and they replied, 'If you don't open it, we will open it for you.' He opened the door against my wishes, and four men came in, and my husband was told to put on his clothes, and they asked him if there was not more men about; they searched for arms, and took a gun and powder-flask, all the weapon that was about the house."*

"I begged them to let Mr. Wilkinson stay with me, saying that I was sick and helpless, and could not stay by myself. My husband also asked them to let him stay with me until he could get some one to wait on me; told them that he would not run off, but would be there the next day, or whenever called for. The old man, who seemed to be in command, looked at me and then around at the children, and replied, 'You have neighbors.' I said, 'So I have, but they are not here, and I cannot go for them.' The old man replied, 'It matters not,' and told him to get ready. My husband wanted to put on his boots and get ready, so as to be protected from the damp and night air, but they wouldn't let him.' After they were gone, I thought I heard my husband's voice in complaint, but do not know; went to the door, and all was still. Next morning Mr. Wilkinson was found about one hundred and fifty yards from the house, in some dead brush. A lady who saw my husband's dead body said there was a gash in his head and in his side; others said that he was cut in the throat twice."[437]

"My husband was a poor man...and was not engaged in arresting or disturbing anybody. He took no active part in the proslavery cause so as to aggravate the abolitionists; but he was a proslavery man."[438]

John Brown's raid then progressed to a third home. Again, James Townsley would be the chief witness to testify about the events. *"We then crossed the Pottawatomie and came to the house of Henry Sherman, generally known as Dutch Henry. Here John Brown and the party, excepting Frederick Brown, Winer, and myself, who were left outside a short distance from the door, went into the house and brought out one or two persons,*

---

436   Robinson, The Kansas Conflict, 267.
437   Ibid., 397-398.
438   Ibid., 398.

talked with them some, and then took them in again. They afterwards brought out William Sherman, Dutch Henry's brother, marched him down into the Pottawatomie Creek, where he was slain with swords by Brown's two youngest sons, and left lying in the creek."

"It was the expressed intention of Brown to execute Dutch Henry also, but he was not found at home. He also hoped to find George Wilson, Probate Judge of Anderson County, there, and intended, if he did, to kill him too. Wilson had been notifying Free-State men to leave the Territory. I had received such a notice from him myself."[439]

John Brown's blood thirst had not been quenched. Townsley's testimony continued. *"Brown wanted me to pilot the party into the neighborhood where I lived, and point out all the proslavery men in it, whom he proposed to put to death. I positively refused to do it."* Brown's massacre had come to an end when Townsley refused to show him anymore southerners who lived in the immediate area. He signed his official sworn statements regarding the massacre, *"James Townsley."*[440]

"At last, it was over. Like some evil mist, Brown and his band dissolved with the dawn, leaving in their wake shattered wives and children to stumble upon the corpses of fathers and sons. Word of the atrocity raced along the Pottawatomie. Within hours, horror-struck proslavery settlers had cleared the valley 'almost entirely,' fleeing the midnight monsters moving in their midst—monsters who not only massacred innocent men and boys before the eyes of their screaming families but who also 'chopped them into inches.'"[441]

At daylight Brown's attack had finally ended and his goals had been achieved, causing many proslavery families to stream eastward across the border of Missouri for protection.

The reaction at Leavenworth following the reports of the slaughter was swift: As G. W. Brown recounted, *"A lady resident of Leavenworth, at the time the news of the tragedy reached the city, told me, ...of its effects on the Free-State population there. She said a public meeting of proslavery men was immediately called, when the account of the Pottawatomie massacre was narrated to the already crazed proslavery mob. The most violent denunciatory and threatening speeches were made. Resolutions were passed of a fiery character, setting forth that first blood had been shed by the Free-State men; that the midnight assassins were not satisfied with simply*

---

439   Robinson, The Kansas Conflict, 267.
440   Ibid.
441   Goodrich, War to the Knife, 128. / Malin, John Brown, 99.

169

murdering their victims, but that they had mutilated them in a shameful manner. They declared that it was impossible for the abolitionist and the proslavery settlers to live together in Kansas, and that the former must leave. She said a body of armed men marched through the streets, visiting each dwelling, and ordered every Free-State man, woman, and child to go at once to the levee. They would not allow her even to close her house; but with her children she was marched to the river, where she found hundreds of others. All were forced upon a steamer lying at the levee, including her husband, whom she found there. The captain was ordered to take these involuntary passengers to Alton, and leave them. She remained in the city until the spring of 1857, when she returned with her husband, and again settled in the Territory."[442]

The first slaughter by abolitionists was completed by Brown and his men. In his eyes, he had done his duty, and it was one which he believed had been ordained and sanctioned by God. This was only the beginning of his strategy to end slavery in America and the interpretation of his actions would receive a wide variation of opinions from the people who heard or read about the unbelievable attack that hideous night.

Many northern newspapers either suppressed the truth about the attacks entirely or devoted a line or two hidden in the middle of their publication. The southern presses, however, were enraged by the madness that occurred that night against innocent men and boys who were sacrificed to fulfill Brown's prophesy.[443]

Enough blood had now been shed by both sides to prime the pump of revenge—and once it started flowing, there was no way to end it.

---

442   Robinson, The Kansas Conflict, 280-281.
443   Nichols, Bleeding Kansas, 116.

CHAPTER SEVENTEEN
Nightmare of Fury

Following the attack on Lawrence, which was succeeded by the grizzly murders committed during the Pottawatomie Massacre, no one on either side felt safe. The gruesome reports of the crimes continued to add to the intensity of the conflict without any justification for the loss of lives reported in the newspapers. The awful accounts detailed both men and boys being shot and hacked to death and needed no embellishment.

As a result of these atrocities, an attempt was made to stop the killings and extinguish the flames of war. Both sides responded and resolutions were written within three days after the Pottawatomie killings. Civil meetings were also called and attended by the political rivals, including some of the most radical Free-State men of the Territory.

One resolution read *"Whereas, an outrage of the darkest and foulest nature had been committed in our midst by some midnight assassins unknown, who have taken five of our citizens at the hour of midnight from their homes and families, and murdered and mangled them in an awful manner; to prevent a repetition of these deeds, we deem it necessary to adopt some measures for our mutual protection and to aid and assist in bringing these desperadoes to justice."*[444]

The resolution also proposed laying *"aside all sectional and political feelings and act together as men of reason and common sense."* It called for the restoration of peace and harmony and pledged both individual and collective intervention to prevent such tragedies. The resolution made it clear that these were criminal acts and the perpetrators would be caught and turned over to authorities for punishment.[445]

The document was signed by a seven man committee.[446] Had the document been accepted and put into action on both sides, the course of history might have prevented the torrent of violence that followed. Neither side, however, could live up to the goals set forth in the resolution. The enmity

---

444   A. T. Andreas, History of the State of Kansas, 132.
445   Ibid.
446   Ibid.

and hateful actions of the preceding years could not be truly forgiven or left behind. Consequently, once the bloodbath began, there was no way to stop the hemorrhage.

During the last week of May 1856, a few days after the Pottawatomie Creek massacre, a southern militia of fifty men, under the command of Captain H. C. Pate, headed toward Osawatomie in search of John Brown and his men. Prior to departing, some of the men were interviewed by the *Lecompton Union* newspaper. One of Pate's lieutenants was quoted as saying, *"We are going down to the southern part of the Territory, expecting to see rattlesnakes and abolitionists, and we are taking our guns along."*[447]

When Pate's militia arrived at Osawatomie, they found two of John Brown's sons, Jason and John Jr. Even though they had not participated in their father's raid at Pottawatomie Creek, they were placed in chains as prisoners. John Junior's house and a store owned by a man who had been with John Brown during the Pottawatomie raid were burned. Later that day, Pate's militia ran into a patrol of federal dragoons and turned over Brown's sons to the soldiers. John Brown Junior's behavior was described by the soldiers as alarming and strongly suggested insanity. According to them, he raved wildly like an uncontrolled maniac and *"lashed his chains in fury till the dull iron shone like polished steel."*[448]

On May 31, another attack led by Pate was undertaken. His men had made camp at the head of Black Jack Ravine. The men became bored and some of them went into the small town of Palmyra to plunder. Two prisoners were taken and arms were stolen in the raid. One of the prisoners taken at Palmyra was a Baptist preacher named William H. Moore, who was a friend of the Still family.[449]

Moore was singled out and tormented because he *"was opposed to drinking, ... they seized* [him] *and putting a tin funnel in his mouth, poured liquor down his throat—the scoundrels swearing they would make the old preacher drunk."*[450]

By Tuesday morning, June 3rd, John Brown had learned of Pate and his militia, and that they were camped at Black Jack Ravine. He and his men quickly joined with another abolitionist force. They attacked Pate and there was an exchange of gunfire that lasted for several hours. During the attack, Pate's prisoners, Reverend Jones and another minister who had been

---

447 Nichols, Bleeding Kansas, 120.
448 Ibid., 121.
449 Clark, Reminiscences, 40.
450 Nichols, Bleeding Kansas, 121.

captured, were tied on top of the barricade wall used by Pate's men for protection. Rev. Moore would later tell the Still family, *"while the bullets were flying around him he was praying as earnestly as he ever had prayed in his life."*[451]

According to Rovia Still, the gunfire at Black Jack could be heard at their home on Blue Mound. As a result, two of her brothers, John and Thomas, started toward Hickory Point, believing that the battle was occurring at that location.[452]

The initial battle at Black Jack Ravine had come to a stalemate with neither side gaining the advantage. The turning point came when one of John Brown's sons, Frederick, rode up to the high ground, brandishing his sword and yelling, *"Come on."* Pate's men mistakenly believed that a large regiment was getting ready to charge them. Many of Pate's militia bolted and ran away. The fight ended when Pate and his men surrendered to John Brown's army. At this point in the battle, there were only twenty-three of Pate's men left, and eight of them were wounded.[453]

On June 6th, following the battle at Black Jack Ravine, John Brown's army was confronted by Colonel Sumner and his federal troops, who were accompanied by U.S. Deputy Marshal Fain. Brown agreed to release Pate and the other prisoners to the federal troops without a fight. Marshal Fain also attempted to arrest John Brown for his part in the Pottawatomie massacre; however, *"he had lost his warrant and Colonel Sumner ruled that under the circumstances, no arrest could be made."* As a result, John Brown avoided capture and was allowed to ride away with his army. [454]

The summer of 1856 was filled with many battles between the abolitionists and the southerners. It was obvious that the Kansas Territory had become engaged in a civil war. Disobedience was raging out of control. Many of the larger battles were stopped by federal troops before active engagement occurred and resulted in the dispersal of the opposing armies prior to shots being fired which created *"the formal warfare pattern of the Territory...all bark and no bite."*[455] An example was an earlier close encounter at Bull Creek at dawn on June 5th. During this confrontation, a large group of abolitionists were facing 300 Missouri militiamen under the command of Whitfield and Coffey. The conflict suddenly ended

---

451   Clark, Reminiscences, 40-41.
452   Ibid., 40.
453   Nichols, Bleeding Kansas, 122.
454   Ibid., 123.
455   Ibid., 142.

without combat when Colonel Sumner and his federal troops interfered in the planned attack.

The federal government, in fact, tried to stop all military conflict and also ordered blockage of any political meetings planned by the Kansas Free-State Government. President Pierce had personally issued a formal proclamation to stop any attempt by Charles Robinson's Free-State legislative group to meet in Topeka on July 4, 1856. This blockade was supported with a dramatic show of military strength when Colonel Edwin Sumner and two hundred dragoons, comprising three full squadrons of soldiers, pulling cannons, rode down Kansas Avenue at a brisk trot. The cannons were set in place, ceremoniously loaded, and matches lighted. Colonel Sumner dismounted his horse and walked into the assembly hall. *"It was high noon... Colonel Sumner got to his feet. [He said] ...Gentlemen, I am called upon this day to perform the most painful duty of my whole life... Under the authority of the President's proclamation, I am here to disperse this legislature and therefore inform you that you cannot meet. I, therefore, order you to disperse."*[456]

The colonel was then asked by members of the free-party legislature if they were to be driven out of the session at the point of a bayonet. The colonel unhesitatingly answered, *"I shall use all the forces in my command to carry out my orders."* [457] The legislature immediately dispersed as ordered. At this point everything looked politically dismal and hopeless for the Free-State Party. Their legislature had been routed, their leaders remained jailed at Lecompton, and even the river routes used for travel by abolitionist immigrants had been shut down with enforcement provided by the Missouri proslavery militia.

On August 16, 1856, another battle was brewing. Sam Walker, an abolitionist, who had the reputation of being a brave military man, had been trying to capture a southern leader named Henry Titus. Titus had the reputation of being fearless. In fact, Titus had become so famous he even had a garrison named after him. Titus' hatred for Sam Walker was well known and he had just raised a bounty on Sam Walker from $300 to $500 in an effort to eliminate him. On this day in August, however, it was Walker's turn to try and eliminate his dreaded enemy. [458]

Prior to an attack on Fort Titus, Walker sent men to Lawrence with orders to return with a cannon. They needed the weapon to break down the

456   Robinson, Kansas: Its Interior and Exterior Life, 313-314.
457   Ibid.
458   Nichols, Bleeding Kansas, 137.

walls of the fort. At daybreak Walker and fifty men began their attack by firing cannon balls at the fort. The six-pound cannon balls had been made out of the lead harvested from the newspaper type which had previously been thrown into the river during the raid on Lawrence. The cannon fire eventually hammered a large hole through the wall of the fort. [459]

Titus appeared at the doorway of the fort covered in blood and with multiple wounds. He surrendered and fell on a bench outside the fort walls. Ironically, on the wall above Titus, hung a handbill offering $500 *"for the head of Samuel Walker, on or off the shoulders."*[460]

Inside the fort, there were many casualties including two dead and two wounded. Titus was one of the most hated of the southerners and Walker's men called aloud for his execution. Sam Walker cocked his pistol and said to Titus, *"Well, Titus, I beat you to it...And I reckon I might as well finish the job."* Titus begged Walker not to kill him, asking for mercy and pleading he had a family and children. Walker was touched by Titus' hopeless situation and took pity on him. As Walker lowered his pistol, one of Walker's men brought up his rifle to shoot Titus. Walker's fist sent the man to the ground before he could fire. Stepping back from Titus, Walker said, *"There Titus sits. If any one of you is brute enough to shoot, shoot."* None of the men took the challenge.[461]

Titus and eighteen of his men were captured. Walker's men then turned their attention to destroying Titus' home. Titus begged Walker to spare his house, but the response from the abolitionist was clear, *"God Damn you, and God Damn your house."*[462] Walker then commanded, *"Men, bring on the hay."* Titus' cabin and a shed were soon wrapped in flames. Walker also told all of Titus' slaves that they were freed and advised them to go to Topeka.[463]

Titus and the captured men were loaded in wagons and taken to Lawrence as prisoners. They entered Lawrence by way of Mount Oread, using the same trail that Titus had previously ridden when he had taken part in the Lawrence invasion on May 21, 1856. When the crowd at Lawrence saw Titus, they *"swarmed around us, clamoring for the blood of our prisoners."* The overwhelming feeling toward Titus was to, *"Hang him on the*

459   Nichols, Bleeding Kansas, 137.
460   Ibid., 138.
461   Ibid.
462   Goodrich, War to the Knife, 154.
463   Ibid.

spot. "[464] Walker was eventually able to cool down the mob and his captives were taken to jail.[465]

The next day, August 17th, Governor Shannon came to Lawrence to negotiate a prisoner exchange. He promised, as part of the bargain, to return the cannon taken during the Lawrence raid in May. The Lawrence citizens became unruly and began insulting the governor. Once again, Sam Walker demonstrated courage when he quieted the mob. He *"leaped on his horse and pulled his pistols. The first man who insults the governor does it over my dead body! He cryed. [sic]. He shan't be insulted. Boys, I am with you, but he shan't be insulted."*[466] When Governor Shannon reached his headquarters that night he was utterly discouraged with the lack of progress toward peace and the unrest that continued to exist in the Kansas Territory. He wrote a letter to General Persifer Smith, the commander of Fort Leavenworth. He told the general that when he was at Lawrence, he had seen at least 800 men who were united in purpose and he feared would try to destroy Lecompton. The next day, on August 18th, Governor Shannon sent his letter of resignation to the President of the United States. Shannon would later say, *"Govern Kansas in 1855 and 56! You might as well attempt to govern the devil in hell."*[467]

The individual carnage between individuals and smaller groups of men were at times even more brutal than the major confrontations. At times, these attacks resulted in large numbers of people killed and showed the lack of any mercy by both sides.

An example of the extreme cruelty of these attacks was exhibited by a band of abolitionists. This group of men called themselves "Danites" and had been organized by James Lane. They were referred to as an abolitionist death squad. In this instance, the Danites had trailed a group of Missourians along Appanoose Creek and slipped up on them as they huddled around their campfire. From the Danites' vantage point on both sides of the banks, they had their enemy positioned in crossfire. The order was given to *"Take aim* [and] *Fire."*[468]

According to an account of the massacre given later by a man named Hinton, he said, *"Hardly had the terrible word been uttered ere the roar of thirty rifles, simultaneously discharged, was succeeded by the wildest,*

---

464   Goodrich, War to the Knife, 154.
465   Robinson, The Kansas Conflict, 312.
466   Nichols, Bleeding Kansas, 139.
467   Ibid.
468   Goodrich, War to the Knife, 166-167.

most unearthly shrieks that ever rose from mortals...I saw two of them leap fearfully into the air."[469]

"*Firing weapons furiously, the Danites poured round after round into the begging, screaming mass. Finally all sound and movement ceased.*" One of the Danites who had passed out at the horrible sight of the men being massacred inquired *"were they all killed, then? Every one of them"* [was the reply].[470]

In another incident on June 5th, a man by the name of Cantrell was captured by a southern scouting party. He was taken to a ravine at Cedar Creek and shot. He cried out, " '*O, God, I am shot! I am murdered!*' " *Then another shot, and a long piercing scream; another shot, and all was still!*" [471]

In the ongoing incidents of brutality, a twenty-man raiding party captured a man named Bailey near Bull Creek. Among this group were Coleman, Buckley and Hargous, who had all been involved in murdering Charles Dow. Bailey was robbed of forty dollars and one of the men demanded him to remove his pants. Bailey gave up his money but refused to have his pants stolen. One of the men in the group shot him and beat him with his rifle. They left him for dead but he somehow survived the vicious assault. Bailey was forced to crawl for miles in search of help and medical care. Fortunately, he was able to reach the home of Abram Still and his family at Blue Mound.[472]

Rovia Still, Andrew's sister, remembered the details of the incident when Mr. Bailey reached their home. "*We had sat down to breakfast when we heard the dogs barking furiously and looking out we saw a man trying to climb a tree and the dogs were nipping at his bare feet. My father went out and made the dogs come to order and spoke to the man. At first he did not recognize the man but on closer inspection after the man had called him by name he found that it was Mr. Bailey of Stoney Point. [Bailey said they took]... him out by the side of the road and shot him. They took all his clothes except his pants and shirt and took his money. He said after they shot him he lay quiet as he could when one of them kicked him two or three times on the head and said, 'I guess the D. old abolitionist is done for,' and went off and left him.*"

---

469   Goodrich, War to the Knife, 166-167

470   Ibid.

471   Robinson, The Kansas Conflict, 284.

472   Ibid., 284-285.

"He said he stayed there till it got dark enough that he thought no one would see him, then crawled on his hands and knees till he got into the thick brush and weeds and stayed there all night, afraid to move or breathe almost for fear the border ruffians would find him. He would walk all night and hide in some secluded place in the day time. When he got to our house he had been out for five days without a morsel to eat except some wild gooseberries he found and as the Bible says, 'Bitter herbs are sweet to a hungry man.' I suppose these gooseberries tasted sweet to him for he said he was so hungry he 'gobbled' them down in a hurry."

"He was in a terrible condition. He had been shot through the shoulder. His feet were scratched and bleeding for they had taken his boots and socks and the weather was quite cool...He was almost demented. He had suffered so from his wound and exposure. My father bathed his feet and dressed his wound and gave him a quieting powder. Mother got him a warm breakfast but it took much coaxing to get him to lie down and take a nap. He would keep saying, 'Oh, I'm afraid they'll come, I'm afraid they'll come.' Father finally got him to lie down. He told him if he saw them coming he would call him. After he laid down he soon fell asleep for he was so exhausted... he carried this bullet to his grave and it often gave him trouble, but he fared better than many of them for he escaped with his life."[473]

One of the most brutal attacks occurred on August 18, 1856, at Leavenworth. A border ruffian, named Fugit, bet his boots against a cash award of six dollars that he could scalp an abolitionist within two hours time. The ruffian left the saloon to find his prey. He soon encountered an abolitionist riding peaceably along a road only a few miles outside of town. He shot and killed the man and went to his work with his knife to complete the challenge. He hastily returned to beat the two-hour time limit and collected his six dollar reward. He proudly flapped the man's scalp around in front of his comrades and boasted *"I went out for the scalp of a damned abolitionist,* [He yelled] *"and I have got one."*[474]

The turmoil continued to intensify when Governor Shannon resigned from office. In Shannon's place, Daniel Woodson, Secretary of State, was named the interim acting governor. Therefore, he assumed the command of the Territorial Militia. Woodson was a strong southern supporter of slavery and he immediately went on the offensive enlisting the help of Senator Atchison who planned to take advantage of the situation while Woodson

473   Clark, Reminiscences, 35.
474   Goodrich, War to the Knife, 156. / Nichols, Bleeding Kansas, 139.

was in charge. Woodson declared the "Kansas Territory in a state of insurrection and rebellion and asked all patriotic citizens' to rally in defense of the law."[475] Woodson urged Atchison to destroy all of the Free-State towns and defeat their militia before the newly appointed governor, John Geary, could arrive in the Territory. Atchison was able to assemble an army of 1150 men. They camped along the Missouri-Kansas border in preparation to sweep in and destroy Osawatomie, Hickory Point, Topeka, and what remained of Lawrence following the sacking attack led by Atchison on May 21, 1856.[476]

On August 30th, a group of men from Atchison's army was split off and assigned to General Reid. General Reid was to lead the initial raiding party to attack the town of Osawatomie. This target was at the top of Atchison's list in retaliation against John Brown for his grisly work on Pottawatomie Creek. Among the attackers was a minister named Reverend Martin White, who had his own axe to grind against the abolitionists. He was a proslavery sympathizer and he had been personally assaulted and abused by the Free-Soilers when he resided at Dutch Henry's Crossing.

Reid's forces were intercepted by ambushers prior to entering Osawatomie. After fighting and repelling this abolitionist resistance, Reverend White was one of the first to ride into town. The first person he encountered was John Brown's son, Frederick, who was walking along the main road. *"Why, I know you," White growled. Without a second thought he raised his rifle and shot young Brown through the heart, killing him instantly. The ball passed clean through his body,"* Martin White would later state with pride. "[477]

It was lucky that Martin White didn't know Frederick Brown had another man traveling with him that day. His companion was John Still, Andrew's younger brother. Frederick had asked John to stay in a cabin and brew coffee and fix something to eat while he went outside to get the horses ready to travel. Again Rovia Still provided details of what happened after Frederick Brown's death. *"Soon after Fred went out my brother heard the firing of guns and as he looked out he saw Fred fall and he ran out to him, He saw he was mortally wounded. He raised his head and held him for a few moments and he passed away and as he laid him gently down he raised up and looked in the direction of the firing and there was a large*

---

475   Nichols, Bleeding Kansas, 141.
476   Trowbridge, Andrew Taylor Still, 71.
477   Goodrich, War to the Knife, 159-160.

company coming into town… They were perhaps a quarter of a mile away. They were shooting at my brother too and he said some of the bullets were falling dangerously close to him. So he pulled off Freds [sic] boots and got his part of the dispatches and he got onto his horse and rode as fast as he could towards Lawrence as he had very important dispatches…but as he turned sadly away from poor Fred lying dead on the ground…he was more determined to fight to make Kansas a free state then [sic] ever before. "[478]

After Frederick Brown was killed and other resistance was eliminated, the southern militia swept through Osawatomie. The town was looted and burned. When Reid's men rode out at the end of their raid, only four houses remained standing with the rest burned to the ground.[479]

The Still family, like the other abolitionist families in the Kansas Territory, was on the front lines of the battlegrounds. They had wounded men crawl to their home for care and support. Without question they were labeled by the proslavery southerners as the enemy. The family, however, never shirked from accepting their responsibility as abolitionists; and now that open warfare had been declared in the Kansas Territory, their lives would be in even more danger.

The abolitionists were outnumbered. They recognized that the Territorial officials, the federal government, and the president of the United States supported the proslavery side. Local militia units and posses were actively involved in driving the abolitionists out of the Territory by creating individual suffering and death.

The cruelty of the conflict and the escalation of force on both sides were beyond reason and understanding. The lawlessness caused many to suffer both individually and collectively. "An eye for an eye, a tooth for a tooth," ruled the men who were fighting the battles.

The atrocities that were occurring in the Territory over the political positions regarding the slavery issue were the ingredients necessary and the prelude to the Civil War looming only a few years away.

---

478 Clark, Reminiscences, 42-43.
479 Nichols, Bleeding Kansas, 142.

CHAPTER EIGHTEEN
On Watch at Blue Mound

The abolitionist forces under the command of James Lane, and the proslavery military forces led by David Atchison, continued to build their armies in an effort to gain control in the Kansas Territory. Their personal goals and ambitions guided both of them in their decisions of where and when to attack to eliminate one another.

The open warfare continued to escalate under Daniel Woodson's authority. As a result there was diminishing governmental protection for the abolitionists. He continued to support the idea of destroying the abolitionists' towns to put an end to their cause. He responded in September 1856 with another public "call to arms" against the enemies of slavery.

Woodson again empowered Missouri Senator David Atchison with the legal authority to respond. On this occasion he was able to accumulate a force of almost 3000 proslavery men to answer the call. Atchison's army quickly moved forward and camped on the Wakarusa River. His army was preparing to launch attacks and deliver a fatal blow on all of the remaining abolitionists' towns by destroying them. Since Lawrence was considered to be the abolitionists' stronghold, it became the main target. Woodson continued the challenge to complete the attacks prior to Geary's arrival to keep him from interfering with the plans and an ultimate proslavery victory. The window of opportunity was short since Geary's arrival was expected sometime during the month of September.

John Geary, however, arrived early on September 9th and assumed command as the Territorial Governor before Atchison and the Missouri militia could begin the attacks on Lawrence, Topeka, and Manhattan. Governor Geary immediately made several crucial decisions to stop the imminent Territorial war. He was acutely aware it was politically necessary to stop the violence in Kansas if the Democratic Party was going to have a chance to win the presidency with James Buchanan as their candidate. Buchanan had, for the most part, been spared from taking part in the slavery issue because he had spent the last several years as an appointed Minister to Great Britain. Regardless, Geary knew that the *"North was a seething caldron of excitement over Kansas affairs, and Buchanan's election was in danger."*[480]

Governor Geary wasted no time. On September 10th, the day after his arrival, he began the process of reducing tensions by releasing the prisoners who were being held in Lecompton. All the abolitionists, and the prisoners charged with treason, including Charles Robinson, were allowed to return to their homes. This was an attempt by Geary to defuse an expected attack on Lecompton that was anticipated to be led by Jim Lane to free the prisoners. Furthermore, the governor issued a proclamation ordering *"all armed bodies of men to disperse"* from the Territory. However, this proclamation had no effect on Atchinson and his army which had previously sacked Lawrence four months earlier. They continued to move toward Lawrence preparing for a second attack.[481]

At the same time, unfortunately for the abolitionists in Lawrence, their defenses were in the process of being weakened. They were unable to defend themselves against any large scale attack because their numbers had dwindled. A further deterioration of their defensive strength took place when General James Lane ordered thirty of the militia in Lawrence to travel with him to Nebraska as his bodyguards. He and his men abandoned the community as the enemy approached. Additionally, Lane had secretly ordered other men to leave the town. He had directed Colonel Harvey and 100 men under his command to join him at another camp site away from the town. Together they would plan to conduct military duties Lane apparently deemed more important than to stay and fight in Lawrence. In addition, Harvey's men made the defensive situation in Lawrence even worse when they took the Sharps rifles that had been issued to them, as well as the only cannon remaining in the town. The end result was that the remaining military force in Lawrence was reduced to 200 men with only fifty Sharps rifles and without any cannons to defend themselves against almost 3,000 proslavery attackers.[482]

The small number of citizens in Lawrence were desperate. Those who remained to fight were against odds of ten to one. They *were short of ammunition...[and] were told to divide their cartridges with their neighbors till ALL WAS GONE, then take to their bayonets, and those who had none, to use their pitchforks, as they were liberally distributed from the stores."*[483]

---

480   Robinson, The Kansas Conflict, 323.
481   Ibid.
482   Robinson, The Kansas Conflict, 322.
483   Goodrich, War to the Knife, 179-180.

According to one report, an additional 200 Free-State Militia soon arrived in Lawrence to join the men who remained, but they brought a very limited amount of ammunition with them. Another man who reportedly came to aid in the defense of the community was John Brown who encouraged the combatants with his advice to, *"Keep cool and fire low."*[484] He also told them, *"don't yell and make a great noise, but remain perfectly silent and still. Wait 'til they get within twenty-five yards of you, get a good object, be sure you see the hindsight of your gun, then fire."* His last advice was *"to shoot low, to aim at their legs instead of at their heads."*[485]

Charles Robinson would later refute the claim that Brown had remained in Lawrence to defend the town against Atchison. To support his claim, he later requested statements from two of the field commanders, Major J. R. Abbott, who was officer of the day, and Lt. Col. Joseph Cracklin, who was the ranking officer in Lawrence. To disclaim the notion that Brown had participated in defense of the town, Colonel Cracklin outlined the events of what had taken place in the initial attack, and that Brown was not involved *"directly or indirectly"* in defending the city.[486]

With Atchison's Army poised to strike at any moment, Governor Geary communicated the gravity of the situation and his concerns in a letter to President Pierce in Washington admitting the situation was worse than he had anticipated. He described the situation without exaggeration when he wrote: *"I reached Kansas and entered upon the discharge of my official duties in the most gloomy hour of her history. Desolation and ruin reigned on every hand; homes and firesides were deserted; the smoke of burning dwellings darkened the atmosphere; women and children, driven from their inhabitation, wandered over the prairies and among the woodlands, or sought refuge and protection even among the Indian tribes. The highways were infested with numerous predatory bands, and towns were fortified and garrisoned by armies of conflicting partisans, each excited almost to frenzy, and determined upon mutual extermination."*[487]

The confusion during September 1856 resulted in both sides having to make decisions under a great amount of stress. Each relented when feeling weak and forged ahead during periods of strength. On September 12th, Governor Geary traveled to Lawrence to meet with Robinson. He reassured

---

484   Nichols, Bleeding Kansas, 156.
485   Trowbridge, Andrew Taylor Still, 75.
486   Robinson, The Kansas Conflict, 325-327.
487   Ibid., 329.

him he was earnestly working to end the armed conflicts in the Kansas Territory. [488]

However, he could not convince Robinson and the town to give up their weapons with the threat of 3000 men approaching. Instead, Geary had to settle for a commitment from Robinson that the weapons would be used only to defend their lives during any attacks. The governor promised an end to the violence and to send the attackers back home.[489]

On the 14th of September, in order to support the upcoming invasion, Atchison moved his army to the town of Franklin so that he would be only a few miles away from Lawrence. He began the attacks by sending an advanced raiding party of 300 men.

Meanwhile, outside of Lawrence, the Still family continued to serve as a lookout for the abolitionist town. Because they lived on Blue Mound, which was one of the highest elevations just outside of Lawrence, they accepted the responsibility to watch from their vantage point for any armies moving toward the town. As a warning signal, they were to run up a large white flag atop the Mound if they observed any enemy forces approaching Lawrence. They also used a captured telescope to give them greater accuracy as they surveyed the area around Blue Mound in their sentry role for the community.

Rovia Still and her sister, Mary, described what occurred on Sunday morning, September 14. They wrote that the Still family had just finished Sunday school and what they witnessed from their vantage point. Rovia said it was *"the largest body of men that ever came up from MO,"* while Mary called *"It a vast army, within four miles of the Mound and ten miles of Lawrence, moving forward at a rapid pace."* Rovia said her *"brother had been appointed by his moonshine company to go upon the Mound and spy out the situation and if he saw any body of men coming, he was to hoist a flag as they had put up a flag pole on top of Blue Mound. My sister, Cassie, and I had gone on to the Sunday school. My sister, Mary, had been sick for several days and was still sick in bed. When we got near the sunday school, my brother had gone on his spying trips and we saw him coming running down the side of the mound as fast as he could. My father was hitched up ready to start to Clinton. My brother said to my sister and I, 'You run home and tell Father to hurry on to Lawrence and give the alarm as*

---

488   Robinson, The Kansas Conflict, 322-323.
489   Ibid., 323.

184

*there is a large body of men coming and they had over a hundred wagons'...
my brother had not raised the flag but was giving the alarm to the settlers.*

*"As soon as we got home and told our story, my sister Mary jumped
out of bed. My mother had been piecing a quilt out of red calico and white
muslin. My sister Mary got out of bed as she had been sick for several days
and picked up the muslin and red calico and a paper of pins and as she ran,
she pinned them together and when she got to the place where the Sunday
school was to be there was a girlfriend of ours there by the name of Sara
Lynn Greenwood...and together they climbed the mound and hoisted the
flag. I have often wondered how my sister could do this as sick as she had
been, but somehow I think in time of emergencies God gives us super human strength. I do not know but I do know that no bad results came from
her lively run."* Mary admitted she had been *"sick in bed...when* [she]...
heard the news...and she had hastily thrown" on her clothes and that the
flag had been hoisted up the pole *"in double quick time."*

Rovia reported that *"during this time my father had gone to Lawrence
and given the alarm but they laughed him to scorn and said, 'You must have
started before you awakened up. We don't see anything of the flag waving
yet,' but he said, 'You had better waken up and get busy or you'll regret it
for there is a large body of men coming.' By this time they saw by their field
glasses that the flag was up and they did get busy and began fixing up their
breast works, making cartridges, cleaning thier [sic] Sharps rifles, etc."*[490]

During the afternoon of September 14th, 300 men in Atchison's raiding party arrived on the outskirts of Lawrence. Charles Robinson and G.W.
Brown, the newspaper editor of the *Herald of Freedom,* sent dispatches to
Lecompton to notify Governor Geary about the impending attack. Fifty of
the abolitionists, armed with Sharps rifles, rode out to challenge Atchison's
raiding party and drove them back in retreat.

When Geary received the news, he immediately requested Colonel
Cooke and his federal troops to start toward Lawrence to prevent further
confrontations with Atchison's men. Cooke's men arrived at night on the
14th and set up artillery on Mount Oread, with dragoons positioned between Franklin and Lawrence to stop any further encounters. The following morning on the 15th of September, Governor Geary and Colonel Cooke
traveled to meet with Atchison and his officers to stop the army from ad-
vancing any further toward the abolitionist towns.[491]

---

490   Clark, Reminiscences, 30-31. / Adams, In God We Trust, 129-130.
491   Robinson, The Kansas Conflict, 324.

Governor Geary, who had known Atchison when he served as the vice president of the United States, warned him that if he continued with his plans to destroy the abolitionist towns, he would be responsible for starting an open civil war involving the entire country. He shamed Atchison into withdrawing his men by reminding him of his responsibility to the country because of his former position as vice president. There were some men in Atchison's army who wanted to continue even if it meant attacking the federal troops as well as the abolitionists. Atchison apparently realized his obligation to the country he had served in the second highest position of the government and relented. The attacks were called off and he sent his army back home across the border. This event ended the call to arms against the abolitionists and once again moved the power struggle over slavery back into the political arena and the voting booths to decide the final outcome.

Governor Geary had met the challenge and accomplished his goals. He had stopped the open warfare in the Territory and restored law and order. He had been in the fields with the federal troops and had personally met with both the proslavery forces and the abolitionists on the battlefield to stop the impending bloodbath. As a result of ending the conflict brewing in the Kansas Territory, he helped Buchanan win the presidency and the Democratic Party remained in power. Geary's victory would be short-lived when Buchanan's administration felt that he sided too strongly with the abolitionists. The administration no longer supported his position. On March 4, 1857, only six months after arriving in the Kansas Territory, Geary resigned from office. There is little doubt that he, with his leadership in the field, postponed the beginning of a Civil War in 1856. Despite his resignation, both sides had respected his integrity and his word. [492]

The fourth governor appointed to the Kansas Territory, Robert Walker, took over leadership on May 27, 1857. He would also remain in the position for only six months and would depart November 16, 1857. Walker had served as secretary of the treasury, and was both a lawyer and an astute politician. His major contribution in helping solve the political situation in the Territory was to convince the abolitionists to have faith in the voting booth and to participate in the election on October 6, 1857. This appeal for trust in the governmental process was not accepted by many of the more radical abolitionists, including James Lane. He was determined to force the acceptance of the Topeka Constitution which had been written and adopted by the abolitionists to become the governing document and legal authority of

---

492   Trowbridge, Andrew Taylor Still, 75.

the Territory. Lane was working behind the scenes making preparations to attack both proslavery and federal troops if they did not accept the Topeka Declaration. He had gone so far as to contact John Brown, who at this time was residing in Tabor, Iowa, requesting his return. He wanted Brown to join him in the planned military raids to force the Topeka Constitution on Kansas. He promised Brown money and transportation and hoped he would bring several of his trusted men with him in the effort to establish political and military control.[493]

However, Charles Robinson continued to gain abolitionist support with his more moderate political tone. He recognized that under Walker's leadership, things were beginning to look favorable. Governor Walker had promised fair elections and the abolitionist population had also been growing because the vast majority of the newcomers entering the Territory were "free-staters."[494]

While the abolitionists won the elections easily in most areas of the Territory, Governor Walker was forced to keep his word and overturn the results in the Oxford election. He deemed the Oxford returns fraudulent and declared the abolitionists the winner.

One of the new legislators elected was Andrew Taylor Still. This was a tremendous change for the Still family because they had always been on the losing end of most political battles. For the first time, the Still family had risen to the top of the political process and were given a powerful position to help keep the Kansas Territory a slave-free land.

Governor Walker still had a major dilemma to deal with since there were two constitutions written for the Territory. One was the proslavery document which had been followed in the past but considered completely bogus by all the abolitionists. The other was the abolitionists' Topeka constitution only recognized by them. Governor Walker again used the democratic process to decide which constitution would be adopted. He called for a special session of the legislature on December 7, 1857, to settle this question.

Andrew Still and his legislative group from Lawrence arrived in Lecompton early. After they arrived, they were challenged by several proslavery men about their intentions. Andrew told the men that he was there to do whatever *"Jim Lane wants done."* Andrew was taken aside and warned that his life was in danger. He pulled back his overcoat so that his

---

493   Robinson, The Kansas Conflict, 359-362 / Arnold, A History of Kansas, 239 /
         Trowbridge, 75.
494   Trowbridge, Ibid.

With the exception of one, Mr. Elliott, these are the surviving members of the first free-state legislature of Kansas which assembled in 1857.
The fiftieth anniversary was celebrated at Topeka, Kansas, December 6th, 1907, and at Lawrence, Kansas, December 7th, 1907.
These are all that are left of both houses, one senator and five legislators.
Still Moore Leonard Steward Morrell
(signed) A.T. Still

companion could see he was carrying two Colt pistols to protect himself. He returned to face the group which now had grown into a crowd. The men were becoming unruly and began to taunt him. Andrew stood his ground. When questioned by Colonel Young, *"What do you expect to accomplish in this assembly, anyway?"* Andrew answered, *"We propose to break every link in the proslavery chain ... required to make Kansas free for all men."* About the time this situation had reached the boiling point, Jim Lane and 700 men rode into town as reinforcements for the abolitionists. Lane caused the proslavery men to run for cover. [495]

The conflict did not end there. According to Andrew, at the legislative session later that evening, the proceedings started off very quietly until one of the proslavery men stood up and *"began a tirade upon us."* The

---

495   Still, Autobiography, 66-68.

proslavery man began calling the abolitionists *"sons of female dogs, pre-fixed by an abundance of brimstone adjectives."* These insults were imme-diately challenged by Captain Walker who leaped to his feet yelling *"G—d d—n you, take that back."* Andrew *"looked about and was surprised to find in addition to my own revolvers five hundred more covering every drop of proslavery blood in the house, from the chairman down. The chairman sprang to his feet crying: 'For God's sake, don't shoot! That man is drunk and don't know what he is doing!'"* Captain Walker responded by order-ing, *"Trot him out of there then, and do it pretty G—d d—n quick, or I will order them to fire, and keep it up until the last dirty proslavery cuss is dead, pitched out of the window, and in h—l."* Four proslavery men jumped up and dragged the man outside. There were no further disturbances. When the assembly reconvened the following morning, there were no incidents. The constitution that was accepted that day supported the abolitionists' position.[496]

On August 2, 1858, the Free-State Constitution was adopted by a vote of 11,300 to 1,788, and peace finally came to the Kansas Territory.[497]

---

496   Still, Autobiography, 70-71.
497   Trowbridge, Andrew Taylor Still, 76.

CHAPTER NINETEEN
The Civil War

During the next two years, the people living in the northern Kansas Territory would begin to experience relatively peaceful living conditions as they worked toward recovering their lives from the lawlessness of the past. Lawrence had finally achieved a peaceful existence through resolution and adoption of the Territorial laws for governance in the new constitution. However, the fighting and raiding continued in the southern part of the Kansas Territory. The conflicts were as bloody as those previously experienced in the Lawrence area and continued to heighten the tension between the abolitionists and the proslavery communities.

A countless number of the atrocities were committed by a former minister named James Montgomery. He was the leader of the "Jayhawks," a gang of thieves and murderers who were primarily radical abolitionists. Montgomery's goal was to drive every proslavery man and woman back across the Missouri border. The attacks were a combination of robberies, beatings, and killings. The "Jayhawkers" reputation of violence singled them out as the most ruthless gang of murderers and thieves. The attacks were so numerous that at one point they were killing the southern settlers *"almost as fast as they arrived."*[498]

The Jayhawkers demonstrated their lack of fear of any authority when they attacked Fort Scott on February 11, 1858, ignoring the fact that federal troops were stationed there. Another attack by the Jayhawkers on the Fort Scott area occurred on April 21st, and this time both southern and free-soil settlers were robbed and tormented. The federal troops tried to intervene in this attack and chased Montgomery and his gang out of Fort Scott. During Montgomery's retreat, the Jayhawkers suddenly stopped running away and turned their horses to face the soldiers and fired their weapons at the federal troops wounding several and killing one of the soldiers.[499]

Montgomery began yet another campaign in the spring of 1858 to again try to drive all proslavery settlers from southern Kansas.[500] The attacks

---

498   Goodrich, War to the Knife, 213.
499   Ibid., 213-214.
500   Ibid.

eventually produced a long line of families fleeing from their homes. A description written in the Fort Scott newspaper captured the magnitude of the uprooting of these families, which was causing them to become fleeing refugees. *"It is a soul-sickening sight to see family after family…flying from their homes, dragging after them the few effects which robbery may have left them…For days the roads have been lined with good, honest citizens, leaving the country of their choice for opinions sake—thus fathers, brothers and sons, have been obliged to leave mothers, sisters and wives, to flee the country from these merciless scamps.—Farms are abandoned with crops planted and everything wears a cheerless prospect."*[501]

The Jayhawkers were not the only group responsible for upheaval. There was a vicious attack committed by proslavery forces in May 1858. This atrocity would be compared in magnitude to John Brown's Pottawatomie Creek massacre. This heinous slaughter would become known as the massacre at Marais Des Cygnes. The leader of the attack was Charles Hamilton, a Georgia southerner, who had been run off his property by Montgomery and his Jayhawkers in their early spring raids. He was determined to return to the Kansas Territory and exact revenge for being routed from his home. He planned to shoot down any Jayhawker *"like wolves"* when he found them.[502] On the morning of May 19, 1858, *"Hamelton* [sic] [and] …*"a band of men numbering between twenty-five and thirty"*[503] swept up the Marais Des Cygnes River, eventually rounding up a group of men who were collected indiscriminately along the way. The captives were made up of farmers, shopkeepers, other men who were captured riding along a road, and one minister.

The act of retribution would later be told by one of the victims, named B. L. Reed, that *"[We] were then ordered to march. After marching half of a mile or there abouts, we were conducted into a deep, narrow ravine, and ordered to halt and form a line. Hamilton gave the command to 'Face front;' he then ordered his own men to form a line and 'present arms' in front of us, the horses' feet being nearly as high as our heads, and about ten feet from us. Someone said 'The men don't obey the order.' Capt. Hamilton gave the order again. They not all obeying, he gave it a third time, swearing terribly."*[504] *"'God damn you, why don't you wheel into line?' shouted*

501   Goodrich, War to the Knife, 214-215.
502   Welch, Border Warfare, 88-89.
503   Ibid., 97.
504   Ibid., 101.

Hamilton to W. B. Brockett. 'I'll be damned if I'll have anything to do with such a God damned piece of business as this,' replied Brockett angrily. 'If it was in a fight I'd fire.' "[505]

"Terrified and trembling, the eleven men in the ravine now knew what was coming as the horsemen finally formed into a line. 'Hamilton drew out a large revolver,' Rev. Reed remembered, '[then] presented it toward the prisoners...and gave the word, 'Fire.' "[506]

"*In a cloud of smoke and dust, Reed and the others dropped down in a heap. When the shooting finally ceased several riders dismounted. As the murderers moved along the ravine, the bodies were kicked over, and when any showed signs of life, they were shot again. Miraculously—though lying absolutely still—six victims remained alive by the time the horsemen remounted.*"[507]

"*Soon I heard no more only the tramp of horses' feet,*" recalled Reed as he lay bleeding from his wound. "*[S]ome began to groan. I spoke very low and said, 'Don't make a noise.' *"[508]

The men were later found lying in the ravine by the minister's wife. Five of them were dead and six of them survived their multiple gunshot wounds. One of the victims had four bullet wounds in his chest, and another, who had taken a shotgun blast to his stomach, had his intestines hanging out from his gaping wound. Unbelievably, another massacre victim stood up and spit out the bullet that had struck him in the mouth and severed his tongue.[509]

Hamilton had completed his revenge against Montgomery and the Kansas abolitionists. However, this did not discourage Montgomery and his Jayhawks or slow down their raids. James Montgomery would eventually earn the reputation among the radical free-state people as a "folk-hero." He continued his raids in the Fort Scott area and harassed the citizens. He attacked Fort Scott again on December 15, 1858, to free one of his men who had been captured and jailed in the town. In a surprise attack, he entered the town and easily regained the jailed man's freedom. Several people were killed during the battle, including Deputy Marshal John Little.[510]

---

505   Goodrich, War to the Knife, 217.
506   Ibid.
507   Ibid.
508   Ibid.
509   Ibid.
510   Ibid., 220-222.

Adding to the aggression of the abolitionists, John Brown would also make another mark across the border from the Kansas Territory on December 20, 1858, to free eleven slaves in Missouri. Again there was bloodshed during the raid and a slave owner was murdered. John Brown would later write an article which was published in the newspaper, "*Trading Post,* Kansas, in January 1859." He wrote about Hamilton's Marais Des Cygnes massacre and the number of men murdered and injured. He then paralleled this event to his last raid where only one man was killed but eleven slaves were given their freedom. Brown attempted to cleanse his actions of lawlessness using the Hamilton attack as an example to justify his means.[511]

In John Brown's last attempt to obtain national attention and involvement in the slavery issue, he and his men traveled to Virginia in preparation to capture the arsenal at Harper's Ferry and attempt to rally the slaves in the state to join and fight for their freedom. He planned to supply the slaves with weapons taken from the arsenal. Brown's men captured Colonel Lewis Washington in his home on October 17, 1859, and brought him as a captive to the Harper's Ferry arsenal. Lewis was a descendant of George Washington, *"and one of the most respected men in northern Virginia."*[512] Reaching the arsenal, Lewis Washington would find himself a prisoner among several of his neighbors who were already inside the armory. Brown and his men barricaded themselves inside the arsenal and were prepared to fight to the last man to achieve his final goal.[513]

Brown had slipped quietly into the federal facility at Harper's Ferry by overpowering the guards. Even though he only had seventeen abolitionists with him, and five former slaves, he had managed to sever all the telegraph wires, which cut off communications and detained a train.

At daybreak the citizens of the town were totally unaware of the circumstances at the arsenal until people in the town began going to work that morning. They encountered gunfire in the area of the armory and several were shot and killed in the streets without warning.[514]

The federal Marines were ordered to Harper's Ferry to roust Brown and his invaders and reclaim it. The commanding officer in charge of the Marines was Robert E. Lee. Lee gave Brown two opportunities to surrender; the first one was soon after he and his ninety Marines arrived at 1:00

---

511   Robinson, The Kansas Conflict, 393-395.
512   Goodrich, War to the Knife, 227.
513   Ibid., 228.
514   Ibid., 230.

a.m. on October 18th. The second was early in the morning on the 19th. Brown gave no ground and said, *"I prefer to die here."*[515] The Marines began the attack on the arsenal and broke down the door, utilizing a ladder for a battering ram. Twelve Marines then charged the arsenal led by Lieutenant [Israel] Green who jumped through the damaged door with his sword drawn and the others with their weapons blazing at the insurrectionists. Lieutenant Green found Brown and attacked him with his sword, striking him in the midsection of his body, and lifting him completely off the ground. Apparently Brown's belt saved him from penetration, even though the sword was bent in half. Green then beat Brown over the head with the hilt of the sword. The majority of Brown's men were killed, including all of his sons who had participated in the attack. After Brown's capture and a military trial, the death sentence was pronounced. John Brown was hanged.

Although viewed as a maniac by most, there would be those who proclaimed him a martyr, *"that by dying he would do more to end slavery than ever he could by living."*[516]

These kinds of attacks and atrocities would set the mood in America by escalating civil unrest and creating political division across the country. There were people who actually hoped that the conflicts and insurrections would ultimately precipitate a war between the North and the South.[517]

During this time of tremendous turmoil in the country, the Still family was dealing with their own personal tragedies. In 1859, Andrew Taylor Still's wife Mary suffered yet another loss of a child shortly after birth. This child, who had been named Lorenzo Still, died just six days after being born. Following the delivery, Mary Still never fully recovered from childbirth, and death claimed Andrew's wife of ten years on September 29, 1859.[518]

Andrew's family would survive without a mother in the house for over a year. He would later marry a school teacher named Mary Elvira Turner, on November 25, 1860.[519]

Andrew and Mary Elvira witnessed the blocked expansion of slavery into the Kansas Territory. The country was now in deadlock, split down the middle politically, and many states felt the time had come to choose one side or the other. On December 20, 1860, South Carolina seceded from the

---

515   Goodrich, War to the Knife, 241.
516   Ibid., 247.
517   Robinson, The Kansas Conflict, 403.
518   Still, Jr., Frontier Doctor, 45.
519   Trowbridge, Andrew Taylor Still, 201.

Union. During the following two months, Mississippi, Florida, Alabama, and Georgia joined in the effort to start a new Confederacy of states.

Kansas achieved Statehood on January 29, 1861, as the national turmoil began to unfold.[520]

On March 16th the new 16th President, Abraham Lincoln, would inherit the monumental responsibility of stabilizing the nation and protecting against further disruption in the country. In April 1861, Fort Sumter near Charleston, South Carolina, was attacked. The Civil War over slavery and other political conflicts were now a national problem. The entire country would soon experience the violence and killing that had occurred in the Kansas Territory beginning in 1854. The attack at Fort Sumter initiated the unimaginable consequence of future loss of American lives and began catastrophic destruction in the country. In preparation for a civil war, President Lincoln requested an immediate increase of 75,000 [521] men to join the military in an effort to end the insurrection in America.

Andrew Taylor Still answered the call for soldiers to serve the Union. He enlisted in the 9th Kansas Cavalry at Fort Leavenworth in September 1861, and was sent to Kansas City. He was assigned to James Lane's brigade and they soon left for Springfield, Missouri. The brigade remained there until November. Six months later, on April 1, 1862, the 9th Kansas Cavalry was disbanded as the Union adjusted their strategic plans and these men were sent back to their homes. Six weeks later, on May 15, 1862, Andrew Still organized a Kansas Militia Company and was commissioned as a captain for D company. He was promoted to the rank of major, and transferred to the 21st Kansas Militia.[522]

There would be many battles and slaughters committed in the cities and towns across America during the Civil War, leaving some with names that would become infamous, such as Gettysburg and Andersonville. There were other non-military battles that would also become ingrained in history. Unfortunately, one of these atrocities would occur in Kansas in 1863. Kansas would join the list of towns where men were massacred in an unbelievable manner. Kansas had not been forgotten and the town of Lawrence remained one of the most hated places by southern sympathizers. A group of former Missouri border ruffians, many of whom were outright outlaws and bandits, had joined up with the regular Confederate forces. These gangs

---

520   Nichols, Bleeding Kansas, 253.
521   Trowbridge, Andrew Taylor Still, 89.
522   Still, Autobiography, 73-75.

were allowed to drift in and out of voluntary military service as they saw fit. The Confederates had little choice but to utilize any force willing to help their cause. Because the Rebel forces were hopelessly outnumbered and overwhelmingly out-supplied compared to the Union armies, they utilized the gangs to help reinforce their strength.

A large number of these outlaws had previously been involved in the earlier border wars between Kansas and Missouri. Many of them were the same ruffians who had responded to the "call to arms" in both the Wakarusa War and the last foiled attempt by Atchison's 3000-man army to destroy Lawrence. Twice the ruffians had marched across the Kansas border only to be denied the opportunity to destroy the abolitionist towns which were their targets and within their grasp. The ruffians had not forgotten the missed opportunities to punish the abolitionist insurgents and still carried a grudge against Lawrence. One man among them, more than any other, despised the town and waited for an opportunity to burn it to the ground and kill every abolitionist male he could find during the attack. His name was William Clarke Quantrill, although he used an assumed name of Charley Hart while living in Lawrence. He had been threatened by the Lawrence sheriff many times for crimes they suspected he had been involved in, including cattle rustling, thievery, and even murder.[523]

Quantrill eventually fled Lawrence to avoid arrest. He formed a gang of desperados, which included some of the most feared men who had earned their reputations as the most cold-blooded killers alive. His accomplices were infamous bandits with names like Bloody Bill Anderson, Cole Younger, and Frank and Jesse James.

During 1863, Quantrill began to lose control of his men and his position as their leader. He decided he would have to do something extremely daring to regain their respect and his control over them. He devised a plan to attack Lawrence and kill all of the abolitionist men in the community. If he were successful, he hoped the Confederate Army would promote him to the rank of colonel or maybe even a general.

Quantrill's plan to attack Lawrence was perfectly timed because of a recent incident. Union troops had rounded up several women sympathizers and relatives of Quantrill's gang. Bloody Bill Anderson's sister was one of the women arrested under suspicion of aiding guerrillas. She was imprisoned by General Ewing, under federal order number 10, along with sixteen other women, for supporting the southern guerrillas. These women

---

523   Thomas Goodrich, Bloody Dawn, 80.

were jailed in the basement of an old dilapidated building in Kansas City on Grand Avenue. While the women were imprisoned, the structure mysteriously collapsed. Among the dead were Bill Anderson's sister, as well as Cole Younger's cousins, and three other women.[524]

Quantrill and his men now had even greater reason to hate the Union. This tragedy increased his leverage to convince his gang that attacking Lawrence for revenge was justified. Quantrill held a roll call with his leaders to decide who would agree with his plan to attack the abolitionists and their town. Anderson's vote left no doubt, *"Lawrence and be damned. Kill all the males."*[525]

Another leader named Shepherd uttered, *"Lawrence should be wiped out. I'm ready now."*[526] The men were all in agreement, and Cole Younger added his final thoughts, *"I say sack the town."*[527] Quantrill summarized the hatred that had been spoken by his men, and said, *"It's Lawrence, Kill every man and burn every house. Saddle up."*[528] He and his gang would attack Lawrence and *"kill every man big enough to carry a gun."*[529]

The Union Army had suspected that the guerrillas were continuing to increase their efforts to destroy the abolitionists and their towns. *"The summer of 1863 witnessed the culmination of the bandit raids. The two years preceding had been bad enough, but proved to have been mere suggestions of the ultimate objective."*[530]

The Union responded by establishing small camps of cavalry located at intervals only ten miles from one another along the state line to guard against any surprise attack by a large force slipping across the Missouri border. The intervals between them were *"to be covered twice every twenty-four hours by [army] mail carriers, and frequently much oftener by scouting parties who were constantly on the alert."*[531]

The Army did not wait for the guerrillas to attack but was aggressively trying to hunt them down. Albert Greene, a Union soldier in the ranks of the Ninth Kansas Cavalry, Company A, which was camped at Westport, described how he and twenty-five men were ordered to leave their horses

---

524 Schultz, Quantrill's War, 142.
525 Ibid., 145.
526 Ibid.
527 Ibid., 146.
528 Ibid.
529 Ibid., 167.
530 Albert R. Greene, What I Saw of the Quantrill Raid, 431.
531 Ibid.

and travel silently on foot. They were to scour the Sni hills in an attempt to locate the guerrilla bands. This assignment had the potential of being a suicide mission. The Major explained the circumstances they would be facing if they were detected. *"This is a hazardous trip boys...for if you can't whip them you can't run away."* The men were heavily armed with two revolvers and a carbine per man and with belts full of extra ammo. [532]

During their reconnaissance mission, no sighting of the guerrillas was made, but what they did find was *"plenty of horse tracks headed west, and they all had the rebel sign of shoeing—three nails on a side instead of four as is the case of ordinary shoeing."* Every road Greene's scouting party crossed was filled with *"evidence of recent use by horsemen, and the three-nail shoes all pointed in the direction of Kansas.* [They] *also found several large deserted camps, one where the ashes were still warm."*[533] They abandoned their mission, suspecting that the guerrilla attack was already underway and hoping Lawrence and Topeka were not in ashes. Greene and the scouting party returned to Westport to report their observations and receive any updates on Quantrill's movement. They learned that Quantrill had been spotted by Union forces in Kansas and Captain Coleman and his men were riding hard in their saddles in an attempt to catch up with him before he attacked his most likely target, the town of Lawrence.[534]

Two days earlier, on the morning of August 18th, Capt. William Clarke Quantrill's men had joined up with Bill Anderson and his raiders in the area of Lee's Summit. Between the two gangs there would be approximately 300 men and Quantrill would be in command.[535] On the second day of the ride toward Lawrence, Quantrill met up with Col. John Holt, who was leading 104 recruits south to be trained as regular Confederate soldiers. Quantrill convinced Holt to join him in the attack on Lawrence. This addition gave him a total of 450 men. As a consequence, Quantrill's army of ruffians was probably the largest independent guerrilla force ever assembled during the Civil War.[536] This army of raiders set out for Lawrence, traveling at night to avoid detection. If they rode hard, it would take Quantrill three days to reach Lawrence, stopping only to feed the horses and allowing the men a few hours to rest. Since there was not much time for sleeping, some of the men tied themselves to their saddles to keep from falling off.

---

532   Albert R. Greene, What I Saw of the Quantrill Raid, 433.
533   Ibid.
534   Ibid.
535   Schultz, Quantrill's War, 153.
536   Ibid., 154.

As Quantrill passed across the Missouri border, he planned to travel through the smallest Kansas towns possible to avoid attention. The group was too big to escape detection, but the majority of people who saw the army moving west thought they must be Union soldiers. Even when they were eventually spotted by two companies of Union cavalry, totaling 100 men under the command of Capt. Joshua A. Pike, there was no encounter. Captain Pike decided he was hopelessly outnumbered. Furthermore, he did not dispatch any riders westward toward Lawrence to warn the town of possible attack. Instead he sent messengers to the outposts along the northern and southern Kansas borders.[537]

Pike's couriers reached their destinations, including Captain Coleman who was in charge of the outpost at Little Santa Fe. Coleman immediately sent couriers to notify General Ewing's headquarters in Kansas City and another toward Olathe. He requested help from the federal commands to warn Lawrence and to help defend the town from the imminent attacks as quickly as possible. Captain Coleman had eighty men under his command and they left their outpost trying to catch up with Quantrill and intervene before he could launch the unsuspected attack on the town. Captain Coleman and his men would eventually reach the area where Captain Pike's men were camped. Coleman took command of the combined force of 180 men to pursue Quantrill and his forces. Unfortunately, the night was so dark *that the scouts had to strike matches to find the trail.*[538] Despite Captain Coleman's efforts to make up for Captain Pike's mistakes, if not his outright cowardly decision, Coleman would not be able to catch up with Quantrill that night. The closest Coleman and his troops ever came to catching up with Quantrill was a distance of five hours behind the invading force.

Quantrill's plans for night travel and sidestepping Union troops had worked unbelievably well. They were getting closer with each potential stumbling block avoided. The plan to sneak through Kansas quietly had worked beautifully as the men passed through Spring Hill unnoticed as guerrilla raiders.

The courier dispatched by Captain Coleman finally reached Olathe. A Union soldier was immediately sent toward Lawrence to warn of the attack. When he reached the town of Gardner, he learned that Quantrill had already passed through the town. The soldier now feared for his own life if he continued toward Lawrence and returned back to Olathe. As a result,

---

537   Schultz, Quantrill's War, 155.
538   Ibid., 158.

he left Lawrence sleeping silently, unaware of the torrent of death that was moving closer with every hoof beat.[539] Another act of cowardice by a federal soldier had turned the tide against the fate of Lawrence.

Quantrill's only delay after leaving Gardner was his unfamiliarity with the countryside. His army had killed about ten men in an attempt to procure a guide to Lawrence. The problem was finally remedied outside of the small German settlement of Hesper. Quantrill's need for a guide ended with a boy named Jacob Rote. The boy was pulled from a farmhouse outside of the tiny settlement in the middle of the night. Jacob would be thrown up on horseback behind one of the bushwhackers. Hanging onto the ruffian's waist, he was at their mercy. This young guide was forced to lead this massive death squad to Lawrence. Quantrill was now only hours away.[540]

Among those who courageously attempted to warn Lawrence, and many who would die in the process, was an Indian named Pelathe. Although he was thirty miles from Lawrence, he was given the best Kentucky thoroughbred sorrel mare to ride in his attempt to race ahead of Quantrill and give the citizens a warning. After running the horse at a fast pace for two hours, the animal began to fail. After a rubdown, he ran the mare all-out throughout the night. In desperation, he cut her shoulders and rubbed gunpowder into the wounds to spur her on. The horse fell dying from exertion, and Pelathe then tried to run the final miles on foot. As he ran, he came upon a Delaware Indian village at daylight and was given a pony to continue his journey. He reached the town of Lawrence at dawn in time to hear gunfire in the distance. Quantrill and his men had already arrived at 5:15 a.m. a few minutes ahead of him and were actively involved in awakening the Lawrence community to one of the ugliest, most base, and cruelest slaughters imaginable. Quantrill's dream had come true and Lawrence's nightmare had just begun.[541]

There was no defense available in Lawrence. The mayor had passed a city ordinance that all firearms were to be locked up in the armory. The weapons would be passed out to the citizens should there be any threatening attack on the city. It was against city ordinance to carry a firearm in the town. There seemed to be little worry about an invasion since the federal troops were encamped only about ten miles apart between the Missouri border and Lawrence. Lawrence believed it would be impossible for a large force to sneak by federal troops. There was also a feeling of safety in the

539   Schultz, Quantrill's War, 159-160.
540   Ibid., 162.
541   Ibid., 169.

town of 3,000 people which had accumulated a substantial wealth of infrastructure in the community.

Every scare of attack by guerrillas, including Quantrill, had proven to be false, and turned out to be a great inconvenience and irritation to the town. It had become more and more difficult to take these threats seriously. Each alarm had proven costly, with two or three nights sleep lost on guard duty. The mayor had been labeled a fool and held responsible for another false alarm.[542]

When Quantrill arrived at 5:15 a.m. in Lawrence on the morning of August 21, 1863, to lead another assault on the town, which had already suffered two previous attacks, the town was asleep and unguarded. Their weapons were stacked neatly in the armory—Lawrence was defenseless. The younger boys in the town, who were not old enough to fight in the war, were camped in white tents together on the east side of Massachusetts Street. They also had no weapons because the townspeople were afraid they might accidentally hurt themselves. There were twenty boys asleep in the tents that morning and they were the first to die. The group of ruffians who attacked that part of Lawrence opened fire on the tents. Their bullets ripped through the canvas, shredding the boy-soldier's bodies unmercifully, tearing them into pieces. Their blood was splattered on the white canvas tents and continued to darken into crimson as the gunfire continued. The assault on the boys was over in only three minutes. Seventeen of the boys were dead with only a few escaping. One of the boys who had made it out of his tent was shot to his knees as he raced to a house close by for cover. In the front yard he begged for his life pleading for mercy with his hands held high in the air, *"For God's sake don't murder me,"* he cried out to his attacker. The ruffian took his life with another gunshot uttering, *"No quarter for you federal sons of bitches."*[543]

Quantrill sent another group to capture the rebuilt Eldridge House Hotel. He rode up Massachusetts Street in columns six abreast with a large group of his men. They shot at doorways, windows, and any man they encountered. When he and his raiders reached the hotel, they waited for the people who were trapped inside the building to make the first move. The unarmed occupants decided their only hope would be to negotiate with the raiders. They tied a white sheet on a pole and thrust the flag out of a window. They

542   Schultz, Quantrill's War, 151-152.
543   Ibid., 170.

agreed to surrender *"if we are treated as prisoners of war."*[544] Quantrill accepted the conditions of surrender. He then released a large number of his army to form small groups to begin the hunt for the Lawrence men on his death list. They were ordered to sack, burn, and plunder the entire town. His charge to them left little doubt of what he expected, *"Kill! And you will make no mistake. Lawrence is the hotbed and should be thoroughly cleaned, and the only way to cleanse it is to kill! Kill."*[545]

The men followed his orders to the letter. The hotel, shops, and the houses were looted of jewelry, money, apparel, and anything else of value. When they were finished looting they set the buildings on fire as they swept through town. The dead bodies were beginning to accumulate in large numbers as the massacre progressed. No man was spared or given mercy if unlucky enough to come into their gun-sights. *"Men died in the houses and shops, their gardens, and fields, in the streets and alleys, and no amount of pleading, of cries for mercy from victims or their families, made any difference."*[546]

Even the people rounded up by Quantrill's men who were only in Lawrence to buy supplies, conduct business, or merely passing through were not spared. It did not matter. Will Laurie's wife, holding her baby, watched in horror as they shot her husband and her brother-in-law again and again until the men finally remained motionless and dead in the street. The business trip that had brought them to town would never be completed.[547]

Before the massacre ended, there were over *"one hundred and eighty-three men and boys* [who had] *met sudden death that morning."*[548] The slaughter during the rampage was brutal, carried out execution style, and without a shred of mercy. It was done by men who had no morals, nor a conscience, and were totally insensitive to any human suffering. It would later be reported that many wives threw themselves over their husbands trying to shield them. They cried and pleaded with the guerrillas for mercy. The raiders responded by raising the women up just enough to aim shots directly at their husbands' heads. The shot fired to kill George Sergeant was so close it burned his wife's neck as she struggled to protect him.[549]

---

544   Schultz, Quantrill's War, 171.
545   Ibid., 172.
546   Ibid., 175.
547   Ibid., 175.
548   Nichols, Bleeding Kansas, 257.
549   Schultz, Quantrill's War, 203.

This attack had been planned and justified by Quantrill. He had convinced his men that the only hope to win the slavery battle was to cleanse the land of northern abolitionists. Quantrill was able to coerce his men to block all human feelings and ignore the victims during the final moments as they begged for their lives. There would be no quarter or compassion shown toward any man found in Lawrence. He was able to somehow bestow on the raiders their obligation to carry out revenge and he was able to replace their human emotions with indifference and cruelty. The raiders' attitudes were as if they were shooting at targets or scarecrows as they went about murdering boys, sons, husbands, fathers, and grandfathers. As the victims were stacked up in the town, their bodies represented a visual, gruesome monument of hate, a massacre that would never be justified or understood.

Quantrill had his way that ugly morning in Lawrence. Although he had not fired a single shot or lit a match, the pile of dead bodies and the inferno that reduced the city to ashes was his accomplishment. It had been Quantrill who had persuaded the raiders to do his evil deeds.

Two of the most wanted men by Quantrill were lucky enough to have escaped the death penalty. One of them was Charles Robinson. He had left his home only a half hour prior to the attack to head for his barn located on Mount Oread to get horses for cutting hay. From his vantage point he could only watch from a distance the people being murdered and the town he had founded destroyed by fire. The situation was hopeless and he knew it.[550]

The man who was at the top of Quantrill's death list was Senator James Lane. Lane jumped out a back window of his home into a tall corn field and ran in his night shirt escaping to a farmhouse outside of Lawrence. He borrowed clothing and a plow horse and rode around outside of Lawrence warning people that Quantrill had come. Lane's escape was Quantrill's only disappointment that morning. Two years later as Quantrill lay dying, he answered the question of what he had intended to do if Lane had been captured, *"I would have burned him at the stake."*[551]

Some of the people trapped in Lawrence that morning would not be as fortunate as Lane had been in his escape from torture. A gunsmith named Dan Palmer and a friend were standing in the doorway of Palmer's small shop at the end of the business district. They were spotted by the guerrillas who rode up to the shop and wounded both of them. The guerrillas

---

550   Schultz, Quantrill's War, 187.
551   Ibid..

dismounted, tied the two wounded men together, and set the shop on fire. As the small shop went up in flames, the guerrillas threw the bound men into the burning building. The men were able to struggle outside only to be tossed back inside the inferno. Palmer cried out, " *'Oh God, save us.' He raised his hands above his head, and as the flames wrapped him in a sheet of fire he sank back, on his face a look of indescribable agony."* There was laughter and cheering as the guerrillas celebrated their feat. They rode away from their victims and the screams.[552]

The Eldridge House was also now on fire, having been looted of everything valuable. A woman was heard screaming that a black baby had been left inside the hotel and pleaded for help to save the child. Her cries for help had no effect on the guerrillas, and one of them expressed their feelings, *"Burn the God damn little brat."*[553]

At around 9:00 a.m., the first of Ewing's Union soldiers were seen by lookouts located on Mount Oread. Major Preston and his thirty troopers had finally arrived at Lawrence. Captain Coleman's 180 men were only seven miles away. Quantrill's men began their withdrawal.

During Quantrill's escape, his army burned farmhouses and crops and continued killing men on their way back home. They came very close to Andrew Still's family and farmhouse located at Willow Springs. However, since Andrew's home was hidden far inside a field, it went unnoticed. Instead they burned down Mr. Gleason's house, a neighbor of Andrew's, which stood only a few hundred yards away. Other members of the Still family were more fortunate. Many were living in Centropolis, which was twenty-five miles from Lawrence.[554] In Westport, Greene's Company A, was preparing to leave for Kansas. They planned to intercept Quantrill and his guerrillas as they tried to escape to Missouri. Many of company A's men had been *"chiefly raised in Douglas county and largely in the town of Lawrence...and the men were naturally anxious to get after the invaders."*[555]

"Two hours passed. The sun was getting high," and the Westport command had not allowed the cavalry to leave and cut off Quantrill in his attempt to escape. The officers and the men in Company A all agreed that General Ewing, *"was badly at fault and responsible for the ravages that*

---

552   Schultz, Quantrill's War, 211.
553   Ibid., 192 / Goodrich, Bloody Dawn, 115.
554   Clark, Reminiscences, 64.
555   Greene, What I Saw Of The Quantrill Raid, 434.

were being committed in Kansas."[556] The officers were swearing and disgusted with the delay and the command's refusal to allow the men to proceed to Kansas and attack the escaping guerrillas. *"Gradually the spirit of jest and expectancy gave way to dejection and sullen silence. Once in a while a man would explode with an overcharge of profanity, directing his remarks to no one in particular but just looking to the front and soliloquizing in a torrent of 'cuss words' until he was out of breath. Thus our command of eighty seasoned cavalrymen (I speak only of one squadron of the battalion, each of which was equally good) with the finest mounts and armed with a carbine and two Colt's revolvers to the man, with belts and saddle-pockets filled with ammunition, stood and waited for fourteen hours. Whose fault was it? Ask Ewing's adjutant general!"*[557]

When Company A finally was released to pursue Quantrill that night, they traveled twenty miles to Olathe and there they were given false information by a messenger that *"Lawrence is in ashes and every man, woman and child in the town is dead."*[558] Greene would offer a picture of the emotional outbreak from the men after being told of the slaughter. *"I know, and say deliberately after knocking about the world in all sorts of company by land and sea for half a century since, that I never heard such a storm of profanity and invective anywhere. Such cordial spontaneous, unaffected fluent, comprehensive and vociferous cussin' is quite indescribable. And Ewing came in for about as many of those elaborate anathemas as Quantrill."*[559]

The tirade was cut short when one of the colonels called out, *"Never mind, men, we will make them smoke when we reach Missouri—we'll settle this account with them there!"*[560] The men were finally on their way to try to catch the guerrillas in Kansas before they could escape across the border. The company traveled throughout the night to a location just south of Spring Hill. Greene was sent to the top of a hill at about sunrise with a spyglass and *"below me and within a mile was Quantrill's whole command"*... *"Turning the glass on the guerrillas I saw that nearly every man had an extra horse and that these horses were loaded with plunder of every description—what appeared to be bolts of dry goods, bundles of shoes, clothing, etc."*[561]

---

556   Greene, What I Saw Of The Quantrill Raid., 434
557   Ibid., 435.
558   Ibid.
559   Ibid..
560   Ibid.
561   Ibid., 436.

Greene also observed that something had stirred Quantrill's men into running for their horses and quickly saddling the animals for another escape attempt. It was at this moment he saw another column of Union cavalry, under the command of Captain Coleman, approaching Quantrill's guerrillas from the west, with a troop force estimated to be about 200 strong. *"It really began to look as if the hour of vengeance had come."*[562]

However, rather than attacking, a council of war was called by Colonel Lynde and an order was given by him to *"unsaddle and graze the horses for an hour,...that the horses were jaded and must have a rest."*[563] The men were again denied the chance to annihilate Quantrill and his guerrillas. *"Captain Coleman and Flesher cursed Lynde to his face for an arrant coward, and repeated it again and again...with profane adjectives that would have shamed a fishmonger."* Other soldiers joined in the verbal attack, *"swearing a blue streak in their impatience to be up and away."*[564]

Years later, Albert Greene would summarize the missed opportunity with the bitterness of the injustice still haunting him. *"Doubtless the exact spot where this command of five or six hundred men threw away the last chance for annihilating Quantrill and his gang is a meadow or pasture dotted over with white-faced cattle, or it may be the site of some stately farmhouse...and it may be that not one of the inhabitants...ever heard of the crime committed there; but if the ghosts of the men murdered at Lawrence ever hold indignation meetings to abhor the arrest of the sword of justice and vengeance, it is there."*[565]

There were additional delays before a detail of only fourteen men in Company A were allowed to pursue the guerrillas in earnest. Greene considered himself lucky to be chosen as one of the fourteen even when it meant they were to catch and *told, to "Bring on an engagement" with three or four hundred desperadoes"* ... *"the boys only laughed as they realized the odds against them."*[566]

In the pursuit of Quantrill, they rode over a trail of packages that lined the pathway of the withdrawing attackers in their retreat for the Missouri border. *"Our horses shied at it, trampled on it, leaped over it; hundreds of dollars' worth of property, but not a man tried to get any of it."*[567]

562   Greene, What I Saw Of The Quantrill Raid, 436.
563   Ibid., 437.
564   Ibid.
565   Ibid.
566   Ibid., 439.
567   Ibid.

The detail under the leadership of Sergeant Davis eventually caught up with the rearguard of the guerrillas and shots were exchanged. Halting at the mouth of a lane between fence corners, they found cigars by the hundreds on the ground, liquor bottles, silks, and fine dress in great quantity. Davis *"suddenly became serious and swore that he would shoot the first man that dismounted."* One of the men in the detail screamed out he had seen a bankroll of greenbacks and was swinging back to get it when Davis repeated his warning. The man turned back to reengage in the skirmish.[568]

The fight was fought with Quantrill's rearguard for the rest of the day until Davis almost led the detail into a hopeless trap. They were saved when the main trailing Union force came forward to enter the engagement, leaving many of the men in the forward detail wondering why the men in the main forces had not joined them in combat sooner.

The Union Army leadership had shown a disgraceful lack of courage from the beginning to the end of the battle. Questions remained unanswered about the delays and the lack of engagement that was allowed to occur against the guerrillas.

Andrew Still and his family had barely escaped the Quantrill disaster in August 1863; however, six months later they would learn that war was not the only enemy. An epidemic of spinal meningitis was ravaging the country. During February 1864, three of his children, Abe, Susan, and an infant named Marcia Ione, died of the disease. The loss of the children would be devastating to Andrew and his family. This tragedy would later profoundly change Andrew's life.[569]

Despite the suffering that the Still family incurred, there was still a Civil War for them to deal with. The conflict would be coming very close to them as the South was in the planning stages of a new offensive, which would be fought only a few miles away and would require Andrew and his Kansas Militia Unit to participate in the battle. This invasion would be led by General Price and his army. Price had also requested the Missouri guerrilla forces to join his attack to increase his army's strength and likelihood of victory. However, General Price, had a huge problem to overcome if the guerrillas were going to join him in his invasion of Missouri. The guerrilla force that had attacked Lawrence the previous year had fallen apart. The leadership under Quantrill had been lost. Many of the men felt the mass killings at Lawrence had been unjustified. Quantrill's leadership had been

---

568   Greene, What I Saw Of The Quantrill Raid, 440.
569   Still, Autobiography, 87.

challenged by George Todd in front of all the men. Todd was one of his former lieutenants, and proceeded to take over command. Unbelievably, Quantrill submitted to Todd's demands.

Eventually, the large guerrilla force would divide up into smaller groups with individual raiders choosing its leader. The choices were between Bloody Bill Anderson, George Todd, or William Quantrill. Each of these men had his own agenda. Each raider had to decide his fate and how to survive in the lawless environment they lived in. Although they were supposedly fighting a war, they had no government contract, no benefits, and no uniforms with stripes or bars. They were essentially outlaws who would live or die without being rewarded for duty, either honorable or dishonorable, as long as they killed the enemy and advanced whichever side they represented. They were guerrillas—to survive another day was the only thing that mattered.

Quantrill had only thirty-three men who would choose to ride with him. Some of the men, however, were the most feared and notorious of the outlaws and included Jim Younger and brothers—Frank and Jesse James.[570]

Those who chose to go with Bloody Bill Anderson as their leader turned out to be the men who had not objected to the mass murders in Lawrence. Anderson and his guerrillas would have yet another chance to duplicate the savagery.

On September 27, 1864, Bloody Bill Anderson and eighty of his men, dressed in Union blue uniforms, entered the town of Centralia. They hoped to get information regarding General Price's location so they could join forces. While they were in town terrorizing the people, the 11:00 a.m. westbound train from St. Louis was forced to a stop. After stealing all the money from the baggage car, the passengers were forced off the train. Twenty-five Union soldiers were among those riding the train and most of them were recovering from wounds and on their way home. They were lined up and Anderson gave the order to fire. All were killed, and some were also scalped and mutilated.

Following the massacre, Anderson and his men rode out of Centralia. They had been gone only about a half hour when the Thirty-ninth Missouri State Militia rode into town. There were 147 raw recruits in the company, untrained, riding plow horses, supplied with old muzzle-loading weapons. The officer in charge was outraged at seeing the dead bodies of the soldiers. The major ignored the citizens' warnings as they begged him not to

---

570   Schultz, Quantrill's War, 293-294.

chase after the hardened guerrillas with these young, inexperienced boys. Disregarding the warnings, the Union officer began the chase, taking 112 of the recruits into the battle with him.

Not far away, Anderson's men had joined up with George Todd's guerrillas. Together they formed an army of 200 experienced and heavily armed raiders carrying multiple revolvers in their belts. As the Union soldiers rode forward, the guerrillas were out of sight up on a hill just on the other side of a crest. The Union militia would not be able to see them until they came up from below, and by that time, it would be too late. The battle was over in three minutes. One hundred thirty-one Union militiamen were dead, including the major. When added to the twenty-four soldiers killed at the train station, 155 Union soldiers lost their lives. Bloody Bill Anderson had been well named. In a grizzly game of victory, some of Anderson's men began beheading victims and switching them to different bodies. [571]

The raids were not over yet because the guerrillas would be joining General Sterling Price in the October 1864 invasion of Missouri. It was too tempting for the gangs to pass up. They had reunited for one last glorious attack. When General Price invaded Missouri with his 12,000 cavalrymen he wanted the guerrillas to create turmoil in advance of his arrival. Their mission would be to cut telegraph wires to interrupt communications, rally the local sympathizers, disrupt the rail services and destroy bridges. The guerrillas were to do whatever it took to distract the Union forces. Price felt this formula would allow his army to gain momentum and allow his passage through the Union lines. General Price planned to go through Kansas City on his way to St. Louis and demonstrate that the Union was not in control of the State. This invasion was felt by many to be the South's last hope of winning the War. The Confederacy needed Missouri if it had any hope of being victorious. [572]

When the Union became aware of Price's plan to invade Missouri, the Yankee's began their own build-up of troop strength to stop him. Major Andrew Still and his company were transferred to Kansas City and placed under the command of General Curtis, who had been chosen to fight General Price's cavalry and the guerrillas at Westport. It would be a battle that Still and his militia would relish. They were about to fight against some of the guerrillas who had joined Price's army and who had been involved in the

---

571   Schultz, Quantrill's War, 289.
572   Ibid., 282.

raid at Lawrence. These men included Quantrill, Anderson, and Todd.[573] This battle involved a large number of combatants with 27,000 to 35,000 Union and Confederate troops waiting to engage one another. The Union's message to their men was absolute and clear, hold the line and stop the advancement of Price's army.[574]

On October 24, 1864, Major Still and his 21st Militia were part of a ten mile line of defenders fighting at Westport. He described the scene as being *"surrounded by fire, smoke, and blood."* During the battle, Andrew Still was extremely lucky to have avoided injury when he later discovered two bullets had gone through the front and back of his coat without striking his body. He had fortunately escaped injury by only a thread.[575]

During the battle *"some of our boys fell to praying for the Lord to save them."* Major Still leaped from his mule *"and planting my foot close behind some of them, I broke the spell."* Andrew's men fought bravely and he was proud of his company *"throughout the remainder of the fight."*[576]

When the battle was over, Andrew and his men had killed 52 of Price's soldiers and captured 127 horses and 28 cannons. Additionally, 140 of Price's soldiers surrendered under a white flag.[577] Following the defeat of General Price, the 21st Kansas Militia was disbanded. Andrew and his men returned to their homes. Andrew's service in the Civil War had come to an end.[578]

Andrew Still returned home, and the survivors of Price's army would retreat back toward Arkansas. The guerrillas would scatter and escape into hiding. Two days after the battle at Westport, however, Bloody Bill Anderson's luck would run out. On October 26, he was ambushed and shot twice in the head by militiamen near Richmond, Missouri. He had lived only a month following the Centralia massacre. A week later, George Todd was picked off by a Yankee sniper outside of Independence. The bullet struck him in the neck and he was paralyzed when he fell from his horse. He lived about an hour.[579]

The only guerrilla the Union army could not catch was Quantrill. Quantrill always remained one step ahead of being killed or captured

---

573   Schultz, Quantrill's War, 282 / Still, Autobiography, 76-77.
574   Still, Autobiography, 75-78.
575   Ibid., 76.
576   Ibid., 78.
577   Ibid.
578   Ibid., 78-81.
579   Schultz, Quantrill's War, 289-292.

regardless of the northern soldiers' efforts. The Union army finally resorted to forming a Union guerrilla unit of their own to deal with Quantrill and his men. Union guerrillas versus southern guerrillas proved to be much more effective. The Union guerrilla unit was led by a man named Edwin Terrill, who was only nineteen years old. He had formerly fought for the South but had switched sides and was commissioned a captain in the Union army. His assignment was to hunt down Quantrill, and bring him back—dead or alive.[580]

Quantrill knew he was the prey and that he would soon be killed. He felt even more vulnerable when his horse, named Old Charley, became lame and had to be put down. He would utter his own premonition, *"That means my work is done, My career is run. Death is coming, and my end is near."*[581]

On May 10, 1865, Terrill's men had tracked Quantrill to a farmhouse where Quantrill and his men were resting in the barn. Terrill shouted to Quantrill to surrender, but instead, he and his men tried to escape. In the attempt, Quantrill's new horse reared and bucked him off and ran away. Left without a horse to ride, he was forced to run on foot after his gang in an attempt to escape. Two of Quantrill's men saw him running behind them. They reined in their horses and turned back to pick him up. Quantrill was shot in the back as he ran toward his rescuers. The bullet severed his spinal cord, paralyzing him from the waist down. Both of the men who had come back to get him were also cut down by the gunfire.[582]

Terrill and his men mounted their horses to chase down the other guerrillas. As they rode by Quantrill, who was lying paralyzed and face down on the ground, one of the men shot off Quantrill's trigger finger. Quantrill was now the one begging for mercy, *"It is useless to shoot me anymore, I am now a dying man."*[583]

Although having received crippling injuries from the gunshot wounds, Quantrill survived. He was carried from the barnyard that night into the farmhouse and cared for by the Wakefield family. Two days later, Terrill loaded Quantrill into a wagon and transported him to the Louisville's military prison hospital. He suffered for almost a month with his painful injuries and died on June 6, 1865, two months after the Civil War had ended. [584]

---

580   Schultz, Quantrill's War, 298.
581   Ibid.
582   Ibid., 299.
583   Ibid.
584   Ibid., 300.

The War formally came to an end on April 9, 1865, when Gen. Robert E. Lee surrendered and signed the documents for the end of the Confederacy. The War had lasted four years and the death toll had been staggering. The economic destruction was unimaginable. For the people of Kansas and Missouri, it had been a War that had lasted twelve years. It must have been hard for them to believe there could be any lasting peace at all.

CHAPTER TWENTY
A New Science

The Civil War had come to an end, but Andrew's personal war against disease without the use of drugs had just begun. Andrew had been devastated by the loss of his children. He felt the war he had fought had been merciful compared to this tragedy. Although he praised the medical attention the children had received during the meningitis epidemic, the deaths had produced a profound effect on him. Andrew felt his heart *"had been torn and lacerated with grief."*[585]

Several of their children had become ill with a fever and headache. Andrew and his family could not have asked for more attentive care. *"The doctors came and were faithful in their attendance. Day and night they nursed and cared for my sick, and administered their most trustworthy remedies, but all to no purpose. The minister came and consoled us. Surely with the men of God to invoke divine aid, and the men skilled in scientific research, my loved ones would be saved. Any one might hope that between prayers and pills, the angel of death would be driven from our door. But he is a stubborn enemy."*

The first child to die was their seven-year-old daughter, Susan, on February 7, 1864. Without any time for the Still family to recover from the shock of Susan's death, a second child would die. Andrew's oldest son, Abraham, age eleven, would succumb to the infection on the following day. Abraham was only an infant when Andrew and his first wife, Mary, had left northern Missouri and traveled by wagon to join the rest of his family at the Wakarusa mission. Now the family had two children to bury. Two weeks later, on February 23rd, Andrew and his wife, Mary Elvira, would be forced to grieve the loss of a third child. Marcia Ione, their thirteen-month-old daughter, would join her brother and sister in the cemetery. The preachers and doctors had only been able to *"Guess [at] what is the matter?" "What to give, and guess the results? And when dead, guess where he goes?"*

---

585   Still, Autobiography, 87-88.

The house at Baldwin, Kansas, in which Dr. Andrew Taylor Still lived is shown in this photograph, made by Dr. H. G. Swanson, K.C.O.S. dean, during his recent visit to Baldwin. The house, although still occupied, bears mute evidence of Dr. Still's sorrow at the death of three of his children. He boarded up a window at which they were wont to stand to greet him on his return home from calls upon patients. *(Caption with photo in Kirksville Daily Express & News, Sunday, Dcember 3, 1933)*

Andrew was driven to his conclusion, *"that God was not a guessing God, but a God of truth."*[586]

Andrew's loss of the three children drove him to search for a better way to approach the treatment of patients who were stricken with many types of illness. He could not separate health from an inherent, built-in recovery process. He also believed that, *"a loving, intelligent Maker of man...* [would have] *...deposited in his body in some place or throughout the whole system drugs in abundance to cure all infirmities."* He was convinced that, *"all remedies necessary* [for] *health existed within the human body."* He postulated that the secret to the healing process and recovery from disease depended upon releasing the mechanisms of these healing substances to *"relieve the afflicted."* His final conclusion was that *"Man should study and use the drugs compounded in his own body."*[587]

Andrew had observed this process personally during the epidemic that resulted in the death of his children. They had succumbed during an epidemic of spinal meningitis. The medications that had been used to treat his

586   Still, Autobiography, 88-89.
587   Ibid.

children had not worked while other children had survived. Some who had survived the disease had not received any medication at all. He was convinced that all humans had their own internal "drugs" and were capable of surviving by conquering the diseases they encountered. It was Still's belief that the recovery from any disease was based on the individual's level of health and the ability of the body to respond by releasing the protective "internal drugs." Andrew felt that both of these conditions were intimately correlated to both structure and function. His view was that surviving any disease process had no correlation to any of the medications used for treatment by the medical profession. He was convinced recovery was based purely on the components already present within the body and that these substances were the integral defense that gave the body the ability to reverse the disease mechanisms and survive. It would take almost another century for medical science to understand what these processes were and how they worked. Still had suggested a concept that would later be named the science of immunology. It was through the immunologic process that the body was able to respond to disease. This process recognized that recovery from disease was dependent on the body's ability to stimulate cellular and humeral components to interact against the invaders. The immune system had the ability to recognize pathogens and form structural antibody substances and specialized cells. It was this protective response that prevented destruction of vital structures necessary for life. But Andrew, at this point, could only offer conjecture.

Andrew had never forgotten an earlier conversation with J. B. Abbott that had occurred in 1855 while the two of them had been hiding out on the banks of the Kansas River. They were forced into hiding because Sheriff Jones had issued arrest warrants for both of them for their participation in the Blanton Bridge rescue of Jacob Branson.[588]

Abbott was a well-educated man and *"a respected naturalist, art collector, inventor and avid reader."* During their conversation, Abbott had told Andrew that he expected a new field of medicine would emerge and replace the current fields of allopathy, eclecticism, and homeopathy.[589]

The Civil War experience had only enhanced Andrew's beliefs that drugs and their side effects were causing people more harm than help. His greatest criticisms were against the opiates and alcohols that caused addiction.

---

588   Trowbridge, Andrew Taylor Still, 63.
589   Ibid.

He had seen *"legions of men and women staggering to and fro, all over the land, crying for freedom from habits of drugs and drink."*[590]

He blamed the Schools of Medicine, the doctors, and druggists for causing this problem. In his view they had created the epidemic in their treatment of pain. He believed that current medical practice was a failure.[591]

Andrew returned to his study of anatomy to try to find the answers for preventing and curing disease. He continued to dig up Indian bodies and freely admitted he desecrated them with his scalpel in the name of science. He *"studied the dead* [so] *that the living might be benefitted."*[592]

Andrew Still questioned and challenged the medical profession and would eventually alienate them. His condemnation and comments against the use of the medicines commonly prescribed during his lifetime would continue to place him in an adversarial position that eventually labeled him as an eccentric if not a lunatic. His comments were scathing but the worst and most damning was that he had noticed children lived longer where medical care was unavailable. As incorrigible as this comment was, it would later be supported. The majority of the medications used during Still's lifetime would be removed because of side effects and patient safety concerns.

One of the most popular medications used was the mercurial compound Calomel. Taken internally, it had extremely toxic side effects, primarily damaging the renal system. Dilaudid was also available. This addictive narcotic, ten times more potent than morphine, could be purchased as a cough syrup in local drug stores without any controls or monitoring. The drug created a major narcotic addiction in the country during this time period. Whiskey and brandy added to the problem because they made up 61.8 percent of ingredients in most of the prescriptions. Probably the only medication that actually had any benefit in providing treatment was quinine for malaria and its efficacy was greatly disputed by the medical profession. The other accepted treatments commonly used were bleeding, purging, and blistering.[593]

Andrew Still was a product of his family's heritage. Once the Stills believed their path was true, nothing would ever change their minds to abandon their cause. Andrew's strongest mentor, the one who had demonstrated perseverance in his life multiple times, was about to depart. His father, Abraham Still, at the age of seventy-one would contact pneumonia. Even

---

590   Still, Autobiography, 82.
591   Ibid., 84.
592   Ibid., 84.
593   Trowbridge, Andrew Taylor Still, 92.

on his death bed, Abram sent for parishioners whom he believed needed to be saved by accepting Christ. They had to come to his bedside because he was too sick to stand. A man named Mr. Minx was Abraham Still's last "trophy for Christ." Mr. Minx promised Abram he would not sleep *"until his peace was made with God."* Abram died the next day; Mr. Minx was dead within a month.[594]

It was in this stage of Andrew's life, at the age of forty-six, having suffered multiple personal losses to illness and the War, that he absorbed himself in a search for a new medical science. He would rely heavily on his decades of anatomical study. His concept of health and the ability of the body to fight disease were based on structure and function in the maintenance of the dynamic process. It was this concept that had been solidified in his thinking. Andrew would announce on June 22, 1874, as the day he realized his discovery had been achieved and his new medical science would benefit the world. [595]

His new science was based on anatomy and physiology. It incorporated both structure and function of the body. He had recognized that the inherent drugs [immune complexes] for curing diseases were already present in the body. He based his treatment on the principles that the body worked as a machine. In his view, the body's anatomical functions could be compared to the operative mechanisms of machinery. The drive-wheels, pinions, cups, arms, and shafts shared the same relationships as those of ligaments, muscles, and the framework of bones. The nerves worked by distributing the electric signals to the distant parts. The heart was a pump and supplied energy by moving the blood to every other part of the body, which allowed the other parts to function. He postulated that if these mechanisms were interrupted temporarily, the body's structure and function would be damaged and this would result in an abnormality—a process known as disease.[596] He believed that all diseases were only effects of mechanical dysfunction and not individual entities.

Andrew lived in a world unaware of bacteria and viruses. Penicillin would not be discovered for 80 years. Therefore, Andrew based his medical science on the knowledge available to him in the mid 1800s. As preposterous as some of his theories were, he would bring a genuine change into medicine. He would modify the way doctors thought about the human body

---

594   Adams, In God We Trust, 193.
595   Still, Autobiography, 85.
596   Ibid., 93-94.

and the treatment of their patients. By treating the entire patient, the holistic approach of structure and function had been born. He believed patients were in their optimal health when structure and function were correct. He also believed this balance would enhance the ability to survive in the environment. Drugs, according to his view, were only palliative and not without side effects. Furthermore, many were toxic and damaging, and narcotics and alcohol were addictive substances and needed to be controlled. He also suggested that alcoholism was an illness rather than a moral weakness; therefore, he was one of the first doctors to contemplate this concept.[597]

Andrew had undergone other scientific changes in his thinking and had embraced both spiritualism and the naturalistic philosophy of evolution. He subscribed to the concepts which had recently been introduced by Herbert Spencer, and was familiar with the works of A. R. Wallace, as well as Charles Darwin.[598]

When Andrew was ready to announce his medical discoveries to the academic community, he chose Baker University in Baldwin, Kansas, as the place for the introduction. The University had been a major part of his life. Andrew's father had been the one who had made the motion to the college planning committee to name the university after the Methodist Bishop, Osman C. Baker.[599] The Still family had donated 640 acres of land for its development, and Andrew and his brother, Thomas Still, were on the committee that had selected the building site on the property. Andrew's generosity to the university exceeded all expectations when he and two of his brothers also donated another 480 acres of land to help establish the development of the town of Palmyra (later named Baldwin). The town would serve as the community for the school.[600]

To support the actual construction of the university, Andrew and his brother, with two other men, purchased a 40-horsepower steam-sawmill. Andrew then learned how to operate the sawmill. For the next five years, when he was not practicing medicine, he milled the wood used to build the college structures.[601]

However, when he requested permission to make the announcement regarding his new medical science at Baker University, they rejected him. Andrew was devastated. *"When I asked the privilege of explaining*

---

597   Still, Autobiography, 115.
598   Trowbridge, Andrew Taylor Still, 116.
599   Ibid., 77.
600   Still, Autobiography, 96-97.
601   Ibid., 97.

Osteopathy in the Baldwin University the doors of the structure I had helped build were closed against me."[602]

Andrew's ideas were too radical of a departure from the normally accepted drug treatments for disease used by organized medicine. In addition, his support of evolution and spiritualism alienated the church, as well as some of his own family members. Some began to question his sanity. There were public prayers offered in church by men and women in the congregation to save his *"soul from hell."* Andrew blamed the unexpected reaction by his former friends and neighbors as the result of a statement he had made that *"God has no use for drugs in disease."*[603]

He stayed in Kansas for three months after being rejected by Baker University and was ostracized by the community. As a result of the criticism he received from the community, Andrew packed his bags and left the state of Kansas. It must have been an extremely difficult decision for him to make. He was leaving his home and the state in which he had served as a Legislative representative. He had fought in the Kansas militia protecting the borders and had practiced medicine among the settlers and Shawnee Indians. He had reached adulthood and had raised his family on the Prairie. Regardless of the past, the insults he now suffered were too great. His dedication and commitment to the University had been unappreciated, and his new medical science was scoffed at.[604]

After leaving Kansas, he visited his brother, Edward Still, who lived in Macon, Missouri. He planned to make a new beginning in Missouri with his family joining him in the future. Most of all, he and his family needed relief from the gossip, the whispers of Andrew's insanity, and the charges of blasphemy against the church doctrines.

Before arriving in Macon, Andrew had been aware that his brother, Edward, had been suffering from a back injury for an extended period of time. After he arrived, he also learned that his brother had been taking seventy-five bottles of opiate annually for the injury. Andrew knew his brother was addicted to the medication and stopped the narcotics. He began treating Edward by utilizing musculoskeletal manipulation for pain relief. Edward recovered and was able to walk again among the people in the town of Macon.

602　Still, Autobiography, 97.
603　Ibid.
604　Ibid., 98.

As the people who lived in the town observed Edward's return to practice and became aware that Andrew was responsible for his recovery, Andrew's reputation as a doctor began to grow in the community. He would be successful in treating a bloody gastrointestinal outbreak, called flux, which had become an epidemic in Missouri. Without the use of drugs he had been successful in controlling the symptoms of this devastating disease. His reputation grew among the citizens and his practice began to flourish until the local Methodist minister heard about *"his miraculous cures and how they had been accomplished by the laying on of hands."* [605]

The minister declared that Dr. Still was possessed by an unnatural spirit and was dangerous. Andrew would also learn during this attack, that even Edward, his brother, had avoided sending him patients. Edward had received a letter from their brother, James Still. In it, James had questioned Andrew's sanity. Eventually, Edward gave Andrew the letter to read in an effort to help him understand the position he was in. From the letter it was clear that James, his own brother, had abandoned him as a result of his new medical concepts and his association with evolutionary beliefs. [606]

Andrew knew his reputation had now been ruined in Macon. He looked northward at the town of Kirksville. This town was located thirty miles north, and was a possible practice site. He had previously traveled there and had become acquainted with some of the residents of the community. They had been friendly and accommodating. He needed a place to live and there was urgency in his decision. Andrew's wife, Mary Elvira, had already sold their farm in Kansas. To make matters worse, the sale had occurred during the 1874 grasshopper invasion. As a result of this agricultural disaster, the sale had not brought in as much money as they had hoped for. The family was now facing a potential economic disaster, and their ability to overcome the difficulties remained totally uncertain. [607]

While in Kirksville, Andrew was fortunate to befriend a woman who would allow him to stay at her boarding house for two months. Furthermore, she was willing to delay any payment. Another opportunity presented itself when a Kirksville doctor helped support him with patient referrals. That doctor had heard rumors of Andrew's success in treating children with flux while practicing in Macon. Then a business owner named Charley Chinn allowed him to rent a small office space in his building. Their terms were based on the principle that other Kirksville residents had extended to him,

605   Still, Frontier Doctor, 93.
606   Ibid., 92-94.
607   Ibid., 95.

pay when you can afford to do so. In addition, Chinn was a constant advocate for Andrew and encouraged him repeatedly saying, *"One day, you will outride the storm."*[608]

Despite opportunities and much encouragement, Andrew continued to struggle with a meager medical practice. After Mary and the children arrived in Kirksville, they were forced to witness the truth. Andrew's reputation as a doctor was still in question, and his ability to earn a living as a physician would continue to decline.

Once again, the will for the family to survive and to persevere when required, would be needed. Everyone would have to pull together. It was a pattern that had been repeated for generations by the Stills. It was their heritage. The Moore family had stood up to the challenge in Abb's Valley against the Shawnee Indians in 1774. Abram and Martha Still had fought every encounter when challenged about being abolitionists. They would not have survived in northern Missouri if the children had not rallied to provide for the family's basic needs. Now, almost thirty years later, Andrew Still and his family were in Kirksville, Missouri. They were faced with economic survival. They had been criticized, maligned, and attacked by the Methodist church for Andrew's views on evolution, and his attacks on the medical profession. It was time, once again, for the members of the Still family to endure hardship. They were again forced to believe in their ability to overcome adversity.

It must have been extremely painful for Andrew to turn his back on the Methodist religion since this church had formerly represented his father's entire life. It was an organization that had permeated their existence. Andrew and his family had dedicated their lives to supporting Abram's ministry regardless of the personal hardships they all suffered.

Now, Andrew and Mary Still's children would have to respond as Andrew and his brothers had done in 1837 when they faced poverty in the wilderness of northern Missouri. Andrew and Mary Elvira's children accepted their role and took on the responsibility of helping the family to survive. The brothers went to work to support each other and their parents. Ten-year-old Charley took a job in the local printing office as an apprentice. Harry and Herman, who were twins, worked at odd jobs after school to help earn money for the family's basic needs. Mary Elvira returned to selling magazines to add to the income.

---

608   Still, *Frontier Doctor*, 96.

These new sets of problems were a direct result of Andrew's outspoken beliefs. He had become a maverick in medicine and had attacked the entire medical profession, calling them all a failure. He had gone so far as to tie the medical treatment issue to religion and had infamously said, *"God has no use for drugs in disease."*[609] Consequently, Andrew and his entire family suffered the direct stigma of his beliefs.

Despite his being labeled a maverick, Andrew's medical practice in Kirksville somehow grew slowly. The obstacles he had created were gigantic barriers for patients to come to him for treatment. He refused to be recognized or associated with the initials "M.D." He would not use drugs and openly criticized the doctors in the community who did. This stance left the patients and the community to only guess at what he was or what to call him other than their doctor. Andrew also struggled with this ambivalence and the advertisement of his medical practice used the titles, "magnetic healer" and "lightning bonesetter" among many others.[610]

Because of Andrew's small number of patients in Kirksville, he was forced to travel to other small communities located in the surrounding areas in the hope of expanding his practice. This strategy proved to be successful and his visit to each community was preceded by handbills and announcements of the date he would arrive. The advertising eventually resulted in creating an atmosphere similar to theatrical entertainment. During these public displays, he would perform manipulation in front of a crowd. The audience would observe him as he performed these treatments: setting displaced bones, realigning spines, and relieving other musculoskeletal problems. The effect of this kind of treatment was powerful. A neighbor would openly witness a friend's health problem being treated. They would see the condition improved or cured right before their own eyes. Then they would hear their neighbor's testimony of successfully being relieved of their pain and discomfort. Eventually, Andrew's medical success gained him notoriety, and it would begin to bring patients from the surrounding areas into Kirksville for treatment.

While the itinerant medical practice proved to be successful, it was exhausting. Andrew's wife saw the effects on her husband's health and encouraged him to stay at home in Kirksville. She believed the patients would now come to see him since he had reestablished his reputation.[611]

---

609   Still, Autobiography, 97.
610   Still, Frontier Doctor, 98.
611   Ibid., 99-100.

Even though Andrew's practice had grown, the income had not improved a great deal. This financial stress was the result of Andrew's kindness to his patients. Many of them were poor, but he would not deny treatment to anyone. Even though he was struggling financially, Andrew continued to buy groceries to help the poor who lived near him, despite the fact that he could hardly afford food for his own family. According to his family the *"wolf was never far from their door."*[612] Andrew had not changed in his generosity since childhood when he had given away the puppies he raised and was supposed to sell to help his family. The poor finances of his medical practice, however, were about to improve.

Ironically, while Andrew's reputation was being compromised by the Methodist Church (to which his family had dedicated their lives), it would be another religious denomination that would come to Andrew's defense. The Presbyterian minister in Kirksville, who had one of the largest churches in the community, had a daughter who was crippled and unable to walk. The minister's wife had requested Andrew to evaluate the girl and possibly offer treatment. Some of the parishioners originally from Macon, who had recently joined the Presbyterian Church in Kirksville, were aware of Andrew's reputation and treatments. They pressured the minister to forbid Andrew from treating his daughter. They considered his healing power to be possessed by the Devil. The Presbyterian minister gave into the pressure of his congregation and denied Andrew the medical consultation. The minister's wife, however, did not give in, and when her husband left Kirksville for a week, Andrew was again asked to examine and treat the girl. Andrew agreed to examine the child at night to protect the minister's wife. Andrew treated her twice during the week her father was absent. After the second treatment, the child was able to walk down a flight of stairs without help. The daughter recovered and joined her father in front of his congregation where the minister praised Andrew and his medical ability. His support of Andrew completely changed the attitude of the people regarding his treatment philosophy. People were soon openly seeking him out. This new confidence in Andrew and his medical practice were also felt by his wife and children who were now respected by the community for the first time since arriving in town.[613]

This recent path of success by Andrew and his family would be short-lived. During the fall of 1876, Andrew was stricken with a severe bout of

---

612   Still, Frontier Doctor, 100-101.
613   Ibid., 101-102.

typhoid fever. He suffered with the complications of the disease for months, and slowly recovered during June 1877. Andrew had become emaciated with significant muscle loss. He was very unsteady on his feet and required a cane to walk. His hair and beard turned gray, and when he was seen in town, the people in Kirksville would affectionately refer to him as the *"old Doctor."*[614]

Since Andrew was unable to practice medicine in his current state of health, he asked for financial aid from the federal government for a hernia he had suffered while fighting in the Civil War. His petition was denied by the Federal Bureau of Pensions on November 20, 1877, because he had fought under orders from the state militia and not the Union army. Andrew was angry and felt his military service had been ignored by his country. He felt he had been denied a pension that he had earned in battle. During this time, he felt helpless and became depressed. He responded in the only way he knew how to express his disappointment. *"If they were going to turn me down, why didn't they let me know sooner?"* It had taken the bureau twenty-three months to respond to his petition. During this two-year span he suffered both mentally and physically.[615]

This period of time was also financially frustrating. Andrew's convalescence was a long one, and his inability to treat patients because of his lack of physical strength resulted in another downturn in his income. He had little choice but to begin exercising to recover his vitality. He took walks for a half-mile each morning and was careful with his diet. He began seeing a small number of patients in an effort to build his stamina. Eventually, he would become strong enough to increase his practice and to travel again to the surrounding communities. By 1880, he had regained his health to the degree that he opened a branch office in Hannibal, Missouri. His success with treating patients in multiple locations resulted in Andrew's practice growing rapidly once again. As his reputation grew, so did his financial strength. One of the local doctors in Hannibal felt threatened by Andrew's success and filed a complaint against him. Andrew was charged with practicing medicine in Hannibal without a license. The case was argued before a jury and the case was dismissed in favor of Andrew. The trial had generated a great deal of publicity, which only enhanced Andrew's reputation and the number of patients who wanted to see him.[616]

---

614   Still, Frontier Doctor, 103 / Still, Autobiography, 112.
615   Still, Frontier Doctor, 105.
616   Ibid., 109-111.

It was impossible, however, for Andrew to take care of all the patients who asked for appointments. The time he took for travel to other communities also interfered. The only choice he had to solve this conundrum was to stay in one location, and to begin thinking about a process to educate other people to administer treatment based on his medical philosophy.[617]

Accomplishing this plan was not going to be easy. It would take time for Andrew to develop a program and the curriculum needed for training other practitioners. In the meantime, he had an even more urgent problem to deal with. There were an increasing number of patients arriving in Kirksville to see him. Andrew often had to reserve all the rooms in the hotels in Kirksville to accommodate them. The burden of the patient load caused Andrew's wife great concern. She was acutely aware of the stress it was causing him to treat the ever-increasing numbers. She pleaded with him to rest and to conserve his strength.[618]

As a result of his success in Kirksville, he also had offers coming in from other communities, requesting him to consider attractive financial compensation to leave and move his practice to their communities. Andrew had no desire to leave Kirksville or the people who had helped him overcome financial ruin. This was the community that had helped him obtain both professional and financial success.[619]

Andrew's patient load continued to increase and provided him with financial growth. Since it was no longer necessary for the Still children to help support their parents, two of Andrew's sons, Charley and Herman, enlisted in the Army. This event was not popular with their father, however, because Andrew counted on his sons to help him with the treatment of the patients in his escalated and growing medical practice.[620]

In 1892, Andrew was approached by two young men who asked him to teach them his new science of medicine. He agreed to accept them as medical students and the tuition was set at one-hundred dollars each. The young men had not had any formal education in anatomy or any other medical sciences. One of the students was a farm boy who would work with Andrew for twelve months. When he left the preceptor training, Andrew felt he had learned to be a "fairly good operator." The second student was a lightning-rod peddler who Andrew had treated for asthma when he was a child and

---

617   Still, Frontier Doctor, 109-111.
618   Ibid., 112.
619   Ibid., 115.
620   Ibid., 118.

Picture of Dr Still

had obtained good results. The young man stayed with him a year or two and left to enter a medical school. Andrew summarized his departure as a person who would know only a *"little about either system."*[621]

This individual student training had not proven fruitful. The education of a Still-trained practitioner was going to require a more formal approach with a curriculum and a school facility. If Andrew was going to educate

---

621   Still, Autobiography, 126.

other doctors to help him, it could not be done efficiently only one at a time. He needed a classroom with multiple students. He also needed help from someone to teach a formal class in basic human anatomy. And he needed a name for his new medical science that defined his philosophy and that set it apart from the better known drug-based treatment, which was called allopathy.

CHAPTER TWENTY-ONE
The American School of Osteopathy

The name of Still's new medical philosophy, which was based on treatment without using drugs, would be called Osteopathy. He would combine two Greek words, osteon, and pathine, which literally meant "bone suffering" in naming the science in 1885.[622] When he was told that the word Osteopathy was not in the dictionary, Andrew countered, *"I know it, but we are going to put it there."*[623]

Andrew had no other choice but to open a school. He was exhausted with the workload and it had become impossible for him to see the number of patients arriving in Kirksville. By 1887, Andrew had patients coming to him for treatment by the wagon and train loads. Patients often had to endure long periods of waiting and at times received their treatment on his porch or lawn.[624]

Whether it was reasonable or financially prudent to begin an Osteopathic school in Kirksville at the age of sixty-three, during the month of December 1891, Andrew Still began the process anyway. The reality of providing individual medical care to the hoards of patients coming to see him was impossible to continue. He had to plan for both the present and future generations seeking Osteopathic care, and there was no other choice than *"to open a small school."*[625]

Andrew asked his son, Charley, to obtain a charter for the school that would serve as the training facility and be called the American School of Osteopathy. Charley had no legal training and he relied on a local judge in Kirksville to assist in the establishment of the Osteopathic School.[626] Although Judge Ellison was very skeptical of the idea, he did not deny that Andrew was a very gifted medical practitioner. However, he had grave doubts that the school would be successful because he was convinced that the treatment methods were powers only Andrew possessed and could not be

622   Trowbridge, Andrew Taylor Still, 140.
623   Georgia Walter, The First School of Osteopathic Medicine, 2.
624   Ibid.
625   Ibid., 3.
626   Still, Frontier Doctor, 137.

taught to others. He expressed his concerns to Charley pronouncing that, *"when he* [Andrew] *dies, his system will die with him."*[627]

The judge voiced many other concerns in an effort to discourage Charley from going forward with the idea. From a business perspective there were too many flaws that had not been resolved to believe that an Osteopathic School could be successful. Among the discrepancies were the absence of a school building and teachers to serve as faculty. The proposed school had not developed goals or a formal medical curriculum. He was concerned that even if a curriculum were developed, there was no guarantee the Osteopathic training philosophy would be recognized by the state. That meant the students who graduated would not be approved or eligible for receiving a medical license. In addition, the graduates of the school would receive a new and unknown medical degree with a title of "Diplomat of Osteopathy" because Andrew Still refused to issue the accepted and recognized "Doctor of Medicine degree." Also, there was little doubt that the Osteopathic graduates would not be welcomed into the medical profession, since Andrew continued to lambast and criticize the MDs and their use of drugs. Charley could not deny any of the concerns the judge expressed about starting the new school and agreed with his assessments and risks of failure.[628]

Against the judge's advice, the application process was started in order to obtain a charter. When the document was completed and the corporate structure had been organized, Charley filed the document with the state of Missouri.

On May 10, 1892, Andrew received notification from the state capital that his corporate charter for an American School of Osteopathy had been approved. The primary shareholders in the corporation, with a capital stock certificate valued at five thousand dollars, would be divided among the Still family and included only two other shareholders who were not relatives. Andrew made sure that he held the majority and controlling interest in the shares.[629]

On May 14, 1892, the Certificate of Incorporation had worked its way through the political process at the Missouri state capital, and the Adair County Courthouse, followed by the filing of the legal document with the Office of the Secretary of State. At this juncture the American

---

627   Still, Frontier Doctor, 137.
628   Ibid., 137-138.
629   Walter, The First School of Osteopathic Medicine, 3.

School of Osteopathy had become a legal corporate body. In the Articles of Incorporation the stated purpose of the school was *"to improve our system of surgery, midwifery, and treatment of diseases in which the adjustment of the bones is the leading feature of the school of pathology. Also to instruct and qualify students that they may lawfully practice the Science of Osteopathy as taught and practiced by A. T. Still."*[630]

The next hurdle Andrew faced to get the school on solid ground was finding a competent academician to teach anatomy. It was serendipitous that William Smith, M.D. happened to be in Kirksville selling medical books and equipment for the A. S. Aloc Company. As he visited the local doctors in Kirksville, he heard many complaints about Andrew Still. They

William Smith
Used with permission of Museum of Osteopathic Medicine℠, [1984.977.14]

630   Walter, The First School of Osteopathic Medicine, 3-5.

accused him of stealing their patients and ruining their business. They were convinced that he was a quack. Dr. Smith, who was a graduate of the Royal College of Physicians and Surgeons of Edinburgh, Scotland, decided to help them expose Andrew and his Osteopathic philosophy. He planned to visit with Andrew and discuss the Osteopathic treatment methods. The local physicians suggested to Dr. Smith that he not reveal his medical background and expertise in his effort.

The meeting between Andrew and William Smith took place, and after a lengthy discussion about the Osteopathic medical philosophy, Andrew challenged Dr. Smith to find a fault with his premise. William Smith embraced Andrew's Osteopathic treatment philosophy, and rather than trying to destroy Andrew, he took a supportive role. He agreed to join Andrew and assist him in his effort to open the American School of Osteopathy in the fall of 1892. One of Smith's conditions was that he had to be a student in the first class. Andrew had found someone he needed, an anatomist who would teach in the new school. Andrew's role would be to instruct the students in the Osteopathic treatment curriculum, and Smith's responsibility was to teach a formal course in human anatomy.

The original schoolhouse.
Used with permission of Museum of Osteopathic Medicine^SM, [1991.1402.02]

First Official Class of Osteopathic Medicine.
Used with permission of Museum of Osteopathic Medicine^{SM}, [2007.09.01]

On October 3, 1892, the first class assembled in a small house that served as a classroom. The American School of Osteopathy had a home. There were initially only ten students accepted in the class, but this number would be expanded dramatically to twenty-one by the winter of 1893.[631]

The term for the first class would last only four months and would end in March 1893. William Smith, M.D. became the only one in the class whom Andrew Still considered qualified, and he became the first graduate of the American School of Osteopathy. He received a handwritten diploma signed by Andrew Still on February 15, 1893. The other eighteen members of his first class would continue their studies and would not complete the requirements for graduation until 1894.[632]

After the entire class had graduated, rather than feeling satisfaction, Andrew felt disappointment with the outcome of the class. He believed that the students in the class lacked the true meaning and understanding of the Osteopathic philosophy. He decided he had made a mistake in his efforts to train other practitioners to administer the use of Osteopathic treatments.

---

631   Walter, The First School of Osteopathic Medicine, 3-5.
632   Ibid., 7.

Andrew made the decision to close the school. However, he was challenged by a local Catholic priest to continue the Osteopathic educational process. The priest advised him to raise the intellectual standards of the students who were selected for admission into the school.[633]

After Andrew reconsidered the admissions requirements, he began selecting the second class. Thirty students qualified and were allowed to enter the school. He also had an additional challenge to overcome. He had to find a replacement for Dr. Smith to teach human anatomy because Smith had decided to leave Kirksville and enter private practice. He was fortunate to enlist a woman named Jeanette Hubbard Bolles, who had graduated in his first class, to fill the position.

When the second class had completed the Osteopathic curriculum, Andrew began to believe in the ability of the school to train others to deliver drugless treatment and became more accepting of the students in the training process.

The rapid growth of Andrew's patient volume continued. This workload was also coupled with an increase in the number of students applying to the school for training. He had created another major problem because it was impossible for him to accommodate all the treatment and educational demands that were asked of him. In an effort to try and deal with their problems, Andrew decided not to accept any new students for enrollment in a third class scheduled to begin in 1894. He needed to take time off to build the infrastructure necessary to serve both the swelling population of students and the number of patients arriving in Kirksville. The initial decision to stop admissions of any new students into a third year class for training resulted in students begging him to reconsider and to change his mind. Reluctantly, Andrew Still gave in but limited the class size drastically. He would only select six students for entrance into the third class. He simply had to have time to supervise the construction of a facility large enough to handle both the student and patient volume that had become insatiable at the institution.

Andrew had begun supervising construction of the large infirmary building, which was erected on the site where the small school building had been located. The initial two-room school building was moved directly across the street to accommodate the new site. After a year and a half, on January 10, 1895, the new infirmary building and training facility was dedicated with a formal ceremony. That October of 1895, the incoming fourth

---

633   Walter, The First School of Osteopathic Medicine, 7-9.

class was increased to twenty-eight students while application numbers continued to explode. Another class of twenty-three students was admitted in January 1896, with the expanded number of fifty-one students.

The year 1896 was a pivotal time of growth for Andrew's Osteopathic School. That year, when the students admitted to the school were added to the existing classes, the total number suddenly jumped to 102 students studying Osteopathy in the small town of Kirksville.[634]

Andrew believed that he had finally achieved his dream of meeting student and patient needs. By expanding the school and the infirmary accommodations, he thought the additions would be enough to satisfy the space needed for the patients and students. The buildings, however, had already been outgrown.

Andrew responded to the continued shortage of building space by adding annexes to meet the overflowing capacity. By July 1896, the space had been trebled in size and was planned to accommodate up to 500 students and provide care for one thousand patients.

After annexes were attached to the main four-story building in December 1896, thirty thousand square-feet, and sixty-seven rooms became available. The cost of the facility was $80,000.[635] Whether he desired to become an entrepreneur or not, at the age of sixty-eight, Andrew had gone from a starving medical practitioner to unimaginable wealth in the last four years.

Andrew and his school would experience another record-breaking success that same year. On November 6, 1896, Vermont passed legislation that granted Osteopathic physicians licensure and the legal right to practice medicine in the state. For the first time Osteopathy was formally recognized as a separate branch of medicine in America.[636]

During the summer of 1896, Dr. William Smith, returned to Kirksville to rejoin Andrew's faculty at the school. He would be reappointed to the position as the head of the anatomy department.

The following year, 1897, brought many other significant changes to Andrew's American School of Osteopathy, which was now frequently referred to as (ASO). He added courses to strengthen the school's curriculum. These studies included the fields of *"osteology, mycology, neurology, angiology, histology, syndesmology, chemistry, and physics."*[637] That same

---

634 Walter, The First School of Osteopathic Medicine, 22.
635 Ibid.
636 Ibid., 31.
637 Ibid., 26.

year Andrew would have the satisfaction of having two more states pass legislation legalizing the practice of Osteopathy within their borders. North Dakota's Osteopathic licensure law was enacted in February 1897, and the state of Missouri, recognized as the home of Osteopathy, would complete the licensure process on March 4.[638]

Obtaining a Missouri medical license had been a difficult political battle for Osteopathic physicians. Past attempts for licensure had been successfully blocked by the state's medical doctors who had utilized Gov. William J. Stone's veto powers in overturning any bill that favored Osteopathic medicine. However, a new bill and a new Missouri governor, Lon V. Stephens, were now in place and his policies supported the Osteopathic medical profession. That year there would be no veto, and Governor Stephens signed the Osteopathy licensure bill into law. For the first time in Missouri, the Osteopathic profession was placed on an equal footing with the medical doctors who practiced there.[639]

Another milestone for Osteopathic organizational development occurred when sixteen of Andrew's ASO students met to discuss forming a national organization. They planned to draft a constitution of uniform governance. The organization's first formal meeting was held on April 19, 1897, and this entity would eventually become the foundation for the American Osteopathic Association.[640]

The following year, in 1898, Andrew's ASO continued to strengthen curriculum by adding course requirements in psychology, pathology, venereal diseases, public health, and medical jurisprudence. These additional classes continued to enhance the curriculum and brought the standards up to the level of traditional medical schools. However, without question, Andrew and many other conservative Osteopathic faculty held firm against adding any course work involving drug therapy. Andrew had to give in and finally allowed surgery to be added to the formal curriculum in 1898, but he was adamant in his belief that surgery could only be performed when all other treatments had failed. Andrew was forced to recognize the patients' surgical needs at the ASO infirmary. Without surgical training his medical faculty had no other choice but to refer the surgical patients to other cities. As the number of surgical patients increased, the referral process was even more burdensome. To meet the surgical challenge, the

---

638   Walter, The First School of Osteopathic Medicine, 31-32.
639   Ibid.
640   Ibid., 34.

maternity hospital was converted into a surgical hospital and named A. T. Still Surgical Sanitarium after its founder. A surgical department was formed and put under the direction of Dr. William Smith, M.D., D.O., and his colleague, J. B. Littlejohn, M.D., both having graduated from medical schools in Scotland. [641]

At the turn of the century Andrew Still's school would continue to experience phenomenal growth. Seven-hundred students had enrolled at ASO with a supporting faculty of eighteen. Andrew would strive to keep the college on the cutting edge of technology and to provide the best care possible for patients. As an example of this, within two years following Rontgen's discovery of the use of x-ray in diagnosis of bone disease, Andrew had x-ray equipment installed in the infirmary. The x-ray machine would be the first one west of the Mississippi. He also organized an entire department of radiology at the ASO facility.[642]

The reputation and success of Osteopathy began to spread across the entire country as hundreds of graduates from ASO began to return to their hometowns to practice. In many cases the graduates moved to new areas to open practices where no medical care had previously existed. The increase in the number of graduates from the Osteopathic schools began to foster other men to think of and experiment with variations in manipulative treatment methods. Many would eventually open their own training facilities. David Daniel Palmer, who visited and studied with Dr. Still would begin a "chiropractic" school of treatment.[643]

Another one of Andrew Still's graduates, Marcus Ward, D.O.M.D., would begin his own competitive school of Osteopathy in Kirksville, which he named the Columbian School of Osteopathy. Dr. Ward would add the use of drugs to his curriculum and if the students stayed for a third year of training in medicine and surgery they would also receive a dual D.O.M.D. degree. The school would ultimately fail and the remaining students were transferred to ASO to complete their training.[644]

Osteopathic schools began to open their doors across the country with many of the schools accused of being diploma mills. These included the initial school in Kansas City and another school located in Milwaukee in 1901. A Denver, Colorado, school opened and failed in 1904, as well as a school located in Chillicothe, Ohio. A troubled Atlantic Osteopathic school

---

641   Walter, The First School of Osteopathic Medicine, 28.
642   Ibid.
643   Ibid., 33.
644   Ibid., 46-47.

was moved to New York but failed in 1905. Many of these schools would sign merger agreements with ASO in an attempt to have their students complete their education. The Des Moines College would undergo several transitions before finally being stabilized. The Chicago College started by the former faculty members of ASO, the Littlejohn brothers, would be successful and remained on solid footing.[645] A later attempt in Kansas City to organize another Osteopathic College in 1916 would be successful.

The voice of the American Osteopathic Association would begin to be heard in 1902, and shifted authority away from the town of Kirksville and its founder, Andrew Taylor Still, to the national organization which had been in existence and growing for five years. The first major change made by the AOA organization resulted when they voted to raise the educational standards for graduation from an approved Osteopathic institution. Their recommendation for graduation raised the training requirement to three years and nine months. With this move in governance, the Osteopathic Medical profession had developed a political national presence and the ability to direct the educational process in a uniform and consistent manner. The Osteopathic training environment would no longer be solely under the control of Andrew Still and his American School of Osteopathy. The AOA would embody the entire professional organization and culture that had grown into a national organization.[646]

In 1907, Andrew Still had reached the age of seventy-nine and he would not be able to keep up the pace he had maintained for almost seventeen years when the ASO had been opened. To add to his responsibilities and concerns, his wife and strongest supporter had become ill. She suffered major health problems which continued to deteriorate to the degree that she could not even leave her home. The American School of Osteopathy and the practice at the medical infirmary would no longer take precedent in Andrew's life. He became completely dedicated to his wife's personal needs as she had been devoted to him throughout their marriage. He had not forgotten her unyielding commitment to him during his time of struggle to promote and develop Osteopathy. As a result, he stopped giving his weekly classroom lectures at the school to give him more time to be with her.[647]

In 1909, Andrew Still witnessed another major change in medical educational standards. The American Osteopathic Association would no longer

645   Walter, The First School of Osteopathic Medicine, 49-50.
646   Ibid., 51.
647   Still, Frontier Doctor, 221.

be the only national authority involved in an inspection process and the setting of standards for Osteopathy schools. This change resulted from the formation of an independent organization, commissioned by the Carnegie Institution, and led by a man named Abraham Flexner. Flexner and his staff waded into the inspection and certification process of all medical schools. He was required to submit a report regarding the quality of the education and training at the institutions. His report was made public in 1910 and would be a scathing one regarding the Osteopathic school in Kirksville. Flexner criticized the lack of a high school diploma requirement for admission to the school, the inadequate number of faculty present to teach the volume of students, and the foul conditions that existed in the dissection room. There were many other derogatory remarks made against the Osteopathic school in Kirksville.[648]

While Flexner's comments were extremely critical of Osteopathic medical schools, he was also extremely critical of almost all of the allopathic medical schools as well. Only 31 out of 155 medical schools were approved by him for meeting the standards for training and licensure.[649]

The American School of Osteopathy reeled at the insulting criticism of the school, but it did bring about many changes. At ASO, a high school diploma for admission was added to the requirements.[650]

The disappointment of having the American School of Osteopathy criticized so harshly by Flexner that year would prove to be a minor event for Andrew Still when compared to the loss he suffered when his wife of fifty years passed away. On May 28, 1910, Mary Elvira Turner Still died just as the graduation ceremonies were about to take place for yet another class. She had been the person who supported Andrew through all the difficult years they endured and had never varied in her support of him. She firmly believed in her husband's medical philosophy even when the entire family had to suffer with shame, even when the communities of Baldwin and Macon questioned his sanity. Mary's loyalty to Andrew and to the Osteopathic profession, which she had seen grow into an unimaginable dynasty in Kirksville, had earned her the title of Osteopathy's "Noblewoman" and she was referred to as "Mother Still" when addressed by everyone in the profession.[651]

---

648   Walter, The First School of Osteopathic Medicine, 71.
649   Ibid., 73.
650   Ibid.
651   Ibid.

Andrew addressed the graduating class members, who were adorned in their black gowns and caps, and he told them he *"could never have survived the early assaults and disappointments but for her optimism and faith.* Following a quiet ceremony, he presented the graduates their diplomas and in the afternoon the class attended Mary's funeral.[652]

At the age of eighty-two, Andrew would have to learn to live without Mary Elvira, who had been his constant companion for fifty years. Andrew's daughter, Blanche, moved into the house to be with him and to help provide care. At least her presence would prevent him from being totally alone. Andrew remained away from the school and infirmary, leaving the management and supervision primarily to Charles Still and other members of his family. As might be expected, without Andrew's dominant oversight, not everyone agreed on the direction the facilities needed to go.[653]

For a man who grew up with so little, he must have felt pride in his latter years as he watched those around him enjoying the success of Osteopathy. During his final years, a groundbreaking occurred for the construction of a mental hospital in Macon, Missouri, in 1913. This facility was built on a 400-acre site located in the country and would be able to care for 200 patients. Andrew's proposed mental health therapy called for healthy food, exercise, music, books, and manipulative therapy three times a week.[654] The mental hospital, named The Still-Hildreth Sanitarium, opened its doors in March 1914 and would be a tremendous success with patients arriving from all over the country to receive care.

This expansion and influence of the Still family continued. In 1914, the Kirksville hospital had to be enlarged to keep up with the patient volume. The addition of a fourth-floor to the existing hospital was completed.[655] Andrew's son, Charles Still and his family, built and moved into a twenty-four room home that took almost two years to construct and furnish. Charles also would be elected mayor of Kirksville that year.[656]

In 1914 Andrew suffered a stroke that left him weak and unable to receive visitors. By the first part of 1915, he had recuperated enough to welcome many famous people who wanted to meet him. Among the visitors were Helen Keller and William Cody.[657] In 1916 the American Osteopathic

652   Walter, The First School of Osteopathic Medicine, 75.
653   Still, Frontier Doctor, 230.
654   Ibid., 236-237.
655   Ibid.
656   Ibid., 239.
657   Ibid., 239-240.

Association held their National Convention in Kansas City and many of the graduates had the opportunity to visit Andrew Still to *"pay their respects to their founder."*[658]

In 1917, a commissioned statue of Andrew Still arrived in Kirksville and he *"joked about being one of the few men who would see a statue dedicated to himself."*[659] He was taken to the site in a wheelchair to observe the unveiling by his grandson, Charles E. Still, Jr., but he was able to attend the event.

Later in the year, on December 12, at the age of eighty-nine, Andrew Taylor Still died from the complications of another stroke. He was given a hero's farewell by the students and faculty who admired him and thousands of friends and family who came to pay him tribute. *"His casket, draped with the Stars and Stripes and surrounded by floral tributes, lay in state at his residence."*[660]

It would have been impossible for Andrew Still to imagine the outcome and magnitude of the profession he is responsible for nurturing into existence. However, it is obvious that the frontier life that he lived resulted in his being unafraid of the unknown or what was on the other side of the mountain. He always seemed to know that even if everything around him failed, he could always get to the top of the peak or find a trail to his dreams. Even though the wind sometimes gets lost in the prairie, he had found his destiny.

---

658   Still, Frontier Doctor, 244.
659   Ibid., 245.
660   Walter, The First School of Osteopathic Medicine, 87.

EPILOGUE

It has been 122 years since Andrew Taylor Still opened the doors to a one-room school building in 1892. He would live for another twenty-five years following that historic event and had the opportunity to witness the incredible growth of the graduates who completed their medical training at Kirksville.

It would take another ten years following Andrew's death before the "no drugs" in Osteopathic training would be changed. This transformation occurred in 1927 at the AOA convention in Denver, Colorado. At that meeting, the Osteopathic colleges agreed to begin teaching a course in the use of drugs for therapeutics. In 1928, additional courses in pharmacology, toxicology, and physiotherapy were added to the curriculum. As a result of adding both drug and surgery courses to the curriculum, the Kirksville school changed its name to the "Kirksville College of Osteopathy and Surgery."

At the time of Andrew Still's death, more than 5,000 D.O. physicians had received diplomas from the school, and were providing health care across America.[661] In 2014, almost a century and a quarter later, more than 87,000 D.O. physicians are practicing medicine and surgery in every specialty throughout the nation. Osteopathic physicians are one of the fastest growing segments of health care providers representing one-fifth of all medical students graduating in the United States. Contributing to this growth is the increase in the number of accredited Osteopathic Colleges. "In the 2013-2014 academic year, the AOA Commission on Osteopathic College Accreditation (COCA) accredits 29 colleges of osteopathic medicine operating in 37 locations."[662] This growth is staggering when considering the fact that in 1972 there were only five Osteopathic colleges in the country. It is anticipated that more than 100,000 Osteopathic physicians will be actively practicing by the year 2020 and the number of osteopathic students graduating annually will be approximately 7,000.[663] The demographics show that over one-third of Osteopathic physicians are female and

---

661   Walter, The First School of Osteopathic Medicine, 87.
662   2013 Osteopathic Medical Education Report, 11.
663   Ibid., 2.

more than half of all Osteopathic physicians currently in practice are under the age of 45.[664]

The majority of Osteopathic graduates choose primary care as their specialty which includes: Family Medicine, 36.9%; Internal Medicine, 13%; Pediatrics and adolescent medicine, 5.8%; Obstetrics/gynecology, 4.6%; Manipulative Medicine 1.9%, and other specialties 37.7%. [665]

The remaining 37 percent of Osteopathic physicians receive their residency training in medical and surgical sub-specialty fields. Those medical sub-specialties include: gastroenterology, cardiology, endocrinology, and neurology to name only a few. The surgery sub-specialties include: orthopedics, otolaryngology, ophthalmology, general surgery, neurosurgery, urology, and other areas.

At the time of Andrew Taylor Still's death in 1917, osteopathic physicians suffered the effects of political discrimination from organized medicine. This professional stigma was highlighted during World War I when D.O.'s were denied military commissioning in the medical corps and were not allowed to provide care as physicians to the mounting casualties. Any osteopathic physician who entered the military service was restricted to provide medical care only as an orderly.

Even when World War II struck the country with the catastrophic attack on Pearl Harbor in 1941, the military and the AMA would not change the continued bias against commissioning or recognizing osteopathic physicians as qualified to obtain the status of medical officers.

Five years after the end of World War II, the Korean Conflict began in 1950. D.O.'s were again denied the privilege of pinning silver or gold bars on their shoulders as medical officers. This situation continued throughout the war.

America became engaged in yet another conflict during 1964 in Southeast Asia, the Vietnam War. This unpopular war divided the country and resulted in a growing population of young adults demonstrating on college campuses across the country in protest. Large numbers of men deserted the country and headed north into Canada rather than respond to the draft notices calling them to enter the military service.

It was during this military conflict, after almost three-quarters of a century of denying osteopathic physicians professional recognition by the medical corps, that the political policy changed toward D.O.'s. Commissioning

---

664   2013 Osteopathic Medical Education Report, 10.
665   Ibid., 8.

status was finally granted, allowing them to serve as medical officers. The acceptance by the federal government of osteopathic physicians to serve in the military as physicians opened the door for an even more radical change. They were permitted to enter AMA approved resident training programs and earn eligibility to receive certification by the American Board. This recognition ultimately forced the AMA to grant osteopathic physicians equality. Civilian residency training programs followed the lead of the military and began opening their doors to D.O. graduates. For the first time in the history of the osteopathic profession, an equal opportunity for D.O.'s to practice medicine in America had been achieved.

Although osteopathic medical education equality had been recognized by both the AMA, and the Accreditation Council for Graduate Medical Education (ACGME), that recognition applied to osteopathic physicians completing an ACGME accredited residency program. Some opposition remained toward accepting the residency training programs accredited by the AOA. This professional/political battle resulted in two separate accrediting processes and residency selection procedures. This has resulted in some fellowship (post-residency) training obstacles, and in some areas of the country, additional hurdles in obtaining hospital practice privileges and with health insurance participation.

In an attempt to finally set aside these remaining residency training discrepancies, the ACGME, AOA and AACOM entered into an agreement in February 2014, to pursue a unified accreditation system for graduate medical education for both D.O. and M.D. graduates in this country. July 19, 2014, was a historic day when the AACOM Board of Deans, the AOA Board of Trustees and the AOA House of Delegates all approved resolutions authorizing both the AACOM and the AOA to enter into negotiations with the ACGME to pursue a new, single accreditation system for graduate medical education under the auspices of ACGME. When fully implemented in July 2020, the new system will allow graduates of osteopathic and allopathic medical schools to complete their residency and/or fellowship education in ACGME-accredited programs and demonstrate achievement of common milestones and competencies.

It is almost impossible to imagine how one man could originate the beginning of the osteopathic medical profession in a one-room school house with ten students. Also unbelievable is that A.T. Still's efforts would eventually generate such an enormous change in American medicine. Furthermore, even more mindboggling is how he achieved a national reputation while isolated in the small community of Kirksville, Missouri. All of these accomplishments were done in direct opposition to the politically powerful American Medical Association.

The Flexner Report in 1910 brought about significant change in medical educational curriculum standards and facility requirements of both osteopathic and allopathic medical schools.[666] Those schools that could not comply with the benchmarks established in the report were doomed to failure. Today's challenges for training physicians, both D.O. and M.D., are to provide a curriculum based on evidence based medicine and demanding acceptable practice management outcomes. Anecdotal treatment advice, such as, "we have always done it that way," is no longer acceptable in clinical medicine. Availability of immediate digital information and unlimited resources online has set a new standard of expectations for our Osteopathic Medical Schools, students, residents and faculty.

As a result of evidence based medicine, drugstore pharmacy shelves are being stripped of useless, if not harmful, medication that has been prescribed for the last hundred years in treating illnesses, such as the "common cold" and a variety of other self-limiting medical conditions. The over-prescribing of antibiotics has been one of the most recent campaigns launched by organized medicine to assist physicians in not using them unless supported by evidence-based information in the decision making process.

Interestingly, Andrew Taylor Still began the osteopathic profession because he lost faith in useless and harmful medication. Today, all of medicine embraces and recognizes the enormous drug problem that exists throughout the world. Narcotic deaths from prescription overdose, one every 14 minutes, killed at least 37,484 people in America in 2009 and surpassed the number of lives lost in automobile accidents that year. The cause of prescription narcotic overdose deaths has doubled in the last decade.[667]

This figure does not take into account deaths from illegal drugs smuggled into the country or manufactured in the hidden meth-labs in America.

There is no question that responsible use of evidence-based medication and treatment is absolutely necessary and has shifted the life expectancy to almost eight decades. The number of people living to one-hundred years is also rapidly growing. Cancer chemotherapy has cured thousands through diligent research. The future promises to be filled with ways to improve the ability to treat conditions that are presently considered hopeless.

---

666   Walter, The First School of Osteopathic Medicine, 71-73.
667   LA Times / Wichita Eagle, September 18, 2011.

However, it is the responsibility of the osteopathic and allopathic medical professions to be vigilant and protect their patients when prescribing drugs. Treatment must be based on safety, risk-reward considerations, and evidence based research. Together, we must unify our common commitment and greatest concern—quality patient care with compassion.

At this juncture in our medical history, who would argue that Andrew Taylor Still was incorrect regarding his judgments of the medications used in the latter 1800s. The time has come for all of medicine to recognize and credit him for seeing the medical world in a different way and providing a medical culture that benefits patients every day.

The world is continuing to awaken to the genius of Andrew Taylor Still. His family must have been very proud of him on April 16, 2014, when he was inducted into the Hall of Famous Missourians in Jefferson City, Missouri, at the state capital building. His great granddaughters and great-great granddaughters and grandson were in attendance and led the induction ceremony in prayer and the Pledge of Allegiance. A bust of the founder of Osteopathic Medicine was unveiled that day during the celebration and a quote from him written in 1902 was printed in the formal program. It read—*"To find health should be the object of the doctor. Anyone can find disease."*

BIBLIOGRAPHY

Adams, Mary Still. *In God We Trust*. Los Angeles. Buckingham Bros., 1893.

Andreas, A. T. *History of the State of Kansas.*

Arnold, Anna E. *A History of Kansas*, Topeka: The State Of Kansas, 1931.

Brewerton, G. Douglas. *The War in Kansas—A rough trip to the border*, among new homes and a strange people. 1856, Reprint. Freeport, N.Y.: Books for Libraries, 1971.

Brown, James Moore. *The Captives of Abb's Valley: A Legend of Frontier Life*, 1854. Presbyterian Board of Publications, 1909.

Connelley, William E. *The First Homicide of the Territorial Troubles in Kansas.* Standard History of Kansas, Vol.1, (1918).

Clark, Marovia Still. *Reminiscences*. Kirksville, Missouri: Still National Osteopathic Museum, 1919.

Everett, John and Sarah Letters, 1854-1864. (Kansas Historical Society).

Goode, William H. *Outposts of Zion, with Limnings of Mission Life* 1863: Poe & Hitchcock, Kansas Historical Society, Topeka.

Goodrich, Thomas. *War To The Knife:Bleeding Kansas*, 1854-1861, Mechanisburg, PA. Stackpole Books, 1998.

_____, *Bloody Dawn, The Story of the Lawrence Massacre*, 1992.

Greene, Albert R. *What I Saw of The Quantrill Raid*, The Historical Collection 13 (1913-1914).

Holmes, Stephen Wondell. *The Political Career of Gen. James H. Lane*. Publications of the Kansas State Historical Society, Vol. 3, 1930.

Leslie, Edward E. *The Devil Knows How To Ride—The True Story of William Clarke Quantrill and His Confederate Raiders*. New York: Da Capo Press, 1998.

J. J. Lutz, "*Methodist Missions Among the Indians in Kansas*," Kansas Historical Collections 9 (1905-06).

Malin, James Claude. *John Brown and the Legend of Fifty-Six.* American Philosophical Society, 1942.

Martin, George Washington. *Early Days in Kansas:* an address. Kansas State Historical Society Transactions 9 (1841-1914): 138-143, 166-167, 186, and 217.

Merrill, O. N. *A True History of The Kansas Wars*, 1856, The Magazine of History with Notes and Queries. Extra Number-No.178. Kansas State Historical Society, Topeka.

Nichols, Alice. *Bleeding Kansas*. New York: Oxford University Press, 1954.

Oates, Stephen B. *To Purge This Land With Blood—A Biography of John Brown*. Amherst, New York. Harper & Row, 1970.

Osteopathic Medical Education Report, 11. AOA, Chicago, IL www.osteopathic.org.

Redpath, James. *The Public Life of Capt. John Brown*: Thayer and Eldridge, 1860.

Robinson, Charles. *The Kansas Conflict*. New York: Harper and Brothers, 1892.

Robinson, Sara T. L. *Kansas: Its Interior and Exterior Life*. Boston: Nichols, Crosby & Company, 1856.

Schultz, Duane. *Quantrill's War, The Life and Times Of William Clarke Quantrill 1837-1865*. New York: St. Martin's Griffin, 1998.

Shoemaker, Floyd C. *Missouri's Proslavery Fight for Kansas, 1854-1855*. Missouri Historical Review 48:4 (July 1954).

Stephenson, Wendell Holmes. *The Political Career of General James H. Lane*: Topeka, Kansas State Historical Society, 1930.

Still, A. T. *Autobiography*, Kirksville, Missouri, 1908.

Still, Charles E. Jr. *Frontier Doctor Medical Pioneer*: *The Life and Times of A. T. Still and His Family*. The Thomas Jefferson University Press, 1991.

The Special Committee Appointed To Investigate The Troubles In Kansas, 34th Congress, 1st Session, House of Representatives, Report 200: Washington 1856.

The Kansas State Nurses Association. "Lamps on the Prairie: a history of Nursing in Kansas." *Emporia Gazette*, 1942.

"Thomas C. Wells—Letters of a Kansas Pioneer, 1855-1860." *Kansas Historical Quarterly* 5:2 (May 1936): 143-179.

Trowbridge, Carol. *Andrew Taylor Still, 1828-1917*. The Thomas Jefferson University Press, 1991.

Walter, Georgia Warner. *The First School of Osteopathic Medicine* (A Chronicle).

Welch, G. Murlin. *Border warfare in southeastern Kansas, 1856-1859*. Pleasanton, Kansas. Linn County Historical Society, 1977.

Wilder, Daniel W. *Annals of Kansas, New Edition*, 1541-1885. Kansas Historical Society, Topeka.

INDEX

Coleman, Franklin 106-110, 112-114, 116, 177
Cooke, Colonel 185
Corbett 23
Cracklin, Joseph 183
Cummins, Robert 92
Curtis, General 209

D

Danites 176-177
Darwin, Charles 218
Davidson, Samuel 25
Davis, Henry 87-88
Davis, Jefferson 135
Davis, Sergeant 207
Delaware Indians 47, 99
Donelson, I. B. 152-154, 156-157, 161, 163
Douglas County, Kansas 113-115, 117, 120, 123-125, 141-142, 144, 147, 155, 157, 163
Douglas, Kansas 86, 88
Dow, Charles 105-114, 116-117, 133, 177
Doyle, Drury 166-167
Doyle, James 166-167
Doyle, John 166-167
Doyle, Mahala 166
Doyle, William 166-167
Dutch Billy 48

E

Eldridge, Colonel 156, 158
Eldridge House Hotel 129, 134, 154, 156-159, 163, 201, 204
Ellison, Judge 228
Elmore, Judge 88
Emigrant Aid Company 59, 63-64, 156, 158

Emigrant Aid Society 58, 63-64, 78, 90
Emigration Aid Society 66, 73
Emigration Society 80
Evans, Martha 35-39
Evans, Thomas 38-39
Ewing, General 196, 199, 204-205

F

Fain, W. P. 156, 173
Farley, Lewis 106, 112
Fish, Cephas 44-45
Fish, Charles 46-47, 52
Fish, Paschal Jr. 43-47, 51-52, 54-55, 75, 79-80, 162
Fish, Paschal Sr. 44
Fish Tribe 43
Fitzsimmons 23
Flexner, Abraham 238, 244
Fugit 178

G

Geary, John 179, 181-186
Gillis House, Kansas City 64
Gleason, Mr. 204
Gleason, Sam/Salem 109, 112
Goode, William H. 55-56, 87-88
Greene, Albert 197-198, 204-206
Green, Israel 194
Greenwood, Sara Lynn 185

H

Halstead, J. D. 25
Hamilton, Charles 191-193
Hargis, Mr. 124
Hargous, Mr. 108, 177
Harmon, Reverend 14, 16
Harper's Ferry 193
Harvey, Colonel 182

54007479R00147

Made in the USA
Lexington, KY
28 July 2016